The
Swift
Years

THE ROBERT OPPENHEIMER STORY

My days are swifter than a weaver's shuttle,
And come to their end without hope. —JOB

Other books by Peter Michelmore

DR. MELLON OF HAITI

EINSTEIN: PROFILE OF THE MAN

The Swift Years

THE ROBERT OPPENHEIMER STORY

BY PETER MICHELMORE
Illustrated with photographs

DODD, MEAD & COMPANY · NEW YORK

1969

Library of Congress Catalog Card Number: 71-88070
Printed in the United States of America
by The Cornwall Press, Inc., Cornwall, N. Y.

Author's Note

My sources for *The Swift Years* were Robert Oppenheimer's complete personal files, now in the Library of Congress, the notes of conversations with his family and friends and enemies, hundreds of items of correspondence to the author, and the publications which are acknowledged at the back of the book. Among the scores of men and women who gave of their time, and their memories, I am particularly indebted to Robert Oppenheimer's brother Frank, son Peter, and widow Kitty. Kitty Oppenheimer kindly gave permission for the use of many excerpts from her husband's published writings and personal letters. This is not, however, an "authorized" biography, nor is it a definitive one. My task was to narrate the story of Robert Oppenheimer's life and to attempt to show how he was fashioned by his times, and his times were fashioned by him.

P.M.

New York City

Illustrations

Following page 150

Julius and Ella Oppenheimer
Robert, aged eleven, with his father
Robert and his brother Frank
Oppenheimer at Caltech with Nobel laureates Dirac and Millikan
At the Alamogordo atomic bomb test site
General Groves and Oppenheimer inspect remains of test bomb
Oppenheimer with Ernest Lawrence
Raymond T. Birge with Oppenheimer in 1946
General Nichols and Henry Smyth with Oppenheimer
The Director of Princeton's Institute for Advanced Study with
     Professor Oswald Veblen
Oppenheimer with Generals Marshall and Bradley at Harvard
Mrs. Frank Oppenheimer
Robert's brother Frank
Oppenheimer in post-war years
William L. Borden
Atomic Energy Commissioners
Oppenheimer at a congressional hearing, 1949
Lewis L. Strauss
Henry D. Smyth
Gordon Gray
Thomas A. Morgan
Ward V. Evans

Roger Robb
Edward R. Murrow interview
Oppenheimer with Albert Einstein
Oppenheimer receives news of Einstein's death
Oppenheimer in his Princeton study, 1957
Robert, Kitty and Toni in Paris
Oppenheimer on the grand tour, 1958
The Oppenheimers on the Acropolis
With Prime Minister Ben Gurion on a visit to Israel
The Congress for Cultural Freedom, West Berlin, 1960
The father of the atomic bomb visits Japan
Receiving the Enrico Fermi Award from President Johnson
An honorary degree from Princeton

The Swift Years

THE ROBERT OPPENHEIMER STORY

1

In its own way, the atmosphere of the apartment where Robert Oppenheimer spent his boyhood and youth in the early part of this century was like Ibsen's Rosmersholm, that aristocratic estate where voices and passions were always subdued, and where children never cried—and when they grew up never laughed.

The apartment was large and richly furnished, facing the front of the eleventh floor of a tall stone residential building on Riverside Drive in New York City. From the windows the view was marvelous—trains puffing up and down the tracks on both sides of the broad Hudson River, ferry boats plowing back and forth, the green Palisades of New Jersey beyond. It was the sort of scene that held limitless magic for two small boys. Robert was the only one at those windows for a long time.

Robert's father was genial, his mother elegant and kind, but there was an air of correctness, of observed decorum, about the household that deprived it of intimacy. One result of this was Robert's total lack of curiosity about his ancestry. He did learn that as recently as his great-grandfather the Oppenheimers were "simple farmers wholly without education." That was enough for him.

Apparently the Oppenheimers survived the convulsive history

of the German district of Hesse without memorable drama until, about the middle of the nineteenth century, some of the sons began drifting off to the towns and cities of western Germany and a few all the way to the New World. Robert's grandfather, Ben, got as far as Hanau, where he had a modest grain business and no doubt took some delight in sharing the same hometown at the same time as the famous Grimm brothers. The boys of his wife's family were more adventurous. At least two of them, a Rothfeld and a Stern, packed a carpetbag and sailed off to New York.

In time these two had established a small company to import cloth and they suggested that Ben's son Julius, barely seventeen years old, should come over and learn the trade. Julius was on the next boat and the sight of him at the Battery one spring day in 1888 must have brought a groan from his uncles. He was awkward in the extreme, as uncoordinated as a puppet, and spoke not a word of English. What he lacked in grace, he compensated for in energy and the ambition to be a man of prestige in that stupendous town. Julius came before the subways, the skyscrapers, the horseless buggies, but Manhattan then, as ever, was a place of opulence and dire poverty, of crusade and corruption; it was a city as romantic as it was rotten. And the evil was all so public. Tammany boss Irish Dick Croker was openly electing tame mayors with his left hand and holding off with his right the Presbyterian preacher Charles Parkhurst who thundered against the chicanery from his Madison Square pulpit. Edison's Pearl Street electricity plant hummed, industry boomed, and the profits put uptown children between silk sheets while those in the lower eastside tenements slept the winter under newspapers.

Rich or poor, the mob had to be clothed. In the lofts downtown, Jewish entrepreneurs could hear the chatter of money as batteries of sewing machines worked for them day and night. Cheap hands for the machine shop were available at the Pig Market, an "informal" labor exchange. Julius was spared this. His uncles put him in the storeroom, stacking and classifying bolts of cloth, learning the business from the basement up.

Like other junior capitalists, the Rothfeld-Stern partners stumbled through the financial panic of 1893 and had some bad moments when William Jennings Bryan threatened the so-called "gilded age," but mostly it was onward and upward on the profit graph, and ever forward for Julius. They specialized in the lining material for men's suits and their English alpaca sold by the mile.

By the turn of the century, when the ready-to-wear fad brought a bonanza to the garment trade, Julius approached his thirtieth birthday as a well-to-do man. Friends were more inclined now to say he looked like a prosperous banker than to note his funny walk. Self-improvement had been an integral part of his trading. Though a friendly man and a keen fighter for better conditions in his industry, his manner could be formal. Employees called him a "proper gentleman." He was learned in history, remarkably good with the English language now, versed in the social graces, and invariably impeccably dressed. Rarely did he have the time to get out of the city, and to make up for the urban shabbiness about him he developed a keen appreciation of art.

Just where and when Julius met Ella Friedman is not recorded; conceivably it was at an art exhibition. She was an accomplished young woman from a Bavarian Jewish family that had been settled in the Philadelphia-Baltimore region for generations. In spite of a crippled right arm, always covered by a long sleeve and glove—some said she was born without a right hand—Ella was a fine artist and had spent a year studying with an impressionist school in Paris. At the time of her marriage to Julius in 1903 she was teaching at her own studio in New York.

Julius prized refinement, and Ella had this in every gesture. She was beautiful: delicately drawn features, large gray-blue eyes, a graceful, slender figure. Women noticed that whenever Ella went out she wore a different pair of chamois gloves.

Teddy Roosevelt was in the White House, and certainly for the Oppenheimers all was right with the New World. They went to live in a sharp-gabled stone house on West Ninety-fourth Street and it was here, a little more than a year after the marriage, on the night of April 22, 1904, that Ella finished a difficult pregnancy by giving birth to a son. The city was shivering in the coldest spring on record and a pneumonia epidemic was causing near panic, but there was no gloom in the Oppenheimer house. The father had first thought to name his son just plain Robert, but he felt this was not distinguished enough, it needed something more. Eventually the new baby was named J. Robert Oppenheimer, the "J" standing for absolutely nothing.

Ella was to bear another two sons—Louis, who came a few years after Robert and who died shortly after birth, and Frank, who arrived on a humid summer day in 1912.

Robert, however, never lost his place as the central figure in the home. From his mother he inherited physical frailty, from his father he got a sort of disjointed vigor. All his own, was a quick, curious intelligence.

Ella had the notion early that his precocity should be channeled into music. She cajoled him into piano lessons, and he did persist with some competence past the exercises and on to simple pieces.

"Robert, play something for us," Ella would say.

"All right," the boy would reply with studied apathy. "I'll play 'Apples' on page nine."

When Robert fell sick with suspected infantile paralysis, Ella nursed him expertly, though constantly asking him how he felt. At last, pale and trembling, Robert raised his head and muttered, "Just as I do when I have to take piano lessons." Thereafter the music instruction ceased.

Robert was still very young when the family moved to the apartment on Riverside Drive. Adult visitors were frequent, for whom a butler opened the door and a maid served tea. On Sunday outings Julius had a Packard automobile, complete with gray-uniformed chauffeur. Summers were usually spent at Bay Shore, Long Island, where Julius first rented and then bought a villa after reading the newspaper advertisements that this was the resort of the future, a beautiful spot "entirely free of malaria."

When he was six Robert had his first Atlantic crossing. They went to see old Ben, who had by then moved to Cologne to be near his daughter Hedwig and her family. Ben was dumbfounded to find that Julius had been transformed into what he called a "royal merchant." Hedwig's boys were intrigued by their rich uncle from New York and by their shy slender cousin who would make a show of reading a book while other children played noisily all about him.

Ben gave his American grandson a small collection of different colored stones and explained their origin. Now it was Robert's turn to be impressed. He rolled them over and over in his hands, asking endless questions. Back home he rummaged for fresh samples along the Palisades, cataloguing them all and studying their descriptions. They were everything to Robert, these rocks. They were his football, baseball, bicycle, and gang. He had no older friends to introduce him to any of these diversions, and no friends his own age to share them with anyway.

Visitors to the house noted that every gap and corner of his bookshelves were crammed with rocks. While they saw it as a solitary hobby for a solitary boy, Julius took it seriously and encouraged Robert with no expense spared.

This was to become the pattern of his fatherhood. Robert, for instance, enjoyed his grandmother reading to him and whenever he showed enthusiasm for a particular book his father would buy a whole set of volumes by the same author.

Excellence and purpose, these were the two bywords in the Oppenheimer family. Julius was not simply a rag merchant, but perhaps the most knowledgeable man in New York on fabrics. His talent for color matching was widely known, and he was proud of the many people who consulted him on it. Ella's ability as a housekeeper was legendary; her accounts were maintained with the same care as a business ledger. Some people suspected Ella ran the family on a timetable, and it was true that when she was away for a day she would leave Robert a list of instructions that she expected to be followed.

Eventually Julius rose to the presidency of Rothfeld-Stern. Now fairly rich, he took his wife for a tour of the galleries to buy some distingushed art for the apartment. By the time they had finished, their walls were hung with several paintings by the most fashionable French impressionists and no less than three large Van Gogh originals.

Friends found it hard to walk into the home, feeling the deep pile underfoot and seeing the great Van Gogh burst of orange on the wall, without lowering their voices and carefully choosing their words. The sense of quietude and perfection carried over to the people; it was expected that Robert should be without flaws, too. At a very early age he learned to curb any excesses of behavior. This was not to say that there were no moments of gaiety in the home. Memorable was the night a train loaded with braying cattle stopped on the railroad tracks that then bordered the river, just down from the Oppenheimer apartment. The trucks were directly in front of the swank Seventy-ninth Street Yacht Club. Julius stood at the window chuckling at the sight of members remonstrating with the train crew, who flatly refused to move the noisy steers. It was a delectable scene to him because the club allowed no Jewish members.

Being nonreligious Jews, the Oppenheimers sent Robert—and later Frank—to the Ethical Culture School on Central Park West. The movement was founded in New York by Felix Adler, a German emigrant and a stout campaigner for social justice, who had one of his greatest supporters in Julius. Adler convinced him that human values do not require dogma to render them important, that goodness is not dependent on theology, that each man should form his own attitudes toward the unknown and the mysteries of life. Men should face life with reverence and zest, accept whatever tragedies occurred without losing faith in the essential goodness of man, without losing the steel that would enable them to live or suffer or die with dignity. It was, in many ways, an heroic mold they had at the Ethical Culture School, and Robert was as much influenced by it as the many other boys of his time who attended the school.

Some years later Robert was to tease his father for his admiration of Felix Adler and the ethical-humanist philosophy. With a mixture of mischief and gratitude, Robert composed a little song for one of his father's birthdays. To the tune of *The Battle Hymn of the Republic,* Robert sang, "And he swallowed Dr. Adler like morality compressed. . . ."

The Ethical Culture teachers considered Robert their star pupil. Classmates were less impressed by the ungainly boy who walked like a bird, always forward on the balls of his feet, and who eschewed games. Robert seemed to spend his life inside a book. His passion for knowledge, indeed for knowing everything, may have derived originally from his loneliness but now it was unassailable. Because he was smarter than any contemporary, and not accustomed to friends, he stood aloof and remained a loner. Whenever he looked back on these years he saw himself as repugnant. He desperately wanted to be liked, even popular, but he had never learned how to let himself go and enter into a full-blooded relationship with other students.

Hunched over his studies, driven everywhere he went, attended by servants, the boy developed a poor physique. At one time the school principal lost his patience because he would not climb the stairs to the second floor, always waiting for the elevator. Home came the abrupt note, "Please teach your son to walk up stairs; he is holding up class."

With the stairs conquered, Robert spent as much time as possible at school. His Greek teacher, a Miss Alberta Newton, kept him after class so they might read together Homer, a little Plato, and fight again the Trojan War. They loved the Greeks but rooted for the Trojans. A chemistry tutor named Augustus Klock, destined to become the Mr. Chips of the place, drew out Robert's talent for science to the extent that he spent one entire summer helping Klock set up a small laboratory.

School days, both elementary and high, were long periods of gorging on the small type of textbooks, interrupted by bouts of sickness. His parents urged Robert into outdoor activity after he suffered an attack of tubercular fever. Tennis was the genteel sport then, and he proved to be a mediocre player. His coordination, like that of his father, was atrocious. Sailing was a different story. It was a sport for loners, requiring skill in reading wind and water and judging a boat's capacity. Through a succession of small vessels, Robert trained himself to rank among the very best yachtsmen on Great South Bay.

By age sixteen he was scooting about in his own twenty-eight-foot sloop, often with his little brother squatting in the cockpit. Robert named his boat *Trimethy,* his shortened version of a chemical compound for which he had particular affection, trimethylene di-oxide.

World War I sparked little interest in young Oppenheimer though it made his father wealthier because he lined the Army uniforms. Shortly after this war, Robert made his first real friends. One was Paul Horgan, later a celebrated writer and then a self-described intellectual brat. The second was a trim, relaxed schoolmate, Francis Fergusson, who was to become a professor of literature. Robert sought to impress them with his two major accomplishments, his fund of book-learning and his sailing.

In skippering *Trimethy,* he had the dash of a Norseman. A summer storm warning would send him to the pier to break out the sails and scud across the bay. Riding the tidal rush through the inlet at Fire Island he exulted in taking the boat right out into the boiling Atlantic Ocean. With the sea breaking over the sides and *Trimethy* heeling to within a plank of capsizing, Robert would then tack back through the rollers to regain the bay. His fix might be a clump of bushes glimpsed through the spray, but he always made it. Shirt clinging to his ribs, hair standing on end with salt and wind, he accompanied his performance with Viking shouts and a look of bliss.

At the Bay Shore villa Ella Oppenheimer stood a constant vigil at the window, her face screwed up with fear. Several times Julius stomped down to his motor sailor and went searching for his son. They would come together at last and Julius would scold Robert, demanding to know why he took such perverse glee in danger, and, with a glance at one of the bedraggled friends, why he was risking other people's lives. "Roberty, Roberty . . ." Julius would say finally, shaking his head. The boy grimaced and headed back across the ruffled water. He hated to be called "Roberty."

He was an enigma to his parents, who wondered how to square a boy who was at once a headstrong adventurer and a bookish introvert, given to periods of sorrowing. His dark spirit was deepened by his reading of T. S. Eliot, Chekhov, Katherine Mansfield, and Aldous Huxley. He lived a fragment of his life in the despairing world of these authors, and he showed signs at home of adopting Hamlet as a brother being.

Frivolity was a good flush for the spirit, but Robert had no talent for this. His habit of propriety and taste for cultivated activities were too firmly fixed.

When Horgan came east in the summer from his home in Albuquerque, New Mexico, the boys would dine at Voisin, then ride in a limousine to a new play. One at the time was *Rain* with Jeanne Eagels. On the journey down to Bay Shore, the two friends might discuss Freud or pause at the Metropolitan Museum to inspect the works of Monet.

A calm day on the bay was an opportunity for Robert to sit in the bow of *Trimethy* and read a book on thermodynamics, smiling every now and again over a clever passage. Horgan sat in the bottom of the boat writing short stories. In their scholarly discussions Robert would punctuate his remarks with a self-deprecatory smile; whether out of inverted vanity or real humility, who could tell.

His last year of high school, ending with the spring of 1921, was an orgy of learning. All the courses available in mathematics and science did not prevent him from taking advanced Greek, Latin, French, and German. His graduation with about ten straight "A's" did not make him any more of a regular American boy than was a fellow called Red Grange who was leaving a midwestern high school at about the same time with sixteen letters in football, basketball, and track. Oppenheimer was as much a champion as Grange; the degree of power and coordination Grange had in his body Robert had in his mind.

To relax him before Harvard, Robert's parents took him across to Germany that summer. Frank went along, too, and it made a lasting impression on both boys to witness the arrogance of the French troops then occupying the Ruhr. By himself, Robert escaped to the Harz mountains, returning after a few weeks with a suitcase full of rocks and a body racked with colitis. He returned to New York in a weakened condition and with a ruined digestion that was to bother him all his days. Harvard was out of the question that year. For the entire winter Robert stayed in the apartment with his books and his somber thoughts. He turned sullen and rebellious at his mother's strict ministrations, purposely ate all the wrong foods, locked himself in his room, and was rude to guests.

By the spring Robert was incorrigible, and Julius begged the tough-minded Ethical Culture English teacher, husky young Herbert Smith, to take the boy west to the mountains to restore his body and spirit. Robert protested, refusing to have a nursemaid, but his father prevailed.

Weeks on end Smith and his charge roamed the mountains of Colorado and New Mexico by train, wagon, and horseback. They camped out or stayed at guest ranches, one being the elite Los Pinos establishment run by Katherine Page north of Santa Fe. Robert was infatuated with the beautiful Miss Page, and his time at rustic and remote Los Pinos was utter joy to him. He would come back often to this place, quite slavishly adoring Miss Page.

Smith's dismay at first that his skinny companion was so clumsy he could not chop a piece of wood without it bouncing off the axe blade into the brush changed into admiration. Axemanship aside, the boy had grit, fantastic stamina, and a marvelous knack with horses. Away from the few dirt roads that snaked through the Sangre de Cristos, it was a lofty wilderness of fast rivers and pine forests and rolling meadows. Santa Fe itself was then a small, time-worn town, while the other places marked on the map were little more than trading posts. Rich visitors from the east came to take the air, and Katherine Page, an eastern schoolteacher herself, catered to these people. There was more than clean air in this mountain retreat, there was a timelessness and a grandeur that lifted the heart.

Hardened and tanned by his summer on horseback, Oppenheimer went to Harvard in the fall of 1922 with buoyant spirits. "It was the most exciting time of my life," he said. "I really had a chance to learn. I loved it. I almost came alive. I took more classes than I was supposed to, lived in the stacks, just raided the place intellectually." What he did not mention was his pleasure at breaking lose from the family and finally having a chance to test himself in the abrasive world outside.

2

—————————

CHEMISTRY WAS Robert Oppenheimer's initial major subject, but he switched in his second year to physics because it seemed more basic. "It was the study of order, of regularity, of what makes matter harmonious and what makes it work," he said.

The courses mixed theory and experiment, and Oppenheimer got up early to be at the laboratory at eight o'clock, long before anybody else. He would stop at a lunch counter in Cambridge to breakfast on what was then called a "black and tan"—wholewheat toast with a layer of peanut butter and a topping of chocolate sauce. The snack, which would have horrified Ella Oppenheimer, was popular at the time because of its concentrated energy. It kept Robert going all day. His other energizer was raisin chocolate. He hoarded huge chunks of it in his rooms, eating it for supper when he would not leave his books to go out.

Physics Professor Percy Bridgman was impressed with Oppenheimer's capacity to learn, though he agreed with other students that young Oppie was prone to ask too many questions, often as a device to show off his considerable knowledge. His energy was volcanic and though aware that his extreme impatience to turn the pages was irritating he found it hard to slow down.

Adjustment to undergraduate life did not come easily to him.

Too often he acted immaturely and he agonized over doing so. Once at Bridgman's home he admired a drawing of an ancient Greek structure. The professor mentioned the vintage and Oppenheimer, impulsively, shot out, "Oh, that is interesting. From the style I would have thought it fifty, a hundred years earlier than that."

Fergusson, also at Harvard, found his friend hard to expain to others. He was an intellectual powerhouse. Doubling the normal student work load still left him with untapped reserves. Walking was his relaxation. Fergusson would be with Robert when relatives visited. Polite now to the courtly degree, Robert would take them to dinner and exchange small talk until Fergusson noticed with alarm that his friend was turning visibly green. Immediately the visitors were gone Robert would hit the sidewalk and pound it for miles, his quiet voice nonstop on some highly technical problem in physics. Eventually the green would fade from Robert's jaw and the boys would go home.

A few others joined these two on weekend excursions to places like Plum Island, a wild stretch of land opposite Ipswich. They trekked over the dunes, with Oppenheimer the one to draw their attention to the perfectly circular tracings in the sand of bent grass blown by the wind. Charming little tricks of nature like this delighted him, frequently moving him to verse. Poetry had become his solace, and apparently he did sell one of his poems to a literary magazine.

Nature's serenity and violence were equally appealing. On a vacation from Harvard Robert returned to New Mexico to go riding with Horgan. They hired two horses, packed them with Robert's books and Horgan's paint boxes, and set off up the mountain trails, heading towards Los Pinos and Katherine Page. Crashing thunder and forked lightning startled the horses at a divide and they reined in. "Just look at those pine trees," said Oppenheimer, pleased. "The tall ones are an excellent conductor of lightning." The rain pelted down and the boys sheltered under the bellies of their tethered animals. Robert hauled a couple of oranges out of his pack and they munched away, waiting for the storm to pass. Unforgettable to Horgan was the sight of his partner, eyes shining with happiness as the juice and rain streamed down his face.

Well into the night they reached the Page ranch, where they unsaddled for a long stay in a cabin that was weathered chocolate brown by a decade of storms.

With Horgan or other companions, Oppenheimer often camped out on the trail. Caught one night without food, he was persuaded to share a friend's pipe as a way to quieten the pangs of hunger. A nonsmoker up to that time, Robert afterwards became addicted to tobacco.

Until he got to the tiller of a sailboat or swung into a big Mexican saddle, Oppenheimer would have ranked as nobody's idea of what an outdoorsman should look like. Although he had grown six feet tall, he was a shade stooped and his spare frame—he never weighed more than 130 pounds—gave him a flimsy appearance. His face, like his mother's, showed fine pale skin drawn over the bones, glossy black eyebrows that almost seemed painted on, eyes that changed from gray to blue. He had large nose and ears and wore his long black kinky hair short at the sides. The hair was coarse and thick, and it was Oppenheimer's secret that he groomed it with a dog's steel comb. His manner of speaking was close to being comically baroque, as were the contorted gestures of his hands and arms.

His intensity about all things made him a prime potential recruit for the political groups at Harvard, yet he evinced marginal interest. Students in the early twenties were excited by the Bolsheviks, by Lenin, by the world ambitions of the Third International. When it got right down to commitment, however, the students shied away. Harvard's Liberal Club of this period had the reputation for being radical and members kept up the pretense because it was more vigorous than the real thing. A senior, John Edsall, roped in Oppenheimer and made him an assistant editor of the new magazine planned by the Liberal Club. Borrowing from Socrates, Oppenheimer named the magazine *The Gadfly,* his sole contribution. On the eve of the paper's publication the *Harvard Lampoon* published a fierce parody of the probable contents. It was a case of over reaction. *The Gadfly* was disappointingly tame and died rapidly.

If Robert had any hours to kill and he did not feel like a trip to Plum Island or Cape Ann, a walk along the Charles River, or an elaborate dinner at Locke-Ober's, he invariably took to his books. He could flaunt his capacity for breezing through the most difficult texts as others might boast of football exploits.

Jeffries Wyman, a science colleague, was once near prostrate with the heat of a late spring day when Oppenheimer came into his room. "What intolerable heat," said Robert. "I have been spending all the afternoon lying on my bed reading Jean's *Kinetic Theory of Gases.* What else can one do in weather like this?"

To nobody's surprise Oppenheimer caught up his lost Harvard year and graduated *summa cum laude* with his bachelor's degree within three years. He declined a scholarship to remain, and dodged the commencement ceremonies. That weekend he and a Harvard friend, William Boyd, were at the Bay Shore villa. *Trimethy* was put in the water, and the two men went across to Fire Island. The way Boyd told it, "We took off our clothes and walked up and down the beach getting a sunburn."

Through the summer of 1925 Robert was eager to be off to Cambridge University, in England, to go on with his physics. He was twenty-one now and his mother felt him grow more distant. She did not mind his withdrawal so much as his continued solemnity. He would sink into an armchair with a book and grow sadder by the minute. This dejection was not so odd considering the literature he read, but Ella thought his unusual intelligence should put some halter on his sensitivity and emotionalism. He had both to an acute degree.

He did take his young brother sailing the Sound and walking the shores, often inventing little adventures. Once they climbed a fire tower. The door at the top was locked, so Robert broke the latch with a stone because Frank wanted to see inside. He left fifty cents for repairs and a note apologizing for the vandalism. Frank adored his brother, found him exciting to be with, though at thirteen he could not really become involved with the sort of books Robert carried in his hip pocket. It was no fun for anyone when Robert hauled out Eliot's *The Waste Land* and quoted aloud:

> But at my back in a cold blast I hear
> The rattle of the bones, and chuckle spread from ear to ear.

The thrust into the cosmos interrupted Robert's grim introspections. Mathematicians and theorists and experimentalists in Europe were exploring the unknown world of the atom, and the challenge of it all was irresistible.

Laymen were aware of the new concept of the atom as a tiny universe all its own, with particles called electrons orbiting a hard nucleus. But since the best microscope could not spot an atom, and it could not have any practical value, the further investigations into the how and why of it aroused little popular curiosity. A separate language and mathematics emerged among the atomic physicists and this served to make the studies totally remote. They were not even pursued in the one place. A German would come up with one theory, which would be extended by a Dane, adapted by a Frenchman, polished by an Englishman, and communicated by a Dutchman. There were few Americans of real note in this extremely select international club, and Oppenheimer went off to Europe in the autumn to see how he would fare.

Grave doubts took hold of him as soon as he settled down at the famed Cavendish Laboratory in Cambridge. The team of physicists there was sensational. Stimulated by fresh theories on the movement and character of electrons (quantum mechanics), the Nobel Prize experimentalists Sir Joseph Thomson and Sir Ernest Rutherford were at work on their verifications with such wondrous young men as Paul Dirac, who was also to win a Nobel

Prize. And the visionary professor from Copenhagen, Niels Bohr, the Columbus of the subatomic world, was a frequent visitor.

Oppenheimer studied theory and mathematics on the side, but his experimental assignment under Thomson was to prepare very thin metallic films to investigate the penetrating power of electrons. To his horror he discovered he was most inept at the job. Jeffries Wyman, his Harvard friend who was at Cambridge doing biochemistry, once encountered him in his rooms lying on the floor and rolling from side to side with a groan on his lips.

His lack of talent in the laboratory drove him to despair, and he was not helped by reading Dostoyevsky far into the night. John Edsall, also at Cambridge, tried to talk Robert around into a better frame of mind. It did not seem out of the question then that he might try to kill himself. In the short passage of time since the summer, he had acquired a tremendous ambition to accomplish something bold and stylish in physics. This goal had taken hold of his imagination and given him a purpose. But where all around him were deft, inventive young men like Dirac, he was failing.

A two months' session with a psychiatrist persuaded Oppenheimer he needed the tranquil perspective of sea or mountains. As a compromise he chose a spring holiday in Corsica with Wyman and Edsall.

They crossed to the Continent on the boat deck of a channel steamer, getting drenched by the wind-whipped spray, then took the train to Paris and Nice, sailing to Corsica for a walking tour. Down the full length of the coast they hiked, sleeping in small inns and peasant huts or out in the open. They forded the streams by jumping from rock to rock, climbed the peaks, listened to the croaking of frogs at sunset as they strolled along the marshy shore near Porto-Vecchio, paused to hear the shouts of the boar hunters off in the mountains. As always, Robert found time to read—on this occasion Proust's *Remembrance of Things Past*.

Once they lay down for a nap and awakened in the rain. Dashing to a nearby inn they hung their clothes by the fire and, swaddled in blankets, gazed into the flames and talked.

"Tolstoy is the writer I most enjoy," said Edsall at one point.

"No, no, Dostoyevsky is superior; he gets to the soul and torment of man," said Oppenheimer. He held the floor for some minutes and remarked on a number of writers. What he despised, he said, was for a fine writer to waste himself on trivia. "Look at Charles Lamb's essay on roast pig," he said with disgust.

With the steam rising from their damp clothes and the fire crackling and turning their faces pink, the three young men talked then about what they would do with their lives.

"My ideal man," said Oppenheimer, "would be one who was good at a lot of things but would still look at the world with a tear-stained countenance."

Edsall and Wyman exchanged glances. Robert's state of mind was improving.

Finally they reached Bonifacio, the little town on the cliffs at the very southern end of Corsica. Edsall approached the fortifications with his camera and started to snap pictures when he was grabbed by a uniformed guard. At the local police station, the tall, rather bashful Edsall was questioned in one room while the two others waited in the passageway and worried whether they would be released in time to eat the lobster dinner they had ordered at a café. Soon the meal was forgotten and Wyman was doubled in laughter at the overheard pleas of their friend to skeptical guards that he was not a spy but a harmless American tourist.

Through tears of mirth Wyman looked up to see Oppenheimer chuckling and slapping his side. He was not collapsed in merriment by any means, but Wyman realized later that Robert had never to his knowledge ever chuckled before.

3

SWINGING A HANDSOME PIGSKIN grip at his side and with a ridiculous metal-stringed tennis racket under his arm, Robert Oppenheimer arrived at Germany's celebrated University of Göttingen in the autumn of 1926 to study for his doctorate under the great theoreticians James Franck and Max Born.

Confidence in his questing spirit had been revived when the august *Journal of the Cambridge Philosophical Society* reprinted two of his papers on aspects of the quantum theory. Born and Franck had already heard of the young American who signed himself J.R. Oppenheimer. Born particularly was pleased to have him in his school because the professor was a man of cultivation, and the American could match him in discussions on literature and philosophy as well as physics.

The scarcely disguised resentments that were to follow Oppenheimer during his life were first noticed in that quiet university town with the medieval architecture and the strains of Bach seemingly everywhere one walked.

Born's excessive interest in the American was a factor, for other students thought they were deprived, but what really rankled were Oppenheimer's wealth and intelligence. Where most students inclined to poverty and shabbiness, the newcomer wore clothes of the finest material. They hung badly on his spare frame, but the quality was still there. Others missed lunch in order to afford books. Oppenheimer had all he wanted, and in leather bindings.

Learned young men and women were in Göttingen from all over Europe to immerse themselves in physics, and among the members of this elite league it was natural for jealousies to arise. At weekly seminars the professors and students engaged in open discussion, and it became routine during that long winter for Oppenheimer to dominate the student benches. The American-accented German, interrupted by the cigarette cough, and the gesturing arms and facial expressions, irked less bright students who felt Born's favorite was putting on a performance. Oppenheimer was just too enthusiastic and too quick in their view. Franck's knowledge of electron laws was not superior to that of Oppenheimer's, though Franck had won a Nobel Prize for the original postulations.

The complexity of Oppenheimer as a person made him an endless subject of gossip. At the villa where he and a few other students rented rooms his manners at the dinner table were so proper that one or two of his colleagues felt like barbarians in comparison. Contrasted with this refinement and genial considerateness of others, it came as a shock, when, in a group, he would suddenly turn his back on one member and shut him out of the conversation. This would happen if a banal remark was made, and Oppenheimer would get that tinge of green in his face. His only excuse for the cussedness was that the culprit should have known better. He could not bear stupidity, and his intolerance was almost violent.

A big, breezy, sharp young American physicist named Ed Condon, who was at the same rooming house as Oppenheimer, saw a touch of arrogance in his countryman. "Trouble is that Oppie is so quick on the trigger intellectually he puts the other guy at a disadvantage," Condon noted then. "And, damnit, he is always right, or at least right enough."

Condon was on a post-doctoral fellowship paid for by the Rockefeller Foundation, but he still found it difficult to keep to a budget because he had a young wife and baby. Oppenheimer was ignorant of the problems of poverty and family responsibilities. He invited Ed and Emilie Condon out for a walk along the river one day. Emilie regretfully said she had to stay behind to tend the baby. "All right," said Oppie, "we'll leave you to your peasant tasks."

This kind of remark was common with Oppenheimer and while it was not meant as scorn and people smiled, they could not suppress a sense of resentment. One more thoughtful student at Göttingen worried why the smart American chafed him. He decided candidly that it was because Oppie frequently invited a mutual friend to dinner, but never himself. It happened that the mutual friend was close to being Oppie's intellectual equal, whereas the uninvited man knew he was a step or two lower. This did not say much for Oppie's well-known grace, but it was a snobbishness that the thoughtful student accepted. It did not prevent him from having an acceptable lifelong friendship with Oppenheimer.

The Cambridge star, Paul Dirac, whose devotion to physics was exclusive, was somewhat puzzled by Oppenheimer's high standing both in his discipline and in other fields, primarily literature. "They tell me you write poetry as well as working at physics," Dirac remarked in a much repeated conversation. "How can you do both. In physics we try to tell people in such a way that they understand something that nobody knew before. In the case of poetry it's the exact opposite." The American was flattered by the comment.

Fritz Houtermans and George Uhlenbeck numbered among the students with developed literary taste. Their relaxation was to read Dante to each other in the original Italian, a pastime greatly appealing to Oppenheimer. He was excluded because he did not know Italian. The other two had lived in Italy and had a command of the language. For a month or so the tall American was missing from the coffee shops and bookstores. Then he reappeared as the third reader of Dante, and his Italian was entirely adequate.

It was no wonder that less brainy students were pleased when

Oppie was seen in some indignity, corkscrewing around the tennis court, his funny racket making a loud twanging noise whenever he hit the ball. Or the time in the tiny flat of Charlotte Riefenstahl, the prettiest of the physics students, when Oppenheimer leaped out of his chair to heat the water so that Charlotte could make tea for a group of them. In Europe the gesture seemed very feminine.

Oppenheimer was immature around girls. As a teenager he had had a mild romance with Rosemary Horgan, Paul's sister, and the previous summer he had visited Amsterdam and had an awkward, agonizing, and unsatisfactory experience with a Dutch girl.

When Charlotte entered his life in Göttingen he was strongly attracted to her. She was warm and gay and highly intelligent, and she liked him, yet his reserve was a barrier for both of them.

They met on a train traveling between Hamburg and Göttingen. A band of young physicists had been in the city overnight for a special semester. Next day at the station all the suitcases were lined up on the dusty platform as the students stood around waiting for the train home and talking over the events of the meeting. Charlotte came in last and eyed the line of cases. All except one were of battered brown leather or cardboard. The exception was the shiny tan leather pigskin grip at the center, and, being a girl, Charlotte forgot the physics and admired the bag.

"What a beautiful thing," she said to Professor Franck. "Who's is it?"

Franck grunted. "Who else but Oppenheimer's."

Later, in the open, bucking carriage, Charlotte had Oppenheimer pointed out to her. She edged to his side and saw he was reading a novel by Gide, an author with whose works she was familiar. They discussed Gide for a time and then Charlotte mentioned how impressed she had been with the beauty of his pigskin grip. The American was puzzled; he had not noticed that others did not have such fine cases.

Charlotte mentioned the conversation to Fritz Houtermans, the man she eventually married, and he said she was foolish because

trunk all strapped up and ready to be shipped. She hefted one side. It felt too light, so she opened it and found inside a few books, a spare pair of pants and some socks. "Look at this Charlotte," she called. "He never takes anything with him anywhere."

Out in the other room, Julius raised his now grey-fringed bald head and remarked with some admiration, "They're both the same, Frankie and Roberty, always away off in space."

Charlotte became convinced that Robert was not ready to share himself completely, not with her or anyone. His attitude prohibited questions about his previous life in New York, and an intimate inquiry, about Ella's covered right arm for instance, was unthinkable. The parents were careful to respect the special privacy of their older boy; Frank was the closest to him and not even he intruded as he pleased.

The study fellowship split the winter for Robert between Harvard and the California Institute of Technology and in both places he produced fine original papers that inched forward the total knowledge of atomic physics. At Caltech, his first lectures to graduate students at the Norman Bridge Laboratory were attended by the chief himself, laboratory director Robert Millikan, who had won a Nobel Prize six years earlier for his work on electrons.

Students were aware, of course, that physics was undergoing a great revolution, that the very nerve of the universe had been exposed. Millikan himself had had an early part in these developments. But the progressive centers of physics were in Europe and the heroes, men like Rutherford and Bohr and Born, were just names in the *Physical Review*. Now back from this tremendous scientific frontier came Oppenheimer, a young American who had ridden with the greatest.

Whatever they imagined him to be like, the man himself was a surprise. Verging on the sickly in appearance, amazingly youthful, and obviously semetic, he stood at the blackboard with a cigarette between his fingers and not a note in sight. Then he began to talk in a low voice about the most intricate theories of the subatomic world in bursts of two or three sentences at a time. The language was so rich, the content so clever, that the classes were mesmerized. As if to make doubly sure he had everyone taut with attention, or maybe as a moment for reflection, Oppenheimer separated his spoken paragraphs with a strange lilting sound, something like "nim-nim-nim," before going on again.

When the lectures ended the students disguised their bafflement by sagely nodding their heads. They had understood him phrase by phrase, but when they put it all together they had nothing. Since it was so easy for Oppenheimer, they figured the fault must be in their own learning, and they went to their books with fresh vigor.

One lone student went on record as openly giving voice to his mystification. "Excuse me, Dr. Oppenheimer, but why are you telling us all this?" he asked frankly.

Oppenheimer was startled. "Why, for your elucidation, I thought," he said. Later, he heard, Millikan's sympathies were with the student.

During this period the idea started to take shape in Oppenheimer's mind that he would like to build in America an advanced school of theoretical physics like Bohr's in Copenhagen or Born's in Göttingen. His preparation, however, was not quite finished. If he was to teach he must have experience under two of the acknowledged best in the world—Albert Einstein's close friend Paul Ehrenfest, who was a professor at Holland's Leyden University, and Wolfgang Pauli, the marvelous Austrian prodigy who was then switching to the Institute of Technology in Zurich.

While he was organizing this pursuit of his career through an International Educational Board fellowship, he took the opportunity to visit Katherine Page at Los Pinos. One July morning they rode a long trail to the high country, climbing to ten thousand feet among the ponderosas and white pine. At the foot of a lifting meadow, matted with thick clover and speckled everywhere with blue and purple button flowers, Katherine unlatched a gate and motioned Robert up the path to a log cabin. It was more exactly a house, carefully built of half-trunks and adobe mortar. Home-

hewn furniture decorated a spare kitchen and there was a fireplace
of seasoned clay in the living room. A narrow staircase led to two
bedrooms on the second level.

"Like it?" asked Katherine.

And when Robert nodded, she told him it was surrounded by
160 acres of pasture, a brook, and it was all for rent.

"Hot dog," said Robert eagerly.

"That's what you can call it, Hot Dog, Perro Caliente," said
Katherine. Within days, Robert had leased the place, acquired
several saddle horses for the corral just down from the house, and
summoned Frank.

By the frail cut of the brothers, they looked the most tenderfoot
vaqueros north of the Rio Grande, but even among the old hands
in the mountains the Oppenheimers won a reputation for expert
horsemanship and ruggedness. They talked while they rode, of
physics, of poetry, of Cummings' recent anti-war novel *The Enormous Room,* of philosophy, of religion, and Frank gained an impression of his brother then that was to be shaken on occasion but
never cancelled. Robert was gentle, trusting of human nature,
honest to a fault, and a genius. Frank was sixteen, Robert twenty-
four, yet they so obviously enjoyed being with one another that
people in the mountains were warmed by the sight of them riding
together.

Among the several visitors who dropped in at Perro Caliente
that summer was his constant friend Francis Fergusson. Reassuring to him was Robert's intellectual distraction, but discomforting
was the low premium both Oppenheimers put on creature com-
forts. After a day on the range, exhausting because of the altitude,
Fergusson headed for the wooden ice box. On the way he remembered Robert's miraculous ability to survive with the barest suste-
nance, and he offered a silent prayer as he swung open the door.
Robert had not changed. The contents were a half bottle of vodka,
a jar of pickled artichokes, a scrape of caviar, and a can of chicken
livers.

The effect of the summer on Frank was to leave him with so

many extended thoughts about the conversations that he wrote Robert a list of questions when his brother arrived in Europe for his final tour. He wanted some guidance on art and greatness and humanity, and a dozen other things.

Robert replied at length in his elaborate sentences without saying anything really original, then anticipating Frank's worry about his own personal direction, he added thoughtfully:

> I haven't answered everything you wrote, nor given you any brotherly advice. That is because it seems to me that you are on the right track and because I think you know pretty well what I should say: Discipline, work, honesty, and, towards other people, a solicitude for their welfare and as complete an indifference as possible to their good opinion.

The latter thought was conceivably inspired by Robert's mixed relationship with his new master, Ehrenfest. Though he was impressed that Robert could give a lecture in Dutch a few weeks after studying the language for the first time, Ehrenfest was irritated by the American's habit of lighting one cigarette from another, of paying little heed to his health and appearance. Furthermore, Oppenheimer was too ready to speed over the detailed structure of a theory, which was necessary to understanding, and go straight to the answers. For lessons on a better paced approach, Ehrenfest was happy that Oppenheimer was going to Pauli.

It was difficult to judge who got most out of the Zurich winter, Oppenheimer or Pauli. The American learned from the Austrian's supercritical mind and precision, and Pauli was stimulated by his new colleague's quickness in getting to the heart of any problem, and then spinning off fresh ideas. On the negative side, Pauli worried over Oppenheimer's impatience with mathematics.

"His ideas are always very interesting but his calculations are always wrong," he complained.

Whatever his shortcomings, Oppenheimer's renown in the high tower of physics was established, resulting in stories about him heard everywhere. Pauli, for instance, called him "the nim-nim-nim man" and imitated his way of speaking and gestures, right down to the nervous biting of fingernails. I. I. Rabi, of New York who was then studying in Europe, also had a memorable crack: "Of course, Robert is a very bright fellow, but terribly purse proud about it."

Sailing home that spring, Oppenheimer sorted through a variety of invitations from American universities. The three-thousand-dollar-a-year assistant professorship at the Berkeley campus of the University of California appealed most because he would have a chance to raise a school of theoretical physics from zero. Another enticement was the presence there of the newest star in experimental physics, a former Yale man named Ernest Lawrence. His concern that he would be cut off from the mainstream of physics was solved when the people at Berkeley agreed to free him each spring to study and teach at Caltech.

In retrospect the whole country seemed to go madcap that summer of 1929; it was the wild night before the bitter morning. Whatever was in the air, Robert caught it, too. Loading a wagon with two gallons of bootleg whisky, two gallons of mineral oil—Robert drank it to ease the pain in his stomach and neutralize the whisky—and inappropriate food like peanut butter and Vienna sausages, the Oppenheimer brothers drove to Perro Caliente for a rest.

Friends who came to visit were astonished at the way the slender New Yorkers relaxed. They rode all day, eating nothing but chocolate, and slept out at night on the porch, warmed by their rotgut whisky and with howling coyotes for company. Robert had personally selected the horses and his own was called Crisis. A strong, huge animal that was only half castrated, Crisis allowed nobody else near him. A stranger saddled him one day and was about to mount when Crisis dug his forelegs in and puffed up his belly until the latigo snapped. One week, the brothers disappeared altogether. They rode clear to Colorado.

Ella and Julius Oppenheimer wanted no part of the ranch and persuaded their sons to meet them in Colorado Springs for a brief stay. From somewhere Julius had picked up a used roadster and the boys spent a week trying to drive it. Never had they been behind the wheel of a car, and it showed. Robert drove up to a gas pump one time, went too far past, backed up, misjudged again, and it seemed an eternity before the car was near enough for the gas hose to stretch to the tank.

They headed off on another occasion, with Frank driving. Rounding a curve too fast, the wheels skidded on a patch of gravel and the car tilted on to one side. They were able to right the vehicle, but it took Frank all night to dig them out of the sand. In the morning Robert was white with pain and sipping from a bottle that smelled like spirits of ammonia. The doctor at the next town found that he had cracked a bone in his arm.

By the end of August, Robert felt sufficiently repaired to go to Berkeley, by way of Pasadena, and start his career as a teacher. He took the car, and there was an inkling that the trip had not been easy when the freshman professor arrived at Caltech with his arm in a sling, his clothes ragged, and several days' growth of beard on his face. Not an inch of the roadster was undented, and someone reported that the same car had been seen mounting the steps of the courthouse of a nearby town a short time before.

All Robert would explain was the sling, "It's a red one," he said shortly, "because I wanted to cheer up my brother."

In Berkeley, Physics Department chief Professor Raymond Birge assigned his new assistant to teach quantum mechanics, and, although he had only one student for credit in a class of twenty-five, he went at it with such crackle and fervor that the young men got the impression he viewed them all as postgraduates. Several complained to Birge that Oppenheimer was going too fast and they could not keep up. They were urged to labor more and strive for their teacher's wave length. After four weeks, Oppenheimer himself came to Birge. "It's no good," he said. "I'm going so slowly in this class we are simply not getting anywhere."

Birge had known the new assistant was brilliant; his mistake had been in not finding out just how brilliant. "It was my first intimation not only of the speed with which Oppenheimer's mind worked," he wrote later, "but also of his complete failure at the time to realize how slowly, comparatively speaking, the minds of most other persons worked."

As a painful act of self-control, Oppenheimer quieted the pace and his reward was to be able to expand his teaching to include general relativity. He also worked far into the night in his quarters at the Faculty Club, trying to extend the theories and ideas he received in the mail from Dirac and Ehrenfest and others of the lofty European school. Nobody who knew him then was surprised to learn that he was completely unaware of the national drama that was being played out on Wall Street. The stock market collapsed, depression spread across the whole fabric of the country and the world like black dye, but Robert did not raise his head. The struggles and pain of the present-day world, of real people in real situations, had never caught his interest.

The atom was yielding its secrets very reluctantly, and if one likened it to a jigsaw puzzle the physicists could be said to have put just a few pieces together at various points. It was an international sport in which anyone could participate and the top practitioners worked at it to the exclusion of everything else. There was glory as well as excitement in advancing the play. Nobel Prizes almost assuredly awaited those who made the breakthrough moves.

If indeed he thought about it all, Oppenheimer would have assessed his chances at the Nobel Prize as rather slim because he was more adaptive than creative, more critic than author. His drive came from his compulsion to know and to teach others what he knew. To bring the new physics to America and to make it flourish, that was Oppenheimer's game. And nobody in the whole nation was better equipped to do it, nobody knew more.

When Oppenheimer clattered down to Pasadena for the spring semester he found a worried letter awaiting him from his brother. Frank, who was in his last year of high school before entering

Johns Hopkins University, where he would major in physics, was discovering what he called "wild variations" in his developing personality. He was alarmed that he and Robert could not *know* each other as before, because he, Frank, was finding so many changes in himself.

In reply, Robert was reassuring and pointed out that "inconstancy and incoherence of personal life" was by no means unique to Frank. And he added, "In mature people there comes more and more to be a certain unity which makes it possible to recognize a man in his most diverse operations."

Robert would not indulge in self-analysis, but simply closed his letter to Frank with the light-hearted remark that, "for the purpose of recognition it will suffice for you to know that I am six feet tall, have black hair, blue eyes, at present a split lip, and that I answer to the call of Robert."

He might also have added that he was still running too fast for his classes. While he had hoped for a snappier group of physicists at Caltech all he got were curious listeners and one lone registered student, young Carl Anderson. After the first lecture Anderson found his way to Oppenheimer's temporary office in the Norman Bridge Laboratory and said he was sorry but he would have to cut out. Though just short of his doctorate, Anderson admitted that he was not in Oppenheimer's league.

"Nonsense," said Oppenheimer. "You'll get good grades whatever happens. You have to; you're my only listed student."

It was a sign of things to come that Anderson stuck and he benefitted immensely. Three years later he discovered a new subatomic particle, the positron, and for this he won the Nobel Prize.

Paul Ehrenfest was visiting Caltech, eager to see—and advise—his former pupil. Hearing that Robert was about to give a colloquium, Ehrenfest hurried to his office and warned him not to drop his voice so low that people could not hear him. It was a habit that bothered Ehrenfest.

"Oh, it won't matter," said Oppenheimer. "It will be just a small group in a small room."

Ehrenfest spread a smile over his face, realizing for the first time that the American used his voice range as a theatrical technique. "Dear Robert," he said, "you do *adapt* yourself!"

The striking of attitudes did not make Oppenheimer in any way a phony; it was perhaps more of a guard for his privacy, a public coloring for his solitariness. While he formed a large circle of friends in his first Californian year, nobody ever claimed to be an intimate comrade. But, then, Julius and Ella Oppenheimer did not make this claim either. They came to Pasadena to see their son at that period. Nothing had changed. Julius noted that Robert had become a keen driver so presented him with a huge Chrysler, which his son named Gamaliel after the Hebrew teacher. Ella made her usual check of her son's living quarters, his clothes, his health. "He still coughs far too often and he needs building up," she reported in a letter to Frank. "But he is in excellent spirits."

The following autumn, Ella died of leukemia, and when Robert went east a family friend, knowing of the reticence between mother and son, said, "You know, Robert, your mother loved you very much."

"Yes I know," he said softly. After a pause, he added: "Maybe she loved me too much."

4

Among the physics graduates in the United States in the troubled year of 1932, one of the best scholastic records belonged to a lean, slow-talking young man from the University of Illinois named Wendell Furry. Born and raised in Farmersburg, Indiana, the son of a Methodist preacher, Furry associated smoking and drinking with the worst kind of brazen living, and he had worked tirelessly, with scant distraction, at his studies since he was a small boy. The reward came late, for he was then twenty-five, but it was fabulous in those days—a National Research Council fellowship to pursue science at the university of his choice on an allowance of two thousand dollars a year.

The previous summer Furry had attended a physics seminar at Ann Arbor and was full of his meeting with the famed European theorists Sommerfeld, Kramers, and Pauli. He had heard at first-hand of the keen pursuits in atomic physics and he vowed then to become a part of them. Only one American had been chosen to share the same platform as the exalted trio and that was a bushy haired man from Berkeley who seemed little older than himself.

This man Oppenheimer was fabulous, related Furry. At one symposium he had been presenting a fresh theory dealing with proton action and had covered half a blackboard with equations.

Suddenly, Pauli had jumped up and erased the entire board, saying it was nonsense. Oppenheimer lit another cigarette and resumed where he left off, adding more calculations. Once more Pauli scrubbed the board clean.

The young American looked about him coolly. "Does anyone here see what I am trying to do?" he asked. "If so, please explain it to Pauli so that I can go ahead." Without waiting for a reply, he continued his exegesis.

Two minutes later Pauli rose again, but this time the heavy Dutch voice of Kramers commanded, "Pauli, sit down and shut up."

Pauli complied while the students beamed with delight. It did not matter to them that the Austrian was right and the American wrong about the theory. Sufficient for them was to witness the rebuke to one of the overlords of physics.

All this was heady experience for Furry, but it raised little awe back at Illinois. "There's a lot of highbrow stuff in physics these days," he was told. "It's not for you to concern yourself with that."

For a whole year Furry carried around the thrill of Ann Arbor inside him, not mentioning it again until he had the first fellowship check in his hand. Then he grabbed his wife Betty by the hand and headed west to California.

Wendell Furry's initiation into the world of Oppenheimer after he stepped off the Berkeley ferry, shivering in midwestern cottons even though it was still August, was to be repeated by many other young men in the years ahead.

The Furrys found Oppenheimer on the veranda of the Faculty Club talking with Ernest Lawrence, a glowing exuberant man who was already a full professor at less than thirty years of age. Oppenheimer greeted them warmly and made such a project of settling them in chairs that the couple from Farmersburg were flushed by all the attention. "Good news, Furry," said Oppenheimer, as if the newcomer was the editor of the *Physical Review*, "Ernest tells me they've just begun to get particles out of the big magnet."

Furry nodded and managed a half smile, while Oppenheimer went on speaking. There was a hesitancy in the speech, but each sentence was emphatic and accompanied by lusty draws on a cigarette. Lawrence broke in a couple of times, but Oppenheimer did most of the talking. Fully aware that his new mentor was including him in a vital conversation, Furry felt panic rise in his throat. He had not the faintest idea what they were talking about. Particles? The big magnet? Only later did he realize that the "magnet" meant Lawrence's fantastic new cyclotron, a device by which atoms of various elements could be bombarded by accelerated subatomic particles. It was a revolutionary research gadget.

With some trepidation, Furry attended his first Oppenheimer lecture. Jabbing at the air with a piece of chalk while he made some elusive introductory remarks, the professor then turned and wrote an equation on the blackboard, inviting discussion. Baffled by the equation, and totally ignorant of where it came from, the brightest boy of his generation in Indiana was surprised when the other students actually had something to say about it. There were only three of them—Frank Carlson, Leo Nedelsky, and Melba Phillips—and they had had at least a year of Oppenheimer. Carlson, in fact, was working on a paper with his master in the area of cosmic rays and would soon earn his doctorate. The newcomer watched the proceedings with a degree of shame. Dumbly sitting there with his gilt-edged fellowship, he remembered that the other three were all subsisting on student grants of a few dollars a week and sharing board and shelter that was said to be largely paid for by the wages of Nedelsky's wife.

Weeks passed and there was so little improvement that Furry went home to his wife one night and said they were going back east. "I don't belong here," he said. "I am hopelessly out of my class." Betty said they were staying.

Before the year was out something occurred to put new spirit into Furry. It was the arrival of a talented young physicist named Glen Camp, who drew Furry aside after his first exposure to Oppenheimer and said how puzzled he was that the others sat around and looked wise during the professor's spiel, when he, Camp, was nonplussed. Wendell was able to tell Betty that night that he had a soul brother.

The pattern of life that was to hold for Oppenheimer all through the thirties developed in those early times. A handful of students taking their doctorate under him pored over their books and figured problems of their own—and Oppie's—conception for upwards of sixty hours each week during the fall and winter. With the spring they would jam into the Chrysler and all drive down to more of the same program at Caltech. Another physics professor at Berkeley sniped at Oppenheimer for acting like a mother hen with his chickens, but the crack bothered none in the group. After the initial terror and doubt they gradually picked up to the leader's pace and were proud that few others in America could match them for competence in the science. In the tight international community of atomic physics, they began to make names for themselves. European experts were reluctant to accept that a prime school was now operating in America, and one of the more arrogant was rebuked by Pauli himself. The man had remarked that there was "no real physics" in the United States.

"Oh," Pauli had said, "you mean you haven't heard of Oppenheimer and his nim-nim-nim boys."

Pauli had noticed that some of Oppenheimer's students were imitating his odd little speech mannerism, even copying the way their master shot his arms about and jabbed the air with chalk. While their regard for him was akin to worship, most called him simply "Opje," a pet name coined by Ehrenfest, which was a Dutch rendering of "little Oppenheimer."

It was Oppenheimer's practise to develop papers on various highly specialized aspects of nuclear physics in partnership with his students and their names were appearing regularly in the pages of the prestigious *Physical Review*.

When Furry labored on a particularly difficult formulation with the boss, it was a common sight to see them pacing the streets of Berkeley, engaged in constant harangue. Colleagues would hoist a thumb in their direction and observe that "the Fuzzy and the Furry are in conference."

Once they paused on a corner while Oppenheimer threw up his arms and said, "Wendell, you *have* to rationalize everything. You seem to be completely incapable of understanding anything that cannot be put into words." Furry smiled, gratified by the remark. Oppenheimer rocked back and roared at him, "I didn't mean that as a compliment."

Their project was finally finished and it was an exquisite piece about the behavior of electrons that helped Furry to his doctorate and to a distinguished career as a professor of physics. Outside the science, of course, the whole exposition was hopelessly confusing and impossible to translate for a layman. Few hints of the revolutionary developments in physics leaked out to the general public at this time. The more dramatic discoveries were reported in the newspapers, but the words were so foreign and the relation to daily life so remote that little attention was paid. There was, for instance, a small article in the New York *American* shortly after Chadwick of Cambridge had found the neutron—the chargeless subatomic particle. It said that a certain J. Robert Oppenheimer and a colleague, Frank Carlson, had put up the idea that cosmic rays may be neutrons. Experimental scientists were deeply interested in neutrons since they could whip through the electron cloud to the very core of the atom. If artificially manufactured, the story said, "they can be used most advantageously to bombard atoms and so reveal the innermost structure of matter and how its stored up energy can be released. . . ."

Preoccupation with neutrons, protons, and electrons made Oppenheimer an unsatisfactory companion on occasion. One night he parked in the Berkeley Hills with his lone female student, Melba Phillips. Excusing himself for a minute, Opje got out of the car to take the air. Somewhere out in the trees a problem of physics caught hold of his mind and he just kept ambling along. He walked all the way back to the Faculty Club and climbed into bed, still pondering. An hour or two later a police patrol found a young woman seething with indignation in an abandoned automobile.

This story made a gossip column in a San Francisco newspaper, much to the relish of the campus. Faculty members were not surprised. Oppenheimer's racing intellect was suspected to go dangerously close to the fever point. Birge, for instance, took seriously the rumors that his youngest physics star would disappear into the woods on occasion and yell at the top of his voice to relieve his feelings. "I am told he has been close to insanity or even suicide," Birge said, dropping his voice.

Only at the Perro Caliente ranch could Oppenheimer be seen in any kind of ease. There, usually with Frank at his side, he rode the mountains for summer days on end. Their mother's death had brought the two boys closer together. When Frank graduated in 1933 and went to Europe to study, Robert wrote him a parting line: "The word between us will necessarily be partial only, but let us keep it."

Julius Oppenheimer saw Robert in California frequently and soon became known to his son's students. His contribution to the school was another Chrysler to replace Gamaliel, which was falling into disrepair. Robert named the new one Garuda, after the mechanical bird the carpenter made for the weaver who loved the princess. "It will go ninety at full throttle," Robert boasted in a letter to his brother, who winced at the thought.

The father got the impression that the men his son most liked and admired in those days were Ernest Lawrence—"a delightful person," said Julius—and Arthur Ryder, the great scholar of Sanskrit at Berkeley. Robert had wanted to read the powerful and beautiful Hindu epic *Bhagavad-Gita* in its original and so took lessons from Ryder. Soon he was proficient at the language and expert on the book, and found the exercise so rewarding he recommended it to his associates. Ryder was a joy to know in himself. "What an astounding person," observed Julius, "a remarkable combination of austereness through which peeps the gentlest kind of soul."

Julius was pushing into his sixties then and slowing down. The market crash had taken some of his fortune and this, plus the combination of his retirement from his beloved fabric business and Ella's death, had simplified his life. His greatest pleasure was to share his son's friends, yet he was careful to keep a discreet distance from Robert. "I am meeting lots of Robert's friends," he said in a letter east, "but I believe that I have not interfered with his activities."

The old man was plump with pride for his son's achievements and most of his behavior. If Robert still showed rebellion against Ella's fastidiousness in his personal haphazard habits, he had responded to the influence of Ethical Culture and to Julius' example of a generous and thoughtful spirit.

One time Robert visited the home of Caltech physicist Jesse DuMond and admired pencil sketches by DuMond's fourteen-year-old daughter Adele. Somehow he discovered the date of her birthday and she received in the mail from him a box of oil colors, brushes, and an academy board. It was the sort of carefully aimed gift he had so valued when he was a child. When Bernice Brode, the pretty and vivacious wife of Berkeley physicist Robert Brode, had a baby, Robert sent her a pot containing a gardenia tree. Bernice counted the blossoms: thirty-five. Gardenia was Robert's favorite flower and it was habitual that whenever he went to a dinner or a concert with a group of men and women he would buy a gardenia for every girl in the party.

While this pleased the women, some of the men resented it and, in this period of the Douglas Fairbanks image of red-blooded American manhood, Robert was regarded as something of a sissy. Husbands did not fail to notice that when Oppenheimer was coming to dinner, the cooking took all day and the best place settings were borrowed for the occasion. Always he would arrive with his overscented flowers and the wives would worry themselves sick all night because he barely ate a thing. His appetite was perilously poor. Once at the New Mexico ranch, Tommy Lauritsen, the young son of a Caltech professor, made it clear that he could not get through the day on a smudge of chicken liver. Full of apology, his host drove him to the store in Cowles and said he could have anything. About the only thing Tommy recognized at the first sweep of his eyes was a sack of potatoes. "Well," he said, "I like potatoes." With a look of triumph, Robert summoned the clerk and said, "Give me one pound of potatoes, please."

The colitis Robert suffered in Europe as a teenager still afflicted his digestive tract, yet he continued to try to eat all the exotic foods he fancied. On a hot autumn day in Berkeley he organized the food for a picnic among friends. At lunchtime he got the campfire going and warmed up a huge dish of Indonesian-style rice and chili, to be washed down with French wine. Except for Robert, who just nibbled, the palates of everyone there protested each spoonful. On the drive home, Ernest Lawrence pulled his car into a roadhouse and bought hot dogs for the survivors.

If he was a flop on a picnic, he was disaster at the beach. While husky colleagues like Lawrence would go bounding into the surf, virtually beating their chests, Oppenheimer would hang back toward the rocks, nothing but skin and bone. It did not happen often because he was self-conscious about his naked body and was rarely seen without clothes. Where Robert shone, and where he captivated women and a considerable number of men, was in an intellectual discussion. He and Lawrence ran a Monday night group called the Journal Club, which Robert tended to dominate. Once, however, he was away in Pasadena, and the members were left to resolve a puzzling question without his help. After an hour or so the subject was finally ironed out to everyone's satisfaction. "I must admit I'm glad Robert isn't here," said Lawrence. "He would have settled everything in thirty seconds and we would have had to go on before anyone else really understood the issue."

Lawrence and Oppenheimer were making Berkeley renowned in both experimental and theoretical physics. Despite differences in taste and temperament they were good friends and devoted to the university. People were to remember the balmy days of these two many years later when events turned them into antagonists.

In some ways, Robert was too close to Lawrence; his respect for laboratory result was impeding his acceptance of new theories that by his standards were only half-tested.

In a letter to Frank, then studying at Cambridge University, Robert expressed his irritation. One did not have to be expert in the language of the science to get the message. "As you undoubtedly know," he wrote, "theoretical physics, what with the haunting ghosts of neutrinos, the Copenhagen conviction against all evidence that cosmic rays are protons, Born's absolutely unquantizable field theory, the divergence difficulties with the positron, and the utter impossibility of making a rigorous calculation of anything at all, is in a hell of a way."

Time would show that Oppenheimer's skepticism was not fully justified—he was wrong about cosmic rays—but his tough, critical approach was valued during a period of rather passionate confusion. First there was the atom, then came the electrons and the nucleus, and before these were properly understood a veritable family of subatomic particles of largely undetermined habit and function began to emerge. It was developing into a crowded little world. When Italy's young Enrico Fermi fired neutrons into various atoms, and unknowingly shattered a uranium atom, the physicists charged on to the next hurdle without so much as tightening rein. They did not realize they were playing a lethal game.

Taking the broadest view of man's history, it could be said that some luck was running with the world. Parallel with the growth of nuclear physics in the early thirties came the brutal gagging regime of Hitler in Germany and the murderous repressions of Stalin in Russia. Many of Germany's best scientists were Jews and they were forced to quit the country, Einstein himself coming to the new Institute for Advanced Study in Princeton. The old master was at odds with the mainstream of physics because he had serious reservations about the imprecise quantum theory, but his relocation had the effect of moving the action to America and many followed him. Because of the influence of Oppenheimer and others, American physics was starting to produce clever theoreticians and expensively equipped laboratories. And with Franklin Roosevelt in the White House the climate for intellectual enterprise could not have been better. For the wave of European scientists it was a Utopia. A few of them tried Russia, but no matter how much communism appealed to some of the physicists in theory, the practise of it then was so aligned with purge and terror that minds as well as souls atrophied. Inevitably, the uranium atom was split again, and the fission recognized as fission. But although this happened in Germany, only in the fertile field of American science did this powerful new seed of knowledge take full root and grow. In Russia the soil had turned sour; in Germany it was arid.

Most innocent of the leading figures in this unfolding drama was Robert Oppenheimer. He held himself aloof from politics to the extent that, while others were burrowing into economics to get a perspective on the Depression or pondering the New Deal or making up their minds about communism, Oppenheimer used his excess mental energy to read Sanskrit and to learn to understand Egyptian hieroglyphics. Communication was obviously his forte, but his interest was all in the past. Colleagues accused him of monumental intellectual uppishness. An appropriate line from *Bhartrihari* would come to him easily in a conversation, and he could quote entire poems by Baudelaire. On the face of it this was not so remarkable, but random verse was part of his everyday vocabulary, and there were many people who had not the faintest idea what he was talking about. The sort of exchange that would send his students dizzy with delight would give some of his faculty contemporaries heartburn.

The fact was that Baudelaire was as familiar to him as Born, Donne was much a part of his life and thinking as Dirac. *Les Fleurs du Mal* transported him. Nobody said it better for him than Edna St. Vincent Millay in her introduction to her translation at the time.

Out of his strange and very unhappy mind Charles Baudelaire made poems of great beauty. . . . His subject matter was often, in itself, scandalous, blasphemous, revolting. He . . . was aware of this. He hated . . . the degenerate, the degraded, the deformed. He hated all that debilitated, defeated, destroyed the majesty of the human mind. It was with this particle that he was at war. He proposed to conquer ugliness by making beauty of it.

And so did Oppenheimer try.

Robert had once written to Frank that there was a certain unity which characterized a man in all his operations.

Berkeley people were hard put to pin down the unity that explained Oppie. They knew he was eclectic, putting together thoughts and motives from a hundred sources, but the product was remote, obviously romantic, at once kindly and warm, abrupt and intolerant. The stupid remark continued to freeze him, the luckless perpetrator hating Oppenheimer for his seeming cruelty.

The problem, as Dirac had seen, was that Oppenheimer was both poet and physicist. He sat at the feet of Bohr and Baudelaire, without Bohr's gift of ease or Baudelaire's tortured genius. One imagined at times that he identified with Baudelaire's Albatross, lured and teased by sailors, and would have liked the poet's self-indulgence.

> The Poet is like that wild inheritor of the cloud,
> A rider of storms, above the range of arrows and slings,
> Exiled on earth, at bay amid the jeering crowd,
> He cannot walk for his unmanageable wings.

As the years rolled on, Robert walked more to applause than to jeers.

5

In 1935, Oppenheimer and Melba Phillips broke new ground with a paper on the activity of deutrons (protons and neutrons bound together in single particles). Fire deutrons into atoms, they discovered, and the neutron is stripped off the proton and penetrates the nucleus.

The Nobel Prize Committee gave the work only passing thought, but it was the latest in a long list of superb Oppenheimer postulates that excited the interest of the physics department chiefs in the big eastern universities. Harvard and Princeton offered to double the young teacher's salary if he joined their faculties. Oppenheimer did visit Princeton's Institute for Advanced Study, which was crowded with talent, but after a few hours he rejected the idea of such a drastic change in schools. He took the train to New York, found a female companion and went to a concert at Radio City.

Frank Oppenheimer had moved to Caltech by this time and was plowing through to his doctorate with the idea of becoming a disciple to his brother, whom he had inflated as his measure for life. A pretty Canadian girl, Jacquenette Quam, an economics major at Berkeley, brought the younger Oppenheimer to earth. Jacky's interests were more contemporary than classical and together they explored the good and bad results of the New Deal, the leftist documents on capitalism, involved themselves in the struggles of labor, and even, at that early time, the savage injustices suffered by red and black Americans. Along with thousands of other intellectuals of their generation they dallied with the Communist Party because it seemed a positive expression of their idealism.

Less of a physicist and poet than Robert, Frank had always been closer to the political realities of America. When he had arrived back from Europe he was horrified to discover the breadlines and to read of strong men being kicked out of the subway stations because they did not have a nickel to ride and sleep the night through. On the Berkeley campus he encountered an active group of Young Communist Leaguers who were sold on the idea of the "classless society" and many more students, generally known as the non-orgs, who sympathized with the cause. Socialist firebrands like Norman Thomas and the Australian longshoreman hero Harry Bridges were banned from the campus, but hundreds of young people attended their meetings outside the gates. When the eggs and ripe red tomatoes filled the air at these crazy gatherings, it occurred to some observers that the students were in it for adventure as well as to right the wrongs of the universe.

Because of the utter disorganization of the communist movement at campus level, party leaders from New York were constantly arriving to try to restore order. Unfortunately for them, one regular pep talk to unruly students used the line, "American workers loyal to the Soviet Union." At this point Jacky would dig Frank and roll her eyes at the idiocy of the thought, the speaker would wait for the hurrahs and get nothing but stony silence.

Over the years Frank had gone to Robert for advice and invariably his older brother's point of view prevailed. Robert's arguments were always so compelling that Frank accepted them, though they proved anything but infallible. Now Frank was off on his own road, and Jacky was at least as important to him as his brother. He married her in September of 1936 and a few months later, for all its transparent shortcomings, he joined the Communist Party. The defection apparently hurt Robert deeply, for he wrote petulantly of his brother's marriage, "It was an act of emancipation and rebellion on his part against his dependence on me. Our early intimacy was never again established."

This dramatization of the facts was a terrible exaggeration of the way things were and were to be, for Frank's love was undiminished. Actually, Robert's even-flowing absorption with physics and poetry had been rudely interrupted, not only by Frank's escapades but by an attractive young woman named Jean Tatlock, whose idealistic gropings were as much inward as Jacky's were outward.

Concerning himself with other people's problems was one way for Oppenheimer to step around his own. The trouble was that his solace, so freely given, invited love and a demand for a kind of soul-sharing in return. Until he met Jean, he had succeeded in ducking away from intense personal involvements, but this time he fell in love. A student of psychiatry, ten years his junior, a marvelously educated girl from an academic family, Jean was tall and slender with luminous green eyes, a combination of dark-haired beauty and intelligent compassion that Oppenheimer found irresistible. The matchmakers among the faculty wives finally were at ease, certain that the redoubtable stag of their dinner parties had found his equal.

Together with Jean Tatlock, it was Robert's turn to try to share the agony that beset human affairs in the mid-thirties. The feeling that he had been keeping himself foolishly distant had been nudging at him for some months. In the first place his students were finding it virtually impossible to get jobs. Then, from his aunt Hedwig Stern, and his cousin Alfred, still in Germany, he learned of the Nazi abuse of the Jews and the march of fascism in Europe.

At campus parties then the talk was of the Italian rape of Ethiopia, of Franco in Spain, of the death rattle of the League of Nations. Literary revolutionaries at these gatherings startled Oppenheimer by attacking Roosevelt as an obsolete defender of capitalism, the gilded politician who refused to acknowledge that Marxism was the wave of the future in America, the panacea for all that was hateful in the country. Roosevelt, said the most bitter of these men, was a secret fascist.

For years Oppenheimer had not subscribed to a newspaper or magazine, nor owned a radio, but it had not really mattered to him that the phenomenon of the Dionne quintuplets and the tragedy of the Lindbergh kidnapping had passed him by. Around the turn of 1937, however, society was trembling to its roots, and he set out to inform himself about the reasons and what might happen next. He bought a radio and started to read into the leftist tracts. It was the start of a brief, intense, perplexing interlude. While he read the communist newspapers and, with Jean, attended left-wing campus meetings, he found the party in America rather gross. His reserved judgment was that it was a fly-by-night outfit, yet serving some very worthwhile humanitarian causes.

Its alien nature was illustrated for him one day when he went with Frank and Jacky to a party meeting to discuss the integration of a Pasadena swimming pool. Negro boys were allowed only on Thursdays, so the communists wanted to take a few Negro boys on Wednesday. One black youngster said he was going to bust his way in. "You can't do that," cautioned a party man. "Lenin calls that infantile reactionism."

This was the first and last time Robert got directly involved with the party itself. Several Berkeley intellectuals, recognizing the young physics professor as a free thinker of renown and his girl friend as a sometime party member, claimed both as keen fellow travelers. Perhaps it was not stretching the facts too much for Oppenheimer was a generous contributor to the various fund drives for such causes as oppressed farm workers and freedom fighters in Spain. And he paid membership dues to all sorts of front societies and organizations.

Basically however, he distrusted movements of the communist size. His idea of a "group" was ten maybe twenty people in which he was the dominant voice. He was an activist, and it seemed rather shabby to him to be off in the eucalyptus-scented hills of Berkeley, angrily denouncing the fat cats of the world at Bohemian gin parties, while automobile workers were laying their life on the line for a better deal in Detroit and youngsters were resolutely standing against Franco. He was an "underdogger," as he put it to Jean, but he would have to settle for the periphery. "Oh, for God's sake," admonished Jean, who so desperately wanted to give herself to something, "don't *settle* for anything."

Oppenheimer's love affair was tempestuous, alternately swinging between bitter scenes and whisperings of love and marriage. But as often as Robert proposed, Jean kept delaying. Robert's adoration for the girl was the core of the problem, at least in the eyes of Jean's friends, for he set her on a pedestal and treated her with reverence. His gifts of flowers and perfume and jewellery came in an unending stream, until she was furious. Her ideal was a virile, robust man, someone both gentle and rough, and she wanted Robert to be all these things. The irony was that he needed these qualities in a woman. They were two melancholic people, and often, while they could not bear to be apart, they were in anguish together. It was Robert who kept his outward control, however, and Jean who gave way to passion.

Once, shortly after she implored him, "no more flowers, please Robert," he arrived to pick her up at a friend's house with the usual gardenias. Jean was dressing and when the hostess appeared in the room with the bouquet, Jean asked quietly, "Robert?" When she was told yes, she took the flowers and threw them to the floor. Her voice was tight. "Tell him to go away, tell him I am not here." Then she waited for Robert to come and get her. But all she heard were muffled voices and the front door closing. He was gone.

It did not end there, indeed the dark romance did not really end until several years later. On a cold, war-gloomy January day in 1944, when Robert was far away and Jean was at home in her studio apartment on San Francisco's Telegraph Hill, she filled her bathtub and piled cushions beside it. That done, she swallowed some pills and sat down to write several letters, the last one without any address. ". . . To those who loved and helped me, all love and courage," she wrote. "I wanted to live and to give and I got paralyzed somehow. I tried like hell to understand and couldn't. . . . At least, I could take away the burden of a paralyzed soul from a fighting world. . . ."

The drugs were taking their effect and Jean's writing trailed off into a jagged line. She left her desk and made it across to the bathtub. Kneeling on the cushions, she plunged her head deep into the water. Days later her father, Berkeley English professor John Tatlock, discovered his daughter's body.

On the other side of the country, one of Jean's closest friends had a telephone call with the news of the suicide. Now she understood with shock and dismay the letter she had just received in the mail, Jean's letter that started out, "Save this for tonight, when I expect to be very lonely. . . ."

And, in the mountains of New Mexico, a tall, slightly stooped physicist had a visitor from San Francisco, after which he left his office and walked alone high into the pines.

6

It was a ragged band of young physicists who came to Berkeley in the second half of the nineteen-thirties to take their inspiration from Oppenheimer and to work their small masterpieces about the atom. The painters and writers of legend who starved in garrets for their art had a parallel in some of these men.

Phillip Morrison, a scrappy little man on fire with his science, hitchhiked from Pittsburgh and lunched on cat meat to stay near Oppenheimer and construct tiers of equations about the subatomic world. Sam Batdorf happily lived in a seven-dollar-a-month hovel, repeatedly and angrily condemned by the fire department, to remain with the group. And then there was Joe Weinberg who had originally started from the lower eastside of New York and eventually found his way to the mecca with the clothes he wore and a spare pair of shoes in a paper sack.

These men, and a dozen others, had four or six hundred-dollar-a-year grants as teaching assistants. It was enough to stay alive, but barely. Oppenheimer, not much more than thirty himself, was both father and mentor to them. He coaxed them through study by day and sometimes fed them at night in his small bachelor house in the hills. Speaking of this era in later years they were all more likely to remember Oppie's speciality of green chile and scrambled eggs than to recall anything he said about social justice. And Jean Tatlock was simply the shy, intense girl who was "around." Every two weeks they clambered into Oppie's car to attend a seminar at Stanford, which they usually succeeded in dominating, or at least looked smug while their master ran things, and then on the way back detoured into a concert or a dinner in San Francisco. At the restaurant, Oppie paid the bill, selected the food, the wine, and on occasion helped the waitress serve.

One student, Russian-born George Volkoff, then fresh out of Canada, felt low one night, so Oppenheimer and Jean found him a date and the four of them toured the bars of San Francisco and ended up dancing to a juke box in the North Beach area at two o'clock in the morning.

Opje, as they persisted in calling him, had a program for his students the year through if they wanted it. With the arrival of spring he jammed the men and often a couple of girls in the Chrysler for the jaunt to Caltech. During the summer they were welcome to visit Perro Caliente, ride horses by day and squat on a Navajo rug before an open fire at night playing their own version of tiddlywinks.

To an outsider they were an extraordinary bunch. If they were engaged in conversation for long they kept saying "like so" instead of "thus" or "in this way," they would drop their shoulders in a stoop, pace around, fidget with a cigarette or pipe, and all had the characteristic of lowering their voice to get closer attention. They were Oppenheimers, and, as Rabi would have said, extremely purse proud about it.

Nothing they did could be described as "Joe College." While others were crowding the football stadium, debating whether Joe Louis would knock out Jim Braddock (he did) and turning to the Chase and Sanborn radio hour to laugh at Edgar Bergen and Charlie McCarthy, the Oppenheimers were reading Arthur Ryder's translations and listening to Beethoven's Quartet in C-Sharp Minor, Opus 131, on Morrison's homemade phonograph.

Joe Weinberg claimed this quartet as the theme song of the

group, which was rather illuminating because Opus 131 is perhaps the strangest and most mystical of all Beethoven's compositions. Only on the fifth or sixth listening does the piece begin to lose its incoherence for most listeners. Weinberg counted the quartet as the highest creation of the human mind. When a little whisky had weakened his resistance one night and his eyes teared at the music, Oppenheimer brushed by quietly and said, "Yes, it's beautiful."

It was quite possible that Oppenheimer and his band of five or ten students were the most intellectual cell in the entire country. They lived a separate life because of their immersion in physics and their deep cultural pursuits. Two of the most brilliant of them, Bert Corben and Julian Schwinger, sometimes worked in tandem on a puzzle, a dusk-to-dawn routine they kept up in Corben's flat at the International House while Mozart played in the background.

None of this would have seemed odd in Europe, but the esotericism stood the Oppenheimers apart at Berkeley. Even to Lawrence's experimental physicists they were a different breed. Corben, who came from the aggressively egalitarian Australia, worried that they were a "self-satisfied, self-centered mob." He found the work too gripping to leave, however.

Eavesdroppers had the notion they used a special code in conversation.

"Opje caught me yesterday," remarked Leonard Schiff, then working as Oppenheimer's research assistant. "I was lecturing on the partial wave series for quantum scattering by a rigid sphere in a short wave-length limit, and ending with the factor of two in total cross section two pi-r-squared. Opje was there in the front row and suddenly looked up and said in that quiet voice, 'I see Dr. Schiff has not yet learned the difference between the order of magnitude of a series and its leading term.' You know, I stayed up all night learning the difference."

The story delighted Weinberg; he had also been honored with what he called the "blue glare" treatment from the professor. Oppenheimer's eyes changed from gray-blue to vivid blue when he was stimulated. Weinberg's lecture had been in the area of subatomic particles and the point to which he was too slowly building related to the movement of the particles.

Oppenheimer, in the front, kept muttering under his breath, until Weinberg finally asked him what the devil was bothering him.

"Eppur si muove!" said Opje.

Weinberg was taken aback. "You mean you expect me to understand Italian, and even then to know that was Galileo's remark at the inquisition, 'Nevertheless it moves!' " demanded Weinberg with mock incredulity.

It was a clever piece of impromptu theatre for the listening students, yet typical. Oppenheimer frequently talked in riddles, challenging his boys to find the answers.

Hartland Snyder, who worked as a truck driver in Utah before coming to the school, once argued loud and long about an aspect of general relativity with a colleague. Opje, as was his mysterious custom, happened to appear and asked the problem. When they explained, the arbiter said, "It seems to me the issue is not one of truth, but of aesthetics, that is what all the shouting is about." So saying, he walked on.

Snyder wrinkled his brow in admiration. "Of course, he's right," he said.

However commonplace the incident or the problem, it was a fad among the Oppenheimers to give it special flair. Opje rarely lectured without a cigarette in his hand. He finished a pack one day and then proceeded to smoke the longer butts in the ashtray. Disgusted, someone in the class offered him a Pall Mall, the new king-size on the market.

"Ah-ha," said Oppenheimer, rolling the cigarette in his fingers. "We have here a sesqui cigarette."

Oppenheimer's office in Le Conte Hall, a giant gray-stone building at the campus heart, was open house to the students and two or three times a week he would hold a graduate seminar there.

Anyone in the group could speak, but Opje, sitting on the desk with his long legs dangling, usually took over after a while.

Hideki Yukawa, the distinguished Japanese scientist who had just discovered there must be another particle apart from protons and neutrons holding the atomic nucleus together (a particle later called the meson), visited once and Oppenheimer invited him to tell his boys all about the missing link.

Poor Yukawa had progressed no more than three minutes when Opje interrupted and finished the explanation. No one, except Yukawa, thought this rude. The assumption was that Opje would know the theory much better than the man who thought it out.

Under his paternal care and brilliant guidance, a dozen men earned their doctorates and took their place among the country's best theoreticians. Others who could not keep up with the pace dropped out after a year and were frequently bitter about the seemingly accepted infallibility of the young Berkeley master.

This was sour grapes, of course, though they did have a point. The team of Schwinger and Corben, who both had doctorates before joining Oppenheimer, once approached him with an idea which he rejected out of hand. "Damn nonsense," was his opinion.

The two dropped their line of inquiry and were miffed some months ahead when another physicist followed it through and produced a useful and valid piece of work.

Corben came to realize that while Oppenheimer was fantastic at fitting pieces of the atomic jigsaw together, at taking numbers from the laboratory and making a theory, his fault was in never looking at the big picture. He did not seek to create, to conceive grand ideas, but to work within the framework of known phenomena. This pragmatism was to have a significant effect on American physics, and Corben regretted its superficiality. It was not the way Einstein had worked. To be with Oppenheimer, however, was to do things his way. Corben learned this early in his association. The Australian became sick soon after he arrived at Berkeley, and Opje advised him to go north to Sausalito to recuperate. When

Corben ignored the suggestion he was surprised to find that his professor was offended.

Schwinger also had niggling doubts about Opje's mammoth reputation, though none at all about his powers of persuasion. Just as Frank Oppenheimer was wary of seeking his brother's advice because it was invariably decisive, Schwinger, a self-assured man himself, made the point after he left the school of not seeing Opje too often.

With some trepidation, the younger man gave a lecture once with the master in the audience. Opje did not say a word until afterwards, and even then there was no criticism. "It's just that I could never find that subject interesting," he said. Schwinger had seldom heard such sweet words.

Outsiders were unaware of the seeds of doubt in the camp, and they never did flourish sufficiently to affect Oppenheimer's stature. Morrison was another who resisted being made over into Opje's image, but, like the rest, he was simply "bowled over."

In a moment of mischief Morrison once imitated the boss by putting a dust mop on his head and pacing about puffing furiously on a piece of chalk. This gesture of irreverence led him to the thought that Opje lacked self-appraisal and was too much a striker of attitudes. Actually, each of the students had occasions when they realized that an invisible gap separated their professor from them. It was more than a student-teacher segregation; Opje could not quite be reached as a total person.

Was he really so stunning? Morrison had the question somewhere in the back of his mind at a party when he was sitting on the floor with Opje watching the dancing in the parlor. Casually, Morrison mentioned trouble he was having with a theory. Opje listened carefully while the roadblock was explained, then took out an envelope and made some calculations. "It should be like so," he said.

Weeks later, when Morrison had puzzled it through himself, he took out the envelope and discovered that Opje had hit upon the solution in those few minutes on the floor at a party.

This sort of performance happened often enough to keep Oppenheimer on his mountain, to make the boys feel tremendous pressure to do their best, and to impel several of them to take notes in relays whenever the master spoke, collating them afterwards with all the care they would give to a prized document. As it was with Wendell Furry so it was seven years later with Bob Christy, the boy wonder from Canada. "The ideas are coming so fast I'm snowed," complained Christy, to which the veterans reacted with a pantomime of violins playing.

A main reason for Oppenheimer's high standing was gratitude and recognition for his accomplishment of establishing a California school of theoretical physics that ranked among the best in the world. Corben, for instance, had earned his doctorate at Cambridge, but his work there had none of the zest and personality it had at Berkeley.

None of the Americans went to Göttingen or Zurich any more, for their own country had become the most active center for physics. Two young professors from eastern Europe, Victor Weisskopf and George Placzek, had chosen the Soviet route early in the thirties, but by 1937 both were in the United States to stay, Weisskopf at Rochester and Placzek at Cornell.

These two, inseparable friends, visited Perro Caliente in the summer to ride horseback and talk things over with their old Göttingen acquaintance. Oppenheimer remembered both as keen socialists and since he was open-minded about Soviet communism himself he wondered why they had quit Russia.

Hadn't Opje heard about the purges, the mass murders, the running fear in Stalin's Russia? Hadn't he been told that intellectual freedom was nonexistent? Oppenheimer said he had vague information on these things, yet it was difficult to know how much was true.

Weisskopf reined in his horse and, with the sun glinting off his spectacles and his jaw thrust out even further than usual, he told Oppie that he had better believe every word of it. "We lived there, worked there, it's worse than you can imagine," said the Austrian.

He searched for the right English phrase, then said, "It's a morass."

Weisskopf, who was to become one of America's most distinguished physicist-citizens, noted that while Oppenheimer took the conversations seriously his interest in communism was at a detached intellectual level. Communism was simply one subject among dozens to which the American turned his mind. It made a more lasting impression on Weisskopf that his friend knew by heart the poetry of Rainer Maria Rilke, the German lyric poet.

Julius Oppenheimer died of a heart attack in September of 1937, shortly after he signed the affidavits sponsoring as immigrants his sister Hedwig, her physician-son Alfred, and Alfred's wife and children. When the liner docked at Hoboken, Frank and Robert met their German relations with the news of Julius's death and assurances that they would stand by them until Alfred had a practice and the family was properly settled. Soon they were residents in Oakland, a mile or two from Robert's house.

To Alfred, who remembered a skinny and nervous youth of bookish behavior, his cousin had developed into a considerably more relaxed and content person. He was encouraged to ask Robert how they would fare in America; what America was really like.

"It is big here," said Robert, as nearly as his cousin could relate later, "not just geographically, but in thinking and spirit. You can move with ease from place to place and among people of all social rank and economic standing. And all people have the possibility to a high degree of influencing their destiny because they have the democratic means. There is a direction for the people and for the country, but this is re-evaluated all the time. You have seen atrocities in Europe and you wonder, can it happen here? I would reply that there is a lack of coercion here, a depressurizing safety valve built into the very nature of a democracy like America's. Totalitarianism is far less likely here than in Europe."

With Alfred Stern as a neighbor, Oppenheimer's foreign interest focused on Nazi Germany. The Russo-German nonaggression pact signed in the summer of 1939 killed any lingering sympathy

for the Soviet Union and the German invasion of Poland in September dominated his thoughts as nothing outside physics and
poetry had ever done before.

There was no way to tell, right at that moment, that he was now
of a warrior profession. He knew that the thrust into the cosmos
in which he had enlisted fourteen years earlier had unlocked the
atom, not only in theory but in fact. But to mobilize those atomic
forces for war, that had not occurred to him . . . not yet.

7

Robert met kitty in the fall of 1939 at a garden party given by Charles Lauritsen, Caltech's celebrated experimental physicist. She had recently moved to Pasadena with her husband, Richard Stewart-Harrison, a young English physician who was working in the Caltech X-ray laboratory. Kitty herself was a graduate student in botany at the University of California. Petite, brown-haired, vivacious, a sparkling thirty, Kitty was described even by women as desperately attractive.

Lauritsen warned Kitty when he introduced them that Oppenheimer was unbelievable. "He gives you the answer before you ask the question," said the experimentalist, who knew his friend as well as any man outside Frank. If this was supposed to put Kitty on guard, it did not work. She spent the afternoon in Robert's company, and by the time she collected her husband Dick for the walk home she realized she had fallen for the chain-smoking professor from Berkeley.

Always recklessly impulsive, Kitty had even surprised herself this time. For his part, Robert was infatuated with the girl and with the little she had told him of her past. In the days that followed he learned more, all of it intriguing. The romantic in Robert was stirred; he called Kitty "golden."

Katherine Puening had been two years old when she emigrated from Germany to America with her parents and settled in the Pittsburgh suburb of Aspinwell. Graduating from the local high school in 1928, Kitty—she never used Katherine—enrolled at the University of Pittsburgh to major in botany. Her high spirits prohibited a conventional student's life. Within a year she was off to France and Germany to continue her studies there and while at the University of Munich she saw the beginning of the National Socialist movement. It so repulsed her that she left her parents in Germany and returned to the United States, entering the University of Wisconsin.

Extremely restless, she tried marriage to a young musician but it did not work and it was quickly annulled.

Back in Pittsburgh for a New Year's Eve party at the end of 1933, she met a dashing young revolutionary named Joe Dallet. Though he had graduated from Dartmouth and his father was an investment banker in New York, Joe was a dedicated communist who wore a cloth cap and spent every waking hour organizing the steel workers in Youngstown. His tough, sometimes bloody occupation frightened a variety of college girls who adored him, but it was an adventure to Kitty. She packed her books in Wisconsin and traveled back across the country in that deep depression winter to share Joe's life.

They married and rented for five dollars a month half a slum house in Youngstown. In the other half lived party stalwarts John Gates and Aarvo Alberg who was to become known as Gus Hall.

Joe and Kitty lived on a small allowance from Joe's father, and relief money, and they steadily got thinner. The house did have a stove, but it was not functioning and they mostly took their meals at a soup kitchen—fifteen cents for soup, meat, potato, cabbage, doughnut, and coffee. After an initiation of selling the *Daily Worker* outside factory gates and passing out leaflets at the mills, Kitty was allowed to join the party. Her duties then were to type letters and mimeograph pamphlets. Suffering the wolf whistles or

insults of steelworkers, she also stumped the grimy town when
Joe ran for Congress on the communist ticket.

Two years of stark poverty killed the excitement for Kitty.
Gaunt with a mixture of overwork and fervor, Joe was not enjoy-
ing it much either but he refused to leave. Tearfully, and still
loving him, Kitty walked out on her husband in the early summer
of 1936 and joined her parents in England. Her party membership died forever when the New York skyline dropped below the
horizon.

Away from the terrible mills of Youngstown, Kitty's spirit revived and she felt ready for another try with Joe. When she wrote
him that she was coming home, he told her to go instead to Cher-
bourg in France, for he was on his way to join the International
Brigade in Spain. Their meeting at the dock and the ten days together in Paris were an interlude that transcended party and Spanish cause; two handsome young Americans wandering the boule-
vards, deeply in love.

When Joe took the train south, Kitty pleaded with him to
arrange for her to come later. Eventually he arranged with a guide
to bring her across the Pyrenees. She hurried out of London in
October that same year and went to a rendezvous in Paris. There
was a message awaiting her: Joe was dead, killed in action.

In agony, hating herself for deserting Joe in Youngstown, hating the party, Kitty walked the streets alone now. She was brought
around to reason by Joe's friend, Steve Nelson. He was American
and he was a communist, but he was a gentle man and Kitty sat
with him and talked of Joe and was comforted. She did, however,
firmly reject his idea to go to Moscow to live.

Her life was rather aimless after that, or vacant anyway. She returned to New York, a forlorn little girl of twenty-seven, and
visited Florida with friends before resuming her botany studies
at the University of Pennsylvania. Out of loneliness she married
Stewart-Harrison, but stayed behind in the east when he went
out to do his internship in Los Angeles. Freshly graduated with
honors, she drove to California to join her husband, and there she

was, almost fully sprung back to her old verve, when Lauritsen asked the new neighbors to a garden party to meet the remarkable Oppenheimer.

The winter and spring dawdled for Oppie. He was anxious to get to the ranch and ride the mountains with his friends, who this summer would include the Stewart-Harrisons. As it turned out the doctor was caught up in research and could not make it, so Kitty went alone. The danger of an affair was there and the other visitors felt it inevitable from the first time Kitty lifted easily into the saddle of a young mare, touched her heels to its flanks and took the east fence at a leap. Oppie watched with undisguised affection.

In the fall of that same year Kitty set up her six weeks' residence in Reno, Nevada, and went straight from the divorce court to a justice of the peace to be married to Robert.

The Berkeley hostesses were aghast when Oppenheimer returned with his bride. Such torrid conduct seemed so out of character for their Oppie and unfair to the much liked Jean Tatlock, that Kitty was openly snubbed by several of them. "Oh, let's face it," said one of the more reasonable wives. "It may be scandalous, but at least Kitty has humanized him."

Oppie had run off with another man's wife, his flesh was as weak the next man's. On campus his stature declined and he was regarded as far less intimidating. Indeed, his social life took a sharp upward turn among what was then called the fast set. Intellectual talk, dancing, and drinking until the early hours of the morning was the usual party format, though the Oppenheimers usually departed early.

It was also a hectic time in physics and Oppie wanted to be at his desk no later than ten in the morning. It could not be earlier, he explained, because he needed a thinking period in bed, a practice he said he acquired from Descartes who attributed his great productivity to the fact that he never arose before noon.

For Kitty it was something of a rebirth. She devoted herself to her new husband and allowed echoes of her former life to intrude only rarely. Once, she invited Steve Nelson and his wife to the house. They had recently moved into the Bay area and although Nelson remained an avid party organizer Kitty liked him for his understanding when Joe Dallet was killed.

Steady companions of the Oppenheimers in those days were Haakon Chevalier and his wife Barbara. The hearty, gregarious Chevalier, then teaching in the French Department at Berkeley, was regarded as an opportunist by many, or, as one of Oppie's oldest friends put it, a "guy with his eye on the main chance." Yet when others were treating Kitty with some disdain, the Chevaliers offered nothing but warmth, and for this Oppie was always grateful.

In later years the French teacher was to write a book about his friendship with Oppie, recalling with enthusiasm how the two of them toiled in the service of the left-wing Teachers' Union. An anecdote related how they sat up half the night addressing and stamping envelopes that carried the latest documents to members. Others were to put a different slant on this episode. Apparently Oppie was indeed a power in the local chapter, but he was so unsure of what to do with it—and what the union should stand for— that his local simply evaporated.

His influence went the way of all the Oppenheimer communist connections, for by now even Frank and Jacky had quit the party. Nevertheless the family was red-tinged on the record and the brand was not easily erased. Certainly there could be no hope of keeping the past a secret. Unerringly, the public spotlight went to the darkest corner of a man's life if he became at all celebrated in America. The new Justice on the Supreme Court, Alabama's Hugo Black, had just gone through hell to clear his name when a newspaper announced that Black had once and very briefly been a member of the Ku Klux Klan.

Oppenheimer's prescience about the communist bogey was nonexistent. Not only did he continue to have Chevalier, an announced radical, as a fast friend, he put himself firmly in his debt. In the early summer of 1941, after an awkward pregnancy, Kitty had been weakened by the birth of a son, Peter. Robert himself had mononucleosis. They longed for the recuperative air of the Sangre de Cristos, but it seemed out of the question until the Chevaliers insisted on taking the baby for a few weeks—not a small favor because Peter was barely two months old and required constant attention.

With Frank and Jacky for company, the emancipated parents drove up to Perro Caliente in July. Quickly strengthened, Robert and Kitty spent a week putting new shingles on the roof. One of their first full riding days ended in a small disaster. Robert was trampled by a horse and twisted his knee. After treatment by a doctor in Santa Fe, Kitty helped Robert into their new Cadillac, named Bombsight, and headed north. At the entrance to Pecos Canyon they had a head-on collision with a truck, ruining the car and bruising Kitty's legs.

Kitty was thus confirmed to be as accident prone as Robert, who at various times at the ranch had been knocked unconscious by overhanging branches, sprained wrists, and, once, wrenched his back when a pack horse he was trailing behind reared up at a creek crossing. The back, like his digestive track, caused him discomfort all his life.

Mishaps notwithstanding, New Mexico always had an expanding effect on Oppenheimer's personality; it seemed to blow clean his arteries, reduce his phlegmy cough, and increase his stride. The big silver-buckled belt he wore to keep up his pants and the strong leather boots gave him a trace of swagger. With Kitty at his side, the vigor was more pronounced. She was a woman of spunk and she proved it in an admittedly frivolous way that summer at the ranch by cantering a horse around the meadow while standing up in the saddle.

They returned to Berkeley in high mood, frowned at their undistinguished rented house, and sought a place better suited to their style. They visited an artist friend in a rambling Spanish American villa high atop the hills, overlooking the Bay. Steps tumbling with ivy hid the house from the road and pines had put a carpet of needles on the apricot-colored tiles of the roof. Inside it was cool with redwood floors and beamed ceilings.

Oppenheimer walked around the place muttering, then came to his friend, a woman, and asked her how much she wanted for the house. She mentioned a figure, and Oppenheimer sat down right there and wrote out a check.

When news of the purchase spread to his associates they said Oppie's sense of theatre had never been more vividly illustrated. It was not the way he made the buy, but the address of the house: 1 Eagle Hill.

Oppie's move into this house coincided with the major turn in his life. In the beginning it was a chance conversation. An Australian physicist, Marcus Oliphant, was in Berkeley to consult with Ernest Lawrence, and Oppenheimer joined them for lunch one day. Unprompted, Oliphant started talking about uranium fission and the chances of using it to make a bomb. He had been working in England and frankly discussed the optimism there of developing such a weapon. Lawrence looked uncomfortable, particularly when the Australian applauded the new cooperation between his country and the Americans on the bomb inquiry. It was September, 1941, and Oliphant had just revealed to Oppenheimer one of the most delicate of all war secrets. Clearing his throat, Oppie mentioned quietly that perhaps the visitor had better not continue because he was not involved in the project.

"But that's terrible," said Oliphant, unabashed. "We need you."

Across the table, Lawrence, who was a key member of the American inner group, nodded vigorously in agreement. Within weeks he had Oppie on the train with him to Schenectady, New York, for a secret progress meeting of the special bomb committee of the National Academy of Science.

With his background as a theorist who greatly respected experiment, the thought of making an explosion by chain reaction splitting of uranium atomic nuclei had occurred to Oppenheimer. What he did not know was that Britain and the United States had been tackling the problem of making an actual weapon for many months, and that the spur to their work was the sinister assumption that German scientists were similarly engaged. Einstein's equation on the equivalence of mass and energy made it fairly obvious that a fission bomb, if it could be made, would explode with terrifying force.

The sequence of events leading up to September, 1941, was this: German physicists Otto Hahn and Fritz Strassmann had bombarded uranium with neutrons in 1938 and split the nuclei of uranium atoms roughly in half. Hahn told his former colleague Lise Meitner, who had just fled the Nazi Jewish purge, and she and her nephew Otto Frisch proved in the laboratory that enormous energy was released when the two parts of the uranium atom flew apart. They wired their friend Niels Bohr to this effect soon after he arrived in the United States in January, 1939. Bohr wrote an account of the discovery in the *Physical Review*, and physicists immediately conjured up the thought of a chain reaction. The splitting of a uranium nucleus would release more neutrons to split more atoms, and so on—causing generation of energy. With the right controls there could be a steady flow of power, or, unchecked, there would be a great explosion. Out in Oppenheimer's smart little group the Bohr article had taken fire instantly. Corben and Snyder spent one afternoon working out a formula for a uranium bomb on Oppie's blackboard. At New York's Columbia University, Italy's gift to America, Enrico Fermi, and others immediately began experiments to try to produce a controlled nuclear fission chain reaction. By October President Roosevelt had been persuaded to encourage explorations into a possible bomb. Technical problems were awesome, and secrecy was a severe handicap in a science that moved best with open communication. There was much activity—more by the desperate English than the Americans—during the next two years, but Oppenheimer still came in close to the beginning after Oliphant dropped his own small bomb at lunch.

The Schenectady meeting of blue-ribbon scientists behind a guarded door at a General Electric laboratory was really the point at which the physicists stopped circling the problem and faced it directly.

In his usual robust way, Lawrence sought to put down the skeptics and insist on a positive approach. Oppenheimer, the surprise guest, backed his Berkeley colleague and, in his own fashion, took over the discussion for some time in exploring the physics of the bomb. Simply expressed, they all agreed that they would get a bomb of "superlatively destructive power" by clapping together sub-critical pieces of the highly fissionable uranium isotope 235 into one mass that would explode. They did not know how much of the rare 235—less than 1 per cent of natural uranium—they would need, how to get it in big quantities, how to fire the parts together, how fast the neutrons would go to work, nor how big a bang would result. It was remarkable that with so many gaps in their knowledge they set a timetable in that fall of 1941 at no longer than four years.

United loosely under the banner of the new Office of Scientific Research and Development, directly responsible to President Roosevelt, the scientists split off in all directions, each working on a piece of the puzzle. In later years even the official historians failed to present a coherent pattern for that period. It was a makeshift operation pushed along by the clever Roosevelt confidant and whip-lean Yankee scientist Vannevar Bush; the austere, razor-sharp Harvard President James Conant; Nobel laureate Arthur Compton; Ernest Lawrence; and several others who rated columns in the *Who's Who of American Science*.

Perhaps the most spectacular performer in the early stages was Lawrence, who converted his cyclotron into a spectrograph to produce the precious 235 isotope by an electromagnetic method. Oppenheimer, meanwhile, was dividing his time between the Radiation Laboratory on the hill, his classes, and snappy calculations into how much of the theoretical energy captured in the uranium nuclei would be liberated on detonation and into more precise figures on the critical mass of U-235 needed for explosion. All this was an unexpected bonanza for student Stan Frankel. Not a brilliant theoretician and therefore excluded to some extent from the Oppenheimer "in" group, Frankel despaired of making his doctorate. He was, however, a gifted mathematician and Oppie sought his help on the nuclear studies. Frankel produced a great sheaf of equations that had his teacher ecstatic.

"You know, Frankel, I think you have just written your dissertation," he said.

When Frankel said it could not be eligible because the work was secret and the examining committee could not see the material, Oppie just waved his hand as he had seen Lawrence do so often and made the successful recommendation.

"What a remarkable display of gall," Frankel told himself as he walked home. Another protégé, a foreigner, was not surprised. He had had to prove himself a student, not a research assistant, to stay in America. At semester's end, Oppie had simply pulled out a phony examination card and marked him straight A's.

It was a cavalier time for the nuclear team at Berkeley, and their exuberance worried Bush and Conant in Washington. There was a danger the atomic bomb would become the talk of the campus. Conant decided to send an Army intelligence officer to Berkeley, under cover of course, to check the security. The assignment went to First Lieutenant John Lansdale, a young blue-blood lawyer from Cleveland and a Harvard graduate. Fresh from field artillery and a novice in spying, Lansdale listened with feigned assurance as his university president talked about the bomb and the need for the strictest secrecy to prevent word leaking out to either the Germans or the Russians. Conant made a few comments about the understandable ignorance of scientists about security matters, gave Lansdale a copy of a Lawrence article in the *Physical Review* about atomic fission, and told him to report in a month.

A few nights later Lansdale, in a well-tailored civilian suit, wedged his athletic frame against the bar in the Overland Limited and struck up a martini conversation with a man who identified himself as a professor of German at Berkeley. Introducing himself as John Lansdale, Cleveland lawyer, the young officer said he felt he should join the Army, but first wanted to complete some legal research at the University of California. It was his plan, he added, to live at the International Club and work in the library.

Delighted by the dedication of the stranger, the professor gave Lansdale a letter of introduction to Max Radin, the head of the University law school. The name made Lansdale smile, for Radin, like a dozen others at Berkeley, was listed as a suspected socialist in the F.B.I. files he had studied. He had not forgotten his instructions about the Russians.

On the first day Radin took Lansdale to lunch at the Faculty Club, where most of the noise came from a long table full of intense young experimentalists from the Radiation Laboratory.

"What's their specialty?" asked Lansdale.

"Something to do with the atom, apparently very important," replied Radin casually.

With a start like this, Lansdale never looked back. Within two weeks he was lunching at the long table and learning all about the uranium work. As an added stunt, he stole a blueprint from the Radiation Laboratory that detailed a cross section of the spectrograph.

Back in Washington, he was promoted to captain and instructed to return to Berkeley as official security officer. For maximum impact, Lansdale ordered everyone concerned in the atom project to the Faculty Club and stood atop the long table. "I'm here to give you hell," he said by way of introduction.

The craziest thing about the Radiation Laboratory, and several in the Oppenheimer group, too, was that key uranium researchers were staunch members of the Federation of Architects, Engineers, Chemists and Technicians, a union that was openly leftist.

Using the membership list as a rough guide, and including the names of non-union nuclear principals like Oppenheimer and Lawrence, Lansdale set up a huge switchboard in the basement of a house in Oakland and put in about thirty telephone taps and room microphones all over Berkeley. Kitty was the first to notice in the Eagle Hill house. When the telephone rang and the conversation began there was a click and then a hollow sound on the line. "We're tapped," she said matter-of-factly. Though the bug stayed with the Oppenheimers for many years to come, both took it for granted and never mentioned it again.

Lansdale's snooping might have been regarded as melodramatic if the Japanese had not attacked Pearl Harbor right then. Suddenly everything was in deadly earnest, America itself was in danger, and those scientists who had looked on the fission experiments primarily as an intriguing, unlikely game, either eased themselves out of the program in favor of higher priority war jobs or they doubled their work load to get some solid results.

The green light to build an atom bomb had actually been given the day before Pearl Harbor, and under the new urgency Arthur Compton called Oppenheimer and the other enthusiastic bomb men to his offices at the University of Chicago—unofficial bomb headquarters—in an attempt to get the project properly organized. There was so much disagreement about the value of what had been accomplished and how to proceed further, Oppenheimer itched for command. If he had one sure talent it was to take the raw milk of theory and experiment and separate the cream. Even his intellectual daring diminished, however, before a panel that included Nobel Prize winners like Compton, Lawrence, Fermi, and the chemist Harold Urey.

A decision was made to centralize chain reaction tests at Compton's Metallurgical Laboratory in Chicago—where Fermi was indeed brilliantly successful—but the work on the bomb design continued without real direction. Gregory Breit, professor of theoretical physics at the University of Wisconsin, had struggled to coordinate knowledge against tough odds of the now crushing security and a personal distaste for administration. After an argument with Compton, Breit quit, and the call went out for Oppenheimer.

While he realized the project was in what he called "bad odor," and the gossips held that it would never get anywhere, he leapt at the challenge. Nor was he deterred when Compton, a steady, reli-

gious man he had known since Göttingen, gave him the responsibility without any means or organization to carry it through.

John Manley, a conscientious young physicist with a fine
background in nuclear studies, became Oppenheimer's associate
—Manley making the measurements in Chicago and Oppie making the theory. The Californian's theatrical manner and lightning
mind had a quite devastating effect on Manley. They worked well
together, grabbing in results from seven different places, as often
as not sorting out the good grain while Oppie nibbled on chicken
livers at Isbel's restaurant in Chicago.

8

THERE WAS ABOUT Oppenheimer then the gravity and enthusiasm of a child, producing in colleagues a desire to please him. At an unguarded moment at Chicago's North Western station, when Manley and his family were seeing him off, Oppenheimer and two-year-old Kathy Manley loitered together at the window of a gift store. A display rack was hung with shiny pocketbooks and Kathy gazed at them to the oblivion of everything else. A few minutes later they came along the platform with Kathy clutching Oppie's sleeve with one hand and hugging a gleaming red purse with the other. A look of wistful sadness never left the scientist's face.

For just an instant it was all there, the nature of this individual at once vivid and unfathomable, a glimpse of a hesitant hero, deprived of a conventional childhood, taught the reverence of life and the goodness of man, who had faltered through to his Corsican conviction of melancholy as a state of grace.

Brooding had ceased to be a weakness with him, preferring to pass off less attractive memories with little jokes. To Kitty's many questions about his early family life, he would say he did not have a childhood and did not really know his mother. When Kitty persisted, Robert finished by telling an anecdote about his penchant for sleeping. His mother had called the doctor and complained that all he ever wanted was to sleep. "Well," said the physician, "let him sleep." Two weeks later, Ella had telephoned the doctor again. "What do I do now?" she demanded. "He's still asleep." Robert chuckled, and the conversation moved on to another subject.

Amazing to Kitty, whose past had brought her into contact with such a wide range of men, was her husband's faith in the lessons of Ethical Culture. He did not believe in the existence of evil; maybe misdirection, ignorance, stupidity, arrogance, but not a definite force called evil. Kitty sought to dispossess her husband of this notion, but, with the exception of foolishness, his habit for a long time was to isolate a man's good qualities and accept these as the genuine article. Purposely blind to the shortcomings of friends, Oppie's intense loyalty was thus less puzzling.

Few injustices, man to man, could not be solved by talking things over and appealing to reason in Oppenheimer's view. His faith in the power of communication was profound. And so it was in the spring of 1942, when he faced obstructions in the approach to making a bomb from nuclear fission, that he gathered together a bunch of top theoreticians at Berkeley to hammer out a tighter program. Among some of his own associates and students were dazzling minds not long out of Europe, ace physicists like the aristocratic Swiss Felix Bloch, the dynamic Hungarian Edward Teller, the thoroughgoing German Hans Bethe.

Security officers, already dismayed at the foreign accents, insisted on locking them inside Oppenheimer's office on the third floor of LeConte Hall. The room had glass doors opening on to a balcony and this, too, was sealed off with a heavy iron netting. Out of the meeting came a more disciplined attack on the essential calculations needed for a practical bomb and one final and horrendous worry about the feasibility of the whole operation.

Oppenheimer called Compton at his summer cottage in northern Michigan and was on the next train east. Compton picked him up at the local station and they drove slowly through the woods while Oppenheimer explained calmly that he and his colleagues were concerned that an atomic holocaust might explode the oceans of the world. While fission released fantastic energy, so did fusion —the combining together of atomic nuclei. Under intense heat, hydrogen nuclei could fuse with other nuclei. An atomic explosion might therefore generate enough heat to set off the hydrogen in sea water, perhaps even explode the nitrogen in the air.

Mercifully out of the public's sight, the scientists checked and double-checked the physics of this monstrous possibility and concluded that it could not happen, an atom bomb was "safe." In their minds, however, and particularly in the brain of Teller, was the possibility of a fusion or thermonuclear bomb.

In view of the firm presidential order to proceed on the bomb, the scientific, industrial, and Army teams charged with various areas of responsibility began to take shape through the summer and fall of 1942. Army counterintelligence ran intensive screens on each man's political and personal background. At Berkeley, Ernest Lawrence and physics chief Raymond Birge were given their top security clearances, and both recommended Oppenheimer without qualification. Agents were uncomfortable at Oppie's own recent Red connections and aghast at the records of his wife and his brother.

Birge's confidence in his young professor was so strong, and his assessment of Oppie's worth so extravagant, that one agent penciled in a tentative "okay" with the comment, "Well, I suppose there is no one else."

Washington had more reservations, however, and Compton received a call in August saying Oppie was not usable. The physicist telephoned Lieutenant Colonel Kenneth Nichols, who had been coordinating with him for the Army Corps of Engineers, and Nichols said the main strike against Oppenheimer was his membership in two or three communistic organizations. The Federal statutes, explained Nichols, prohibited Government funds going to anyone who advocated the overthrow of the United States Government by force. Compton, a shade bemused by the official jargon, replied that he would vouch for Oppie's loyalty whatever his political or humanitarian views. All right, said Nichols, who was on uncertain ground himself, maybe the answer to the problem was to get Oppenheimer to sign an affidavit saying that he did not seek to overthrow the Government by force.

The next dialogue in the telephone drama, which was all tapped by intelligence anyway, was between Compton and Oppenheimer. "I'm cutting off every communist connection," said Oppie. "I want to work for the Government and don't want anything to interfere with my suitability." He agreed to sign the affidavit suggested by Nichols, then rang off to figure out what organizations he still belonged to that could be Red.

On the ineffectual intellectual fringe during the Spanish War, an anguished bystander through the German atrocities, Oppenheimer was determined to take a combative role in this war. Nobody could be allowed to interfere.

Impatiently he waited while the Army Corps of Engineers cranked the whole bomb operation into the highest priority, started construction of the laboratories and plants to get the raw material, purposely found an innocuous name for the project, the Manhattan Engineer District, and produced a managing director, Brigadier General Leslie Groves. A husky, conceited career officer in his middle forties, the son of an Army chaplain, Groves was generally disliked and actually challenged by Vannevar Bush because of his lack of tact. Groves stayed put, however, as he usually did, and visited Berkeley to talk with Lawrence and Oppenheimer.

Behind the burly front of Groves was an extremely shrewd and single-minded man, who knew enough in his judgment of other people to subordinate personality to talent. To his mind, Lawrence was top score in both departments and the two became close friends and companion rooters at the football game on every available winter Saturday. On the other hand, Oppenheimer fell immediately into the Groves category of intellectual eastern Jew with no morals, a pigeonholing that came easily to him when he heard the gossip about Oppie's hasty marriage and his flirtation with communism.

Having sized up his man, Groves then put his estimation to one side and asked Oppenheimer in his role of super scientist what was needed to hurry along the actual bomb design program.

"We've got to find a way to open the lines of communication between the physicists," replied Oppie. "The secrecy is slowing down everything. This thing will never get on the rails unless there is a place where people can talk to each other and work together on the problems of the bomb. There's just got to be a place where people are free to discuss what they know and what they don't know and find out what they can."

Groves liked the idea, which he saw manifested as a laboratory under tight Army rule in a remote section of the country. Turning it over in his mind as he traveled to Chicago to check with Compton and Fermi, he kept thinking of the slender theorist with the direct gaze. "Those blue eyes," he said to nobody in particular, "they look right through you."

In Chicago he called Oppenheimer to join him and they continued the discussion about the secret laboratory in Groves' roomette on the Twentieth Century between Chicago and New York.

Within the month, Oppenheimer and another young nuclear physicist, Edwin McMillan, rode out from Santa Fe on horseback with one of Groves' staff, a Colonel Dudley, to find a place to devise and assemble the bomb. Dudley chose a hidden valley, which Oppie rejected for the simple human reason that it would give the scientists an oppressive, hemmed-in feeling. Groves joined them late in the day and at Oppie's suggestion they left the horses and drove to Los Alamos, a mesa high in the mountains northwest and around twenty miles crow's flight from Santa Fe.

Huddled on the mesa were the timber and adobe buildings of a boys' school, which was barely struggling along. "Here," said Oppenheimer, sweeping his arm in the direction of the snow-topped Sangre de Cristos and his own distant ranch of Perro Caliente. Groves nodded affirmatively.

When the general moved, he really moved. By November he had acquired Los Alamos and set Oppie to work on designing the laboratory and houses and recruiting personnel. It was Groves' notion that an experienced administrator like Lawrence or Compton would head the laboratory, but neither of these two could be released from their present duties and nobody else seemed to fit the order. Oppie more or less got the job by default and then only after Groves and Nichols personally guaranteed his indispensibility. Military intelligence, which still had not finally confirmed his security clearance, objected to the choice. It was clear when it was given that if Oppenheimer transgressed Groves would go down with him. Meanwhile the files on Oppenheimer were kept in the current cabinets, and Manhattan security men trailed him twenty-four hours a day.

Delighted at the appointment and deeply grateful to Groves, Oppie submerged everything else in his life to get Los Alamos into action. He wore himself down from a reedlike 125 pounds to a skeletal 113 pounds in stumping the country and coaxing physicists to join what was still envisaged as a military post in the wilderness. In the joy of being hired, Oppie had quickly agreed to an Army commission, but others turned thumbs down on wearing a uniform and living under Army regimen. To get the reseachers he wanted, Oppie realized it would have to be a civilian laboratory. He felt foolish at ever believing otherwise.

From university to university he went, his pipe sending off plumes of smoke, his trench coat flapping and his new pork pie hat—"now I'm married I should wear a hat," he had told Kitty—slanted forward against an imaginary wind. He was asking the best creative scientists he could find available to pick up their wives and children and live for a few years in the mountains. The enthusiasm he exuded was contagious and he recruited excellent department heads—Cornell experimentalist Robert Bacher, chemical whiz-kid Joe Kennedy, industrial scientist Cyril Smith for the metallurgical division, and Hans Bethe for the theoretical department.

The volatile Edward Teller had hoped for this last job and Groves, the student of human nature, always imagined that what was to become a famous enmity between Teller and Oppenheimer really began when the Hungarian was passed over. Teller came anyway, though he was never a team man and tested Oppenheimer's patience with his odd working hours and separate lines of inquiry.

Harvard's Ken Bainbridge, who knew firsthand of the British work, was one of the anchor physicists, and among the others were John Manley, a Princetonian named Robert Wilson, who shared Oppenheimer's love of horseback riding and became a close friend, Oppie's Berkeley research assistant Robert Serber, a fellow Berkeley professor Robert Brode, and another old acquaintance Victor Weisskopf.

They came singly and in pairs and then virtually by the dozen, mostly young men with pony-tail wives and often babes in arms. Fourth generation Americans were intermingled with recent emigrants from Europe. Later, they were joined by Englishmen and then even the great Dane himself, Niels Bohr. One day they were at home tending the garden in places like Englewood and Birch Valley; the next day they had disappeared, sometimes traveling under assumed names and all bound for New Mexico where their address would simply be Box 1663, Santa Fe.

Oppenheimer himself could not keep track of all their specialties and identities at first. His old friend from Göttingen, Ed Condon, was there as associate director trying to get some order in the makeshift quarters in both Santa Fe and Los Alamos. Confronted with a list of fifteen young physicists to assign, Condon collared Oppenheimer striding by in the converted schoolhouse.

"Robert, who are all these guys?" Condon asked waving his list.

Oppie grabbed the paper, glanced at it, handed it back, and strode on. "I don't know," he said over his shoulder. "I got them as a job lot in Princeton."

Condon was the first casualty. Robert had encountered him by chance in a Union Pacific coach and asked him to help establish

Los Alamos. For a month Condon labored like a beaver, but his irreverent and breezy manner offended Groves. Condon argued about security, thought it ridiculous to keep everyone confined within the Los Alamos fences, and worried about where his daughter would go to high school.

"Thousands of our boys are dying out there in the Pacific," fumed Groves. "Can't you make some sacrifice?"

"Of course, I can," Condon shot back, "but I'm not going to make any damn fool sacrifices." With that he wrote a long letter of resignation and went to fight the war in another laboratory.

The sight of soldiers riding the Los Alamos barbed wire fences on guard duty always struck Oppenheimer as rather bizarre, although he himself had begun to pay some attention to security. When he and Kitty had moved out to New Mexico with young Peter to live in March of 1943 he felt he owed some explanation to his brother Frank.

"We won't be around for some time," he said. Then he added limply, "We're going into a cooperative venture."

Jacky grinned at the obvious subterfuge. "You mean the Twin Pines." (This was the name of a local cooperative grocery.)

Robert's eyes snapped to Charlotte Serber, the physicist's wife, who was also there. His immediate thought was that Charlotte had been dropping clues about their destination because one of the main landmarks at Perro Caliente was the Twin Pines gate. Jacky intercepted the angry look and quickly explained her joke.

Another incident just before he left Berkeley aroused him more. Haakon Chevalier stopped by the Eagle Hill home for a drink and when the two men were alone in the kitchen Chevalier mentioned a conversation he had had with a British friend, George Eltenton, a Shell Oil Company engineer who had recently moved into the area.

Eltenton, who had lived in Russia and still felt sympathetic to the Soviet cause, moved with the rapid Berkeley left. This clique included several scientists and Radiation Laboratory technicians whose indiscretion, as Lansdale found, was grotesque. Eltenton had heard that Oppenheimer was involved in a top secret war job and he suggested that in the interests of Soviet-American cooperation Oppenheimer might be persuaded to give details to the Russians, no doubt meaning the Russian consulate intelligence officers in San Francisco.

Chevalier said he was horrified at the idea but still he carried this extraordinary proposition from friend to friend, seeking to make Eltenton sound a little more substantial by mentioning that the Englishman's wife Dolly was a first cousin to Sir Hartley Shawcross. Actually this was untrue, and it was the one part of the story about which Eltenton ever got angry, but then Chevalier was very impressed with titles and celebrity. Oppenhemier's reaction was to become "visibly disturbed," as Chevalier remembered it, and when the physicist had to recall the incident he remembered saying something like, "But that would be treason. . . ."

If it occurred to Oppenheimer that he should report this conversation to Manhattan security officers, he soon rejected the idea. Attempted Soviet spying was not to be equated with German espionage in his view. Russia was an ally and it did not seem impossible to Oppie that the United States Government would inform Moscow about the atomic bomb project as a friendly act, perhaps as reassurance that America was working to match any super weapons that the Nazi military scientists might develop. His objection was to Eltenton's bid to get the information out of the back door.

The heroic stand of the Red Army at Stalingrad in January of 1943, and the counteroffensive that was bringing the Axis forces to their knees, had sent gusts of admiration for the Russians through Berkeley. The Communist Party members and fellow travelers, including some of Oppenheimer's students and friends, were outspoken in their pleas for closer alliance with the gallant Soviets. It was common knowledge that Berkeley scientists were engaged in the development of new weapons, and the Soviet consulate officers in San Francisco, embarrassed at being so far from the real action, were aggressive in their quest for details.

In the emotionalism of the time it seemed that only the Amer-

ican security establishments, whether F.B.I. or Army counterintelligence or Manhattan's separate squad, kept doggedly insisting
that the Soviet-dominated Communist Party was the avowed
enemy of the American Government. Lansdale, now the colonel
in charge of all atomic bomb security, was fighting a side battle in
Washington against commissioning party members as military
officers.

Dozens of the scientists recruited for Los Alamos and the other
atomics laboratories around the country had left-wing back-
grounds. Accepting them was always a calculated risk, measuring
their discretion against their value. In these circumstances it was
virtually impossible to preserve the secrecy of the project itself,
and, in fact, the scope and aim of Manhattan were known to Moscow early in the program.

Oppenheimer was not aware of this leak, but there could be no
question in his mind that the Eltenton probe was not an isolated
incident. His wife's old friend, Steve Nelson, was still moving
freely about Berkeley on his assignments for Soviet communism—
and Oppie could reason that there would be far more obvious and
sympathetic marks than himself for information among those who
were in some way connected with the project. Whether or not
these people would leak information would be, to his mind, a
matter of character, and he completely trusted the people closest
to him who had once been party enthusiasts, his brother (now at
the Radiation Laboratory), his wife, and his friends, Robert and
Charlotte Serber.

He might have been less sure about some of his students and
research associates except that it had become practice among the
theorist group to go to the master in case of trouble or doubt.
Oppie served a priestlike role, everything in strictest confidence.
Several even consulted him on their love affairs. Without question
his word was trusted and this confidence gave him great pride.

Chevalier passed on the Eltenton approach to his friend without
a moment's fear that Oppie would ever implicate him. While simi-

lar incidents were never specifically recorded, Oppie almost certainly was told privately about other potential spy attempts.

Trust in Oppenheimer gave Los Alamos its special impetus right from the start. He arbitrated the personal differences, directed the construction of housing, made the final decisions on what lines of inquiry to follow and what to reject, told the scientists when to get up and when to go to bed. A certain mystique was attached to the man, for time and again when a group would reach a dead end Oppenheimer would uncannily appear on the scene to open a fresh avenue. He was the man who stood between the cloistered scientists and old "Iron Pants" Groves, and he kept away the irritations of Army interference.

In the first few weeks of the laboratory on the mesa, when most of the men and women were still living a barracks life, a Colonel Herman became disturbed at the romantic appetite of the young scientists. He prepared a general order which read, "Male callers to the women's dormitories will be received only in the recreation rooms. Their presence in the sleeping rooms is prohibited."

Oppenheimer saw the order before it went up and dashed off a memo to Herman saying, "I sincerely hope that no such rulings will be posted. I can assure you that they will not be obeyed." The order never reached the bulletin board.

Nothing had changed with Oppie. Despite the weight of his new responsibility and his new prestige, his own judgment was king with him. He was still the same man who faked examination papers for foreign research assistants and awarded doctorates on a freelance basis. He was the Great Protector.

In the wartime scatter of his students only one was left stranded and lost. Oppenheimer went back to pick him up and get him settled down for the duration. This was not an easy task, for although this Oppenheimer protégé had a fresh doctorate, few colleges relished the idea of hiring Shuichi Kusaka.

Shu, as the Berkeley crowd called him, had been born in Osaka, migrated to Canada at age five and come to Oppenheimer from Vancouver around 1940. He was in America on a non-work visa and could not return to Canada because he was not a citizen there either. Oppenheimer coaxed the American immigration authorities into changing his visa, explaining that Shu could not go home to a Japan whose policies he abhorred. Oppie then found him a job as physics instructor at Smith College, in Northhampton, Massachusetts, warning Shu that he would have to turn the other cheek to a lot of insults.

The people at Smith did not flinch, and Shu survived the catcalls downtown. "My arrival in Northhampton caused quite a row," he wrote to Oppie in New Mexico. "Some people and certain organizations objected strongly to the invasion by a Jap."

Even after a time at Smith Shuichi Kusaka could not get his citizenship, so, again with Oppie pulling strings, he managed to enter the Army. This made him a surer candidate for his papers, and when they did finally come through—this was after the war— he asked Oppie to get him out so he could teach physics at a university. Oppie came to the rescue for the fourth time and Shu ended up at Princeton.

It seemed a particularly senseless cut of fate when on Shu's first summer vacation from his proud position as assistant professor of physics at Princeton, he drowned.

For Oppenheimer, who had been at Shu's side through the torments and trials of the previous years, it was a cruel death. He had loved the indomitable little Japanese. Within a few days he received a letter from Canada, from Shu's sister Haruko, and he preserved it always. With no attempt at Oriental formality to a stranger, Haruko wrote, "Shu loved you so much, much more than anybody else in the world."

And Shu was not alone. When everything else was breaking loose, there was always Oppie to seek out and talk to. One of the earliest of his students, Sid Dancoff, was teaching at the University of Illinois in later years when the doctor diagnosed in him terminal cancer. Dancoff kept the tragedy to himself, not wanting to give his immediate family and friends unnecessary pain. But he had to tell someone, and it was Oppie.

"You have been an important, even decisive influence in the lives of many of us," Dancoff wrote Oppie shortly before he died. "I suppose you occupy a special position for us, even after we have left your immediate protection and it seems natural to confide in you things that affect us deeply."

9

Cooperative was the right word for the Manhattan district; American industry had never seen anything like it. Corporations, big and small across the nation, were enlisted by Groves to turn out special products and often to assign large staffs to develop entirely new gadgetry and equipment.

The most pressing problem was not so much in the early stages with Los Alamos but with making the raw material for the bomb, either the uranium 235 isotope or plutonium, the savagely fissionable element discovered at Berkeley by chemist Glenn Seaborg. Scientists thought in terms of micrograms of these substances; for the bombs they needed pounds. Groves ordered construction of giant multi-million dollar plants to separate the materials from the parent natural uranium.

In the hills of Tennessee, fifteen miles from Knoxville, mushroomed the secret town of Oak Ridge. Its purpose was to build and operate two 235 factories, one to separate the precious isotope by Lawrence's electromagnetic method and the other to get it by gaseous diffusion.

Lawrence's way was to shoot uranium gas into a strong magnetic field, which divded the paths of the lighter 235 atoms and the bulk 238 atoms, and in this way collect the 235. It was cumbersome, expensive, and the end result was a speck of the isotope, but then the second technique was equally troublesome. Uranium gas was forced through a filter and since the lighter molecules traveled faster the gas on the other side was richer in 235. Repeat the process a thousand times and there was some degree of purity.

Later, at Oppenheimer's suggestion, a thermal diffusion plant was added to the Oak Ridge complex. While this was the simplest method—uranium gas was passed through a chamber containing a hot and a cold pipe, causing light 235 to separate to the hot pipe —the purity of the resulting uranium was not sufficient for use in the bomb. However, by using the enriched material from thermal diffusion in the electromagnetic plant the technologists were able rapidly to accelerate their production.

Hanford, a village on the west bank of Washington State's Columbia River, was taken over for nuclear reactor plants. In December of 1942, under the west stands of Chicago's Stagg Field, Enrico Fermi had demonstrated the world's first self-sustaining chain reaction of fissioning uranium nuclei. He did it by piling up natural uranium and graphite blocks, the graphite to slow down the lightning fast neutrons so they could split more nuclei. Fermi needed fifty tons of uranium to get to the critical level, but he had proved that chain reaction could and would happen. It would happen in a far more instant and explosive way in a small quantity of the sensitive 235 isotope. It was also a fact that some of the sluggish 238 was transmuted into plutonium in the reactor pile. Since plutonium had fission properties similar to those of 235, Groves had no hesitation in organizing its production at Hanford. Nobody could guarantee success at either Oak Ridge or Hanford, and certainly not at Los Alamos. It was a two billion dollar gamble.

Oppenheimer and his brilliant coterie of scientists figured they must get an explosion of tremendous force as soon as either 235 or plutonium reached a critical mass where the chain reaction sustained itself. How to get that mass without premature explosion, how to detonate it, and how to fit the whole works into a bomb casing that could be carried on an airplane was an immense and complex problem. With only a few hundred grams of the 235 and plutonium trickling into their laboratories the experimental work was frustrating.

They had an idea of using the gun method to explode the bombs—to fire one subcritical piece of the metal down a six-foot gun barrel into the second piece. But then they discovered to their horror that this would be all right for 235 but not for the quicker, deadly plutonium because the time lapse, as infinitesmal as it was, could lead to a fizzle. It was suggested then that they would surround a separated ball of plutonium with explosives, detonate them to send the pressure inwards and not outwards, and compress the plutonium halves to the critical density that way. Through the weeks and months the chemists and physicists traveled down a dozen false trails before hitting on the right one.

Los Alamos grew from a population of hundreds to thousands, yet still a strangely ingrown community. Up there on the mesa, more than seven thousand feet in the sky, it was an artificial, even adventurous life common to shipboard. Oppie was the skipper and he was given the same soaring respect as any Cunard liner captain enjoyed from his passengers.

Instead of deck tennis and shuffleboard there were horses to ride and slopes to ski in the winter, square dances, concerts, and private parties. There were no idle rich, no invalids, no unemployed, and few people over forty years of age. The birth rate was spectacular, and Kitty Oppenheimer was to add to the number with a girl, Katherine, whom everyone came to call Toni.

The inhabitants wandered the pine-floored valleys and scaled the pastel pink escarpments, marveling at the purity of the white clouds against the rich blue sky. Once a week the women went shopping in old Santa Fe, gunning their jalopies along the dusty road that snaked down and through the mountains. The ponderosa gave way to pinion and juniper and down further to the aspen that flooded the hillsides with gold. A rickety wooden bridge crossed the narrowing Rio Grande and then the road passed Spanish pueblos, thickets of cottonwood, roughly made sapling corrals, tumbledown adobe houses, and a scatter of excited chickens and skinny dogs.

Privations of living in square four-family houses that lacked adequate water and heat and real privacy would not have been tolerated anywhere else, but on the mesa it was part of the romance. The sinister purpose of Los Alamos was hard to keep in the mind as month followed month in this postcard land. Scientists looked on it as an epic laboratory experiment.

Oppie was one of the few who journeyed regularly to Berkeley, Chicago, Washington, and Oak Ridge, and at least away from the mesa his perspective returned—and it troubled him. Unalterably he wanted to build the bomb and he wanted it to be a success, meaning a gigantic explosion, because in a way the size of the bang would measure his achievement. He was now a munitions maker, a dealer in death as they called it. He pondered the ethics and the justification of seizing on the great fund of world nuclear physics knowledge and turning it into a destructive force. Usually, the justification won out—the Germans could be after the same thing. Some of his thoughts he wrote to Jean Tatlock, the most sensitive person he knew outside the project, but since he could give no context to his muse, nor say where he was or what he was doing, Jean found his notes mystifying. She told her friends she did not know how to reply. In any event she was more concerned with her own personal torments. After several anguished letters she implored Oppie to return from wherever he was and give her the comfort of his compassion and understanding.

In June of 1943, on one of his trips to Berkeley, tailed as he well knew by a security man—one of them foolishly wore a bright yellow scarf—Oppenheimer visited Jean Tatlock in her apartment in San Francisco and talked all through the night. The agent's report to his district chief, Lieutenant Colonel Boris Pash, was dynamite when the girl's identity was checked and matched with her past.

Even if Pash, a former high school football coach, had not

been so violently anti-Soviet himself, his report to Washington
might have been damning. As it was he did not stop short of
recommending Oppenheimer's immediate dismissal.

Again Groves came to the rescue with a flat order that Oppenheimer stay; it was either that or admit that he had been wrong
about the trustworthiness of the Los Alamos director, and Groves
was not a man to admit error. "Decision making in a hurry is the
key to success," he had once explained. The Berkeley professor
was proving to be an excellent administrator and every scientist
Groves spoke to at Los Alamos congratulated him on his choice of
Oppie. It was the general's firm opinion that Oppie was the most
intelligent man he had ever met. The faith he put in him, however, was a matter of pure hunch—a hunch he was willing to back
with his career. When Lansdale asked the general what he would
do if Oppenheimer was indeed a spy, Groves said without hesitation, "I'd blow the whole show."

Lansdale took it on himself to become personally acquainted
with Oppenheimer after this and visited Santa Fe for a long,
though general discussion about the importance of security with
the Los Alamos head.

He also sought Kitty's company on subsequent occasions and
the two of them came to enjoy their dialogues, stimulated by
whisky and given the bite of quick, aware minds at work—one trying to get to the core of motive and commitment and the other
knowing it. The message Lansdale received from Kitty was that
Robert was going to deliver an atomic bomb to the Army, and
nothing mattered but the desire of both Oppenheimers to win
and deserve celebration in their own country.

The on-base security man at Los Alamos, debonair young Captain Peer de Silva, had apparently decided to follow the same tactic
as Lansdale. He sought to divine Oppie's true character by pumping Kitty. Several times when the husband was away the captain
escorted Kitty to parties at the camp. Her signals must have been
strong, for de Silva's first conclusion reported to Washington, was
that "Oppenheimer is deeply concerned with gaining a worldwide

reputation as a scientist and a place in history." The captain kept up his chivalry to Kitty, but unaccountably grew tougher on Oppie, finally telling his superiors he was a Russian agent.

Toiling night and day to get the design for the bomb on a half-way promising tack, Oppenheimer paid scant attention to the cat-and-mouse security game. Los Alamos was a closed shop, once a man came he stayed, and since Oppie knew everyone privy to the vital information he was convinced there was no leak to either the Germans or the Russians. That was enough for him.

However, he was indebted to Groves for giving him the job and vouching for his veracity, and since secrecy was a passion with the general Oppenheimer did his best to indulge him in this respect.

One of his most brilliant students, Rossi Lomanitz, who had been detached to Lawrence's crew at the Radiation Laboratory for nuclear calculations, had run afoul of security because of his alleged loose tongue and quite openly expressed left-wing sympathies. Lansdale's office had seen to it that Lomanitz was served with draft papers to get him into an Army boot camp and away from classified material. Lawrence had complained that this was madness; he needed Lomanitz and if he went then Lawrence would have to take two mathematical physicists from Los Alamos to compensate.

Typically, Oppie thought he could solve the whole problem by talking to Lomanitz, a young man who looked on him as a God-head. He did visit Berkeley and reasoned with Lomanitz, in company with his friends of like mind, Joe Weinberg and David Bohm, but first he checked with the local security man, Lieutenant Lyall Johnson, to make sure this meeting was in order. As he was leaving, he made a casual comment that was to haunt him for the rest of his life. The real troublemaker in Berkeley, he said, was the union, the Federation of Architects, Engineers, Chemists and Technicians. This organization had stirred up Lomanitz and the others, putting damn fool notions in their head. It was as pink as sunset and while most of the members were probably 100 per cent

loyal, some must be spy prospects. In particular, said Oppenheimer, he was thinking of one of the union organizers, the Englishman George Eltenton, who was an enthusiastic Red. In his
opinion Eltenton should be watched closely.

Johnson was young, a lawyer fresh to the intelligence service,
but he was not stupid. When Oppenheimer went off to plead some
sense into Lomanitz—not very successfully in the light of the end
result, for he was drafted and shipped out to the Pacific as a private
—Johnson called Boris Pash to tell him of the random remark
about Eltenton. Pash immediately sent word to Oppenheimer to
see him the next day.

The microphones were on and the hidden dictaphones whirring
silently when Oppie came in to face his hunter. They exchanged
pleasantries and talked of Lomanitz. Pash was after bigger game
and Oppie sensed it. As a favor to the man, he sought to make the
Eltenton tip worthwhile.

Oppie mentioned hearsay evidence about a man in the Soviet
consul who had indicated he could transmit information by microfilm without danger of leak or scandal. Indirect approaches had
been made to people in the project and the one name he had
heard as a possible intermediary was George Eltenton.

"He has probably been asked to do what he can to provide information," said Oppenheimer. "Whether he is successful or not,
I do not know, but he talked to a friend of his who is also an acquaintance of one of the men on the project and that was one of
the channels by which this thing went. . . ."

Oppie realized he was talking too much. The last thing he
wanted to do was to throw a fresh shadow over himself, and he
was honor bound to keep Chevalier out of it, so when he touched
dangerously close to his own specific incident he smoothly backed
away and said that to go beyond this point "would be to put a lot
of names down of people who are not only innocent but whose
attitude was 100 per cent cooperative."

Years of student-teacher relationship had accustomed Oppie to
have the last word and when Pash continued to bore in for more

detail, his reaction was briskly and firmly to instruct the colonel, that, apart from Eltenton, there was nothing to worry about. Pash was conceding that the people who brought Oppenheimer the information must be trustworthy, when Oppie interrupted for the third time in mid-sentence and said he had known of two or three advances to men who were very closely associated with him, therefore beyond doubt.

Up to this point Oppenheimer had stayed near to his true assessment of the events that had happened some months before and were already vague in his mind. His dominant thought of that period was of Chevalier. He could not mention him, but the name was there, the mental picture of the tall French teacher in his Eagle Hill kitchen.

And Pash was saying, "These people . . . were they contacted by Eltenton direct?"

"No," replied Oppenheimer, remembering his friend's awkwardness.

"Through another party?"

"Yes."

The damage was done; he had admitted a middle man between Eltenton and the scientists, which was not the true nature of the operation at all. Chevalier had spoken only to him, he was sure of that.

Pash had the scent and there was no stopping him. Oppie puffed on his pipe and fidgeted, but beyond saying that the intermediary was a member of the faculty at Berkeley and not connected with the project he would not further identify him.

The two agreed that it was Pash's job to be a bloodhound. Oppie countered with the opinion that it was his own duty "not to implicate these people who are acquaintances or colleagues and so on of whose position I am absolutely certain—myself, and my duty is to protect them."

By the end of the interview Oppenheimer had satisfied himself that Pash had given up and the issue was closed. His concern as he headed back to Los Alamos was Lomanitz and whether Lawrence would raid his staff when the boy was drafted. Johnson had said Lomanitz was dangerous and Oppie was inclined now to give him up as a lost cause. Two weeks later, when he was in Washington, Lansdale called him around and he just assumed the subject was Lomanitz again.

Lansdale disposed of the side issue quickly and then eyed the physicist with a stern friendliness. Pash's latest angry memo had convinced him that Oppie remained pigheaded and naïve about security. He would shake him up. He drew from Oppie a concession that the most dangerous information to leak to Russia would be the extent of the commitment on the bomb and the time schedule. Then Lansdale directed his blow: the Russians already knew these things from spies, and clearly the informants were men and women still loyal to the Communist Party, whether or not they declared themselves members.

One confidence invited another, as Lansdale well knew, and Oppie volunteered that his brother Frank had made a definite severence. Lansdale agreed, though he admitted reservations about Jacky, which Oppie did little to contradict. Then the intelligence officer came to his key question, the name of the intermediary Oppie had mentioned to Pash, the man now noted in the security files as having approached three members of the Manhattan project on behalf of Eltenton. Oppie refused once more; to name Chevalier now would be recklessly unjust, and to backtrack on the error and reduce the Chevalier contact to one, himself, would reveal what looked like deviousness and threaten his position.

Fighting to keep his temper, Lansdale asked if Oppenheimer would expose the man under any circumstances.

"If I had any evidence or anything came to my attention which was indicative that something was transmitted. . . ." His voice was so low then that Lansdale could not hear and did not wait for him to finish. The arrogance of this statement, this dogged Oppie-knows-best attitude that Lansdale heard whenever he visited Los Alamos was too much for him.

"I'm telling you it is," Lansdale snapped. "Right today I can't tell you the last time information was passed, but I think it was about a week ago."

Though he remained adamant about not telling the name, the rebukes softened Oppenheimer to the extent that he answered fairly and frankly every other question Lansdale put during the long morning dialogue. The scientist kept lighting and relighting his pipe and often got up to pace the room. The colonel smoked cigarette after cigarette until the room reeked with the stale smell of tobacco.

Lansdale excelled at cross-examination and his witness could not twist away from the tough, direct questions. The pressure was new to Oppenheimer, and his personal code of honor began to crack.

His intellectualism took over, balancing the supreme importance of the bomb project to himself and his country against the reputation of a few friends.

Agreeing that membership in the Communist Party was incompatible with employment on a secret war job, he told Lansdale that Rossi Lomanitz and Joe Weinberg were still members, that Charlotte Serber was formerly a member and her husband Robert may have been, that Hannah Peters, the wife of project physicist Bernard Peters, was once very close to the party, that Jean Tatlock was at one time a member, and ironically that his friend Haakon Chevalier was "quite a Red." It was Lansdale who introduced Chevalier into the discussion.

These names, and several others mentioned, were not new to Lansdale but he had known little of Bernard Peters, who was then working with Lawrence. Oppie said the German-born Peters had always expressed great interest in the communists and had been imprisoned in Dachau concentration camp by the Nazis for his activities. Peters escaped and brought his wife to the United States. About four years ago Peters had enrolled with him as a student, and had been a very good one.

The conversation moved away from Peters then, but his name was added to the list of suspects. About a year later, in another security briefing, Oppie conceded that Peters could be a "danger-ous Red" for all he knew. He lived to regret he had ever men-tioned him in the first place, but the fact was that Oppie had developed an intuitive dislike for Peters.

Towards the end of his talk with Lansdale, after he had given so much secondary information, Oppie relaxed and confessed that he wished he could give the one name the colonel wanted. "But I would regard it as a low trick to involve someone where I would bet dollars to doughnuts he wasn't involved," he said.

To which Lansdale, who had already expressed his personal re-gard for Oppenheimer, responded with a brisk, "Okay, sir."

A paramount thought in Oppie's mind as he took the train west was just how much harm he would do Chevalier if he did name him. He did not know even where he was and what he was doing. From the meeting with Lansdale, however, it was obvious that his friend was already on the files as a possible Soviet sympathizer. This meant that he would not be hired on to responsible wartime work in any case. As with Eltenton, the worse that could happen would be that he would be put under surveillance. They could not draft him, as they were doing with Lomanitz, because Chevalier was too old.

His question was answered shortly afterwards, for he received a note from Chevalier, postmarked New York. None of the cordial bluster of old was there, just misery. "I am in deep trouble," he wrote. "All my foundations seem to have been knocked out from under me and I am alone dangling in space, with no ties, no hope, no future, only a past. . . . I am close to despair and in such a mo-ment I think of you and I wish you were about to talk to. . . ."

Unknown to Oppenheimer, the French teacher had taken a year's leave from the University to work for the Office of War Information. The west coast office had sent him to New York for assignment in September, but since then he had been waiting around in cheap hotels and attending literary cocktail parties while his security clearance was considered.

While none of this was indicated in the note, Oppie could assume that Chevalier's forlorn state was attributable to his Red-tagged dossier in the security files, to difficulties in his rather tempestuous marriage, and probably to inaction in his true love, novel writing. He replied with a friendly, encouraging letter suggesting that Haakon was just a victim of the malaise of the times, and barely a week after he mailed it off he obeyed General Groves' order to name the mysterious middleman in the Eltenton affair.

It was apparent that Chevalier was a suspect and could not be in a more demoralized state than he was now. By naming him and assuring Groves that Chevalier, by his nature and competence, could not be seriously considered as an atom spy, Oppie did not feel that he had done his friend a disservice. In general terms, he also told Groves that the entire Eltenton affair had been distorted far beyond its importance.

Oppie's reasoning turned out to be dead right. Chevalier was denied his security clearance, and thus freed was able to concentrate on his writing and teaching, which he did happily and with some success until the war's end.

The adolescent wrangling that had gone on for months revealed much about the naïve view Oppenheimer had of world politics, and of human nature. Kitty still had not taught him enough about evil.

While many American scientists and statesmen secretly hoped the atom bomb would never be a reality, the chances were strong that it would be. Oppenheimer's own conservative estimate was that the first rudimentary bomb, if it worked, could raze a city center and kill twenty thousand people. The first country to possess the bomb could tyrannize the world if that was its policy. And Russia, under Stalin, was capable of just that. Temporary allies or not, Soviet knowledge in 1943 of any scientific details of the Manhattan district would be disastrously premature. Understandably, Groves stoutly maintained that nobody in Russia could duplicate his feat in under twenty years. More objective forecasts by Vannevar Bush and James Conant were four years. It was not utterly impossible for Russia to beat America to the punch.

The time would come, when success was closer—and this could be within months—to inform Moscow so that east and west could devise some formula where they could live in peace with the monster. But certainly not in 1943. Oppie's men had not perfected a thing, and Oak Ridge and Hanford were yet to produce. In this context, Oppie's name game was absurd and dangerous.

Right then Bush and Conant were joining with other key policy men in Washington in resisting the full exchange of atomic information with Britain itself. Early impetus for the program had come from England but now that country was being shut out. The Americans worried about the blatant favoring of one ally over another, and the repercussions this would have later, and about Britain's commercial exploitation of the American atomic work.

Prime Minister Churchill argued that if the two nations did not cooperate on the weapon production, Germany or Russia might win the race to develop it for international blackmail. The Americans insisted they must reserve the right to limit England's commercial and industrial application of atomic energy after the war. In August, 1943, Roosevelt and Churchill signed the Quebec Agreement, authorizing collaboration but leaving postwar atomic initiative in the hands of the United States.

By December, the first English scientists arrived at Los Alamos. Soon there would be twenty, including the morose young theoretician who was assigned to Bethe's vital department, Klaus Fuchs. His mother driven to suicide by Nazi persecution, his father in a concentration camp, Fuchs had turned to aggressive communism long before he escaped to England from his native Germany. In his sallow face burned the eyes of a revolutionary, in his belly was the fire of a martyr. His talent as a physicist earned him a place on the British atomic team and he was an asset at Los Alamos. There could be no suspicion that he would pass on the most intricate details of bomb design to Soviet couriers. He said nothing, just watched and worked, and fed on his passion to serve the cause of Soviet communism.

10

The year 1944 saw Groves barreling about the country refusing to take no for an answer on anything. With majestic authority and priority, he was able to appropriate men, money, machines, and brainpower to stagger the imagination. He was like an Atlas holding the whole project on his shoulders. Dismay at Hanford, distress at Oak Ridge, a succession of wrong guesses and backtracking at Los Alamos—nothing could diminish his confidence that he would deliver atomic bombs in the first half of 1945.

But time was running out for Groves and his dream of the Sunday punch to bring victory for America on all fronts and make his country, whose morals he trusted as implicitly as his own, the supreme power in the world. Allied bombers reduced Cologne, Hamburg, and Berlin to rubble. Then came the fall of Rome and the June 6 Normandy invasion. Russia punched through Finland, Rumania, Bulgaria. Germany was crumbling and it had nothing in reserve.

Reports from on-the-spot intelligence teams, which included Boris Pash, revealed that Germany had not really started work on making an atomic bomb. The original motive for the American program was gone, but there was no thought of stopping. The genie was halfway out of the bottle. Russia was aware of uranium fission and chain reaction, and Washington knew that the Soviet's American spy apparatus had given basic information on the mammoth Manhattan district complex. Was it time yet to inform Moscow—and the world—officially of the bomb and to begin negotiations on a new postwar order of disarmament and cooperation, based on the total unacceptability of a competitive race to arm with doomsday weapons? The point was, could America expect Russia to leave it with a monopoly on atom bombs?

Niels Bohr was one of the first to see clearly the peril ahead and he personally urged Roosevelt as early as August, 1944, to tell the world about the bomb and initiate international control of atomic energy. Soon afterward Roosevelt and Churchill discussed the issue at Hyde Park and flatly rejected Bohr's proposal. Their thought was to take an Anglo-American approach to the postwar atom world. The miscalculation was that the technical details could be kept secret. The formidable team of Bush and Conant, who thought Bohr's proposal a shade premature, was nevertheless generally in favor of international control after the war. In their view a policy based on the hope of continued secrecy was the height of stupidity. When French scientists who had been attached to a phase of the bomb program in Montreal returned to Paris and passed on their knowledge, the need for a postwar plan became all the more urgent, yet nothing was resolved.

The diversion, of course, was the war in the Pacific and the growing assumption that the bomb might be used to force a Japanese unconditional surrender.

In the Chicago laboratories, scientists led by the veteran James Franck and Leo Szilard, the physicist who had coaxed a letter from Albert Einstein to help persuade Roosevelt to build an atom bomb in the first place, were becoming restive about America coveting its future atomic weapons. They, the scientists, were helping to make the bomb and they demanded a voice in evolving American policy. Specifically, they wanted guarantees from Roosevelt that he was committed to international control. The bomb must not be used on Japan unless Japan, and the world, was fore-warned of its devastation.

But the mainstream of international physicists was not now in Chicago or Oak Ridge or Hanford. It was inside the barbed wire fence of Los Alamos. And what they thought about the political implications of the bomb was largely lost in the more engrossing quest to finish their momentous laboratory experiment and see what it produced.

Oppenheimer was everywhere, encouraging, flattering, lighting cigarettes, darting in and out of offices and laboratories with suggestions. Once he stopped a pregnant wife on the dirt road and asked her how she felt. Before she had two words out he interrupted and listed her ailments, then strode off hurriedly down the path.

"How the devil," said the woman catching up with a friend, "does Oppie know how a pregnant woman feels." Then she grinned and added, "You know, he was dead right."

In such ways did Oppie charm the mesa. He got impossible results simply by kindness and communication. The smallest detail, the most minor functionary, got his undivided attention. It was brief, but it was there. A Spanish-American cleaner who tidied up Oppie's office each day made the peculiar boast to friends that he and the boss were such pals that he could spit on Oppie's floor without fear of discipline.

Frank Oppenheimer, who came to Los Alamos by way of the Radiation Laboratory and Oak Ridge, made the mistake in his first week of speaking abruptly to a purchasing agent who was having trouble getting a piece of equipment Frank needed. The man was so obviously offended that Frank backed away muttering apologies. The mesa was not Oak Ridge.

Creative work moved along faster if everyone knew the whole picture, so Oppenheimer, to the anguish of security, held weekly colloquia for every scientist with an academic degree. He told them of fresh progress, of new problems, and each man went away determined that his particular department would not lag behind.

Group leaders took part in regular sessions of a coordinating council, where discussions ranged from gripes about the Army to intricate problems of the implosion method of exploding the plutonium bomb.

It was a paternalistic society on the mesa, few could deny this,
but the regimen and strain noticeably aged the scientists and
brought out flashes of temper in the more highly strung wives as
1945 dawned with its July deadline for the bomb.

They were an individualistic crew in the first place, of a half
dozen different nationalities and a variety of religions, and the
miracle was that for all this the spirit of the place did not flag.
Groves himself treated the luminaries at Los Alamos with unac-
customed tenderness, which he gruffly explained to his officers was
because "at great expense we have gathered on this mesa the larg-
est collection of crackpots ever seen."

Physicists took it as a compliment when they heard the remark.
Being called prima donnas did not worry them either. They
counted themselves as special, and if anyone wanted convincing
they could point to Enrico Fermi riding by on his bicycle, Edward
Teller thumping on his piano, Niels Bohr careening down the
ski slope. Any one of these individuals had an IQ that was beyond
measuring. But the real stunner was their leader, Robert Oppenheimer.

A visiting scientist, Ralph Lapp, could not forget his meeting
with Oppie at this time. In his book *Atoms and People,* he was
to record:

A full week's growth of beard plus his general scrawny appearance made him look like one of the traditional sourdough pros-
pectors. I gazed in astonishment at his face. "Don't mind this," he
said, indicating his face. "I've had a case of measles and can't
shave." He kept chain smoking and talking, hooking his fingers
into a large Mexican silver belt buckle—a fashion which much of
Los Alamos imitated. I found him a most fascinating character and
had I not known his profession I would have guessed that he might

have been a great actor. His eyes, particularly, struck me as reflecting a sense of tragedy. This impressed me at the time and many times thereafter.

As a very young man in Corsica, Oppenheimer had said he wanted to do many things well yet still regard the world with a tear-stained countenance. By the early months of 1945 he had done many things well and his face was etched with fatigue and that haunting melancholy.

There would be two bombs, with the strangely gay names of "Fat Man" and "Little Boy." The rotund bomb would be plutonium, the skinny one uranium-235. "Little Boy," which was more likely to succeed, would be handed over for military use. "Fat Man" would be finished first and have to be tested. A site was chosen on a sere desert landscape a hundred miles south of Albuquerque, in the Jornada del Muerto Valley.

Oppie called the test Project Trinity. The physicists thought it an appropriate name, signifying the explosive union of the toil at three centers, Los Alamos, Chicago, and Hanford. Actually, Oppie got the name from John Donne:

> As East and West in all flat maps—and I am one—
> Are one, so death shall touch the Resurrection.

Plutonium, the angriest metal known to man, arrived at Los Alamos from Hanford in sufficient quantity for "Fat Man" before the sharp winter winds had gone from the mesa. The time had come for the tortuous assembly, the journey to the Trinity camp at the Alamogordo range, and then the final countdown to the world's first atomic bomb.

Groves' message to his crackpots was insistent, "Faster, faster." Allied forces were slugging through the islands and atolls, inexorably converging on Japan. Germany was down and would soon be completely out. At Yalta, Stalin promised Roosevelt and Churchill that Russia would invade Manchuria three months after the Ger-

man surrender. He extracted a price, of course, but the Pacific
Allies wanted to force a Japanese unconditional surrender and
they needed Russia. In San Francisco the founding conference for
the United Nations convened to safeguard postwar peace. The
American organizer there was a young State Department officer
named Alger Hiss.

Events were moving too fast for their managers. The Chicago
scientists, away from the obsessed atmosphere of Los Alamos, became shrill in their demands to Washington to reveal the atomic
secret to the architects of the future in San Francisco.

Roosevelt was their hope, but their hope was exhausted. The
President died on April 12.

High on the mountain in New Mexico the bomb makers heard
the news and wandered with gaunt faces to the center of the compound, not saying anything, just closing in together for comfort
and looking to the American flag whipping in the cold wind. Oppie appeared at the foot of the flagpole, hatless and coatless. He
spoke softly to the men about the dead President and though none
could remember afterwards what he said, the words were simple
and strong and they loved Oppenheimer for saying them.

The quick footfall of history faltered around the world, then
picked up and was more rapid than before. Germany capitulated.
Russia drove its stakes into eastern Europe. Casualty figures in the
drive against Japan were sickening on both sides. Fire bomb raids
on Tokyo had killed more than eighty thousand civilians, yet
there was no break in will, no real hope of avoiding the bloody
invasion.

In Washington, the firm hand of Harry Truman had taken
over. For the first time he learned of the Manhattan district, of
"Fat Man" and "Little Boy," vital details of which had been
passed to the Russian leaders by Klaus Fuchs months before. Secretary of War Henry L. Stimson, who at seventy-eight was still the
wisest man in the Administration and who was the power behind
Groves, briefed the new President on the far-reaching political

implications of the bomb. Should they tell the Russians? Should they use the bomb on Japan?

At the end of May the most eminent of the working scientists were brought to the Pentagon and asked their opinions. Arthur Compton, Ernest Lawrence, Enrico Fermi, and Robert Oppenheimer met with General George Marshall, James F. Byrnes, soon to be Secretary of State, Groves, Bush, and Conant. The physicists were there, said Stimson, because the Administration did not see atomic energy just in military terms but as opening a new age in mankind. He wanted their views.

Group discussion was Oppie's game, and soon it was his voice and his measured sentences that held the attention. "Our basic goal in this must be the advancement of human welfare," he said, rising above the specific points of debate. He developed his theme: America must share its atomic information with every nation for the purpose of securing the peace and for the encouragement of world cooperation on peacetime uses of atomic energy; and to strengthen the moral position of the United States as the leader in this new endeavor the interchange should begin before the bomb was used.

Bush's eyes sparkled at Oppie's proposition. He was articulating the vision of Niels Bohr, from whom he had learned, and now this was Bush's thinking, too. Stimson was more tough-minded, worrying over the difficulties of a free flow between democracies and totalitarian states, but he was impressed by Oppenheimer. He vowed then to know him better. Byrnes, the no-nonsense southerner, was less concerned with words than with facts. Throw a few crumbs to Stalin at this point and he would want the whole cake. The preliminary to all this was improved political relations with Russia. With Byrnes' influence, it was obvious he would prevail. Russia would not be told yet.

Discussion on whether or not to warn Japan if and when the bomb was to be used dealt not with morals but with practicalities. Lawrence leaned towards a prior demonstration, but Oppenheimer said this would not in his opinion convince the Japanese to surrender. And what, he asked that suddenly silent room, if the bomb were a dud?

Through that long day there had been worked a subtle change in the relationship between Lawrence and Oppenheimer. Oppie had left Berkeley as the number two star to Lawrence. In that day's interplay, Oppie had more than once cut in on Lawrence and disagreed. At one point the eager, driving Lawrence had said that whatever happened the strenuous research levels of wartime must be continued to keep America ahead in atomics. Oppenheimer not only pointed to the wrong-headedness of this notion but took the luster from Lawrence's considerable wartime contribution as well as his own. Nothing fundamental had been done during the war, said Oppie, simply the plucking of fruits from earlier discoveries. The postwar need was for unhurried, deeper research, devoid of deadline pressures.

When the meeting adjourned Oppenheimer was established as the spokesman for the four-man scientific panel and it was he who sent to Washington within three weeks their final suggestions. While some colleagues at Los Alamos, Berkeley, and Chicago differed, Oppie said, the Big Four had agreed that a military demonstration of the bomb on Japan was best. Before this was done, however, Russia, France, and China should be told of the atomic progress and be invited to recommend ways of postwar cooperation in the field.

Top policy advisers, including the dogged Bush-Conant duet, accepted the proposal of the Oppenheimer group to use the bomb without warning. They would tell Britain of the decision, forget France and China, and suggest to Truman that he tell Stalin at the scheduled Big Three meeting in Potsdam in July that America was working on the bomb and expected to drop it on Japan. Truman could say that he would welcome Stalin's ideas later on how atomic energy could be best controlled to make a peaceful world. Stimson endorsed this approach, and after he had carefully presented it at the White House, so did Truman.

Troubled scientists in Chicago knew they had lost the battle to keep the bomb from combat use. In a last desperate plea Leo Szilard wrote to his friend Edward Teller to intervene, not aware that Teller agreed with Oppenheimer that perhaps the only sure way of convincing the world of the future implausibility of war was military use of the bomb. Teller's reply to Szilard put the Los Alamos philosophy succinctly.

"The things we are working on are so terrible that no amount of protesting or fiddling with politics will save our souls," Teller wrote.

> The accident that we worked out this dreadful thing should not give us the responsibility of having a voice in how it is to be used. This responsibility must in the end be shifted to the people as a whole and that can be done only by making the facts known. This is the only cause for which I feel entitled in doing something: the necessity of lifting the secrecy at least as far as the broad issues of our work are concerned.

Szilard was inconsolable, and many others were too, yet he realized that to judge his colleagues at Los Alamos and in Washington as callous would be wrong.

At a quiet dinner at Eagle Hill in Berkeley early in July, Vannevar Bush and Robert Oppenheimer sat alone sharing a brief interlude before Alamogordo. The fire and vinegar had gone out of the rugged little Yankee. Both men had paused and faced the reality of the weapon they were about to introduce into a warring world.

Oppenheimer toyed with his wine glass and began to recite a verse he had memorized from *Bhartrihari*. He stopped and suggested Bush might take comfort in the poetry too. Then, almost in a whisper, he spoke these lines:

> In the forest, in battle, in the midst of arrows, javelins, fire
> Out on the great sea, at the precipice edge in the mountains
> In sleep, in delirium, in deep trouble
> The good deeds a man has done before defend him.

The two men sat in silence then. What they had wanted to say to each other had been said two thousand years before.

Bush and Oppenheimer reasoned that the alternative to using the bomb on Japan was more grotesque, for this meant an invasion and a hand-to-hand fight to the death on Japanese soil.

Out in the Pacific the battle-weary American forces looked around at their already badly depleted units and regarded the weeks ahead with alarm. To conquer Japan could cost a million lives, foe and friend. It would take a miracle to prevent the most savage slaughter in the history of war. They did not know that their miracle was in waiting, and, in fact, the Joint Chiefs were not counting on it. The bomb could indeed be a dud. Plans for the invasion had to proceed.

Suffocating July heat drained the physical energy from the scientists toiling at Alamogordo and they kept going on salt tablets and nerves. July 4 had been the target date for "Fat Man," but there had been delays in delivery of vital parts for the implosion mechanism that could compress the two separate hemispheres of plutonium together for the critical mass.

A week passed. Tension was at the breaking point.

Truman, Churchill, and Stalin cleaned their desks and prepared to head for Potsdam, near Berlin, to get down to the business of the Japanese invasion. They would meet on Monday, July 16. This was the new deadline.

If "Fat Man" functioned, then "Little Boy," although using uranium-235 and of different design, must work too. And the uranium bomb was nearly completed. Within days it would be on its way by sea to the Pacific Island of Tinian, where Colonel Paul Tibbets and his crew were waiting with their modified B-29.

On Thursday, July 12, young Louis Slotin, who had babied the plutonium and Phil Morrison, Oppie's old student, loaded the separated eighty-pound core of plutonium into the back seat of an Army sedan and drove down to the Trinity site. Friday the plutonium was encased with explosives and the bomb shell—a fat slug, five feet across the girth. Saturday the weapon was hoisted atop a one hundred foot steel tower.

Scientists slept fitfully through these feverish days. It was spooky in the desert.

Before dawn one morning someone let out a yelp. "Look, look, whazat, whazat." Men stumbled outside pulling on their pants. There it was, low in the sky, a bright white light. Urgent calls were put through to the nearby air base; could the object be intercepted and identified? Something close to hysteria was taking hold in Trinity.

The slap in the face came drily from one of the physicist-astronomers. "Venus," he said, "will you stop trying to shoot down Venus."

"Fat Man" squatted sullenly in his shed on the tower that Sunday while Oppenheimer checked Groves into the dugout observation post more than five miles to the south. They decided to explode the bomb at 4:00 A.M. Monday, which would be about lunch-time in Berlin, where the Big Three would meet at any hour.

A light rain started to fall at midnight and did not stop until four. The new time was five thirty. Ken Bainbridge armed the bomb and drove slowly back to Oppenheimer.

Oppenheimer stood motionless, gripping the post of the shelter. He was thinking of the complex implosion device. "I'm afraid it will fail," he muttered.

George Kistiakowsky, the Russan-born chemist who had spent months perfecting the technique, overheard his chief and yelled, "Bet you ten it works." Oppie accepted the bet without the trace of a smile. He was alone, turned off from the people around him. Groves, who earlier had been walking him backwards and forwards in front of the dugout to keep his mind off the bomb, left and returned to the base camp a few miles distant.

Twenty minutes before zero hour Oppie heard the familiar voice of Sam Allison, a project leader, start the countdown over a crude public address system. As the minutes ticked off several people spoke to Oppenheimer. He did not reply, at least not consciously. His knuckles showed white on the post. His face was drained, taut.

The minutes gone, Allison counted down the seconds. Oppie shut his eyes tightly and put his hands over his protective dark glasses. Allison shrieked, "Now!"

The hot fury locked inside those billions of plutonium atoms burst forth in one instant of blinding yellow glare. Oppie's fingers dug into his eyes to keep out the pain no lens could stop. Slowly his fingers, wet with tears, crept down his cheeks. He could see it now, the world on fire.

The radiance of a thousand suns.

The line came into his head from the *Bhagavad-Gita.* The yellow ball of fire hovered, bellied out, rose, then turned to pale orange, to red, to blood red, rising now in a column, darkening and burning.

The end of the verse came to him: *I am become death, The Shatterer of Worlds.*

The dark plume billowed into a great gray mushroom and as they all looked up the roar filled their ears and the heat blast nearly toppled them off balance. The entire astounding display had taken seconds—savage seconds in which an entire city could be obliterated. Breathless voices were heard in Oppie's dugout. "My God, it worked!" "Dear God!" Only this invocation seemed appropriate.

Kistiakowsky slapped Oppenheimer on the back. "Oppie," he said, "you owe me ten dollars."

Oppenheimer was hollow-eyed and unshaven, but his face had relaxed and he looked less ghostly. There was no whoop of glee from him; his mind was working ahead. The blast had far exceeded his expectations. He had thought it could be as low as the equivalent to two thousand tons of high explosive. It was much higher. He would find Fermi, he would know. The estimate, correct, was a fantastic twenty thousand tons.

He kept his mind off Japan, off death. The roar of the "Fat Man" which had turned its steel tower to gas, still reverberated across the desert and against the distant mountains when he swung into a jeep and was driven to base camp. They were all there, hands extended to him, Groves and Bush and Conant. He did not want to be alone now, but he did not want to talk. Then he saw Frank and his eyes came alive. The brothers sat together, sharing a brandy, and when the telephone was free he put in a call to Los Alamos to get a message to Kitty. "Tell her she can change the sheets," he said in the prearranged code that meant they had won.

Weariness came over him when he hung up and he remembered Ken Bainbridge's phrase as he drove away from the dugout. Bainbridge had gripped his hand and said, "Now we're all sons-of-bitches." Oppie felt nobody then or ever expressed it better.

"Little Boy" was already on the way to the Pacific and a second "Fat Man" would join it shortly. They would be used to incinerate thousands upon thousands of anonymous civilians in Japanese cities. They would be sacrificed for the dawn of a better world. Oppie could only look at it that way. He could not say Trinity was too successful, the bombs too murderous. Groves was sending the message to Washington to relay to Stimson and Truman in Potsdam. Truman must tell Stalin. In that Oppie put all his trust.

Stalin was late in arriving at the conference so nothing had been done by the Monday evening when the coded bulletin came to Berlin from Washington: "Operated on this morning. Diagnosis not yet complete but results seem satisfactory and already exceed expectations. . . ."

Truman and Stalin began their horse trading on the Tuesday, with Stalin predictably wanting concessions from the Chinese before undertaking the Manchurian invasion.

Wednesday saw another message from Washington: "Doctor has just returned most enthusiastic and confident that the little boy is as husky as his big brother. . . ."

Truman's confidence grew by the day and when Groves' detailed report came at the weekend he knew he would not have to beg favors from Stalin, could resist the Russian dictator's fresh demands in Europe, and simply encourage him to enter the war as part of the overall strategic invasion of Japan. In everybody's minds, and certainly strongly in Churchill's, was the real chance that the dropping of two atom bombs on Japan early in August would bring an unconditional surrender short of invasion and short of destroying Japan's honor.

When the session ended on July 24 Truman walked up to Stalin and said casually that the United States had a new weapon of unusual destructive force.

"Glad to hear it," said Stalin evenly. "I hope you make good use of it against the Japanese." Truman said no more, and as he walked away Stalin must have been burning inside. He knew of the work on the atom bomb. Soon he would be informed of Alagomordo because he had a man there, Klaus Fuchs.

Three days later America issued its ultimatum to Japan to surrender or face "prompt and utter destruction." Japanese Premier Suzuki said he would just ignore it. His rejection was broadcast as the finishing touches were put to "Little Boy" on the island of Tinian. Colonel Tibbets and his crew were ready; the weather was the only holdup.

At 6:00 A.M. Monday, August 6, Tibbets gunned his motors and set his course for Hiroshima. The city of a quarter of a million people, the town they said had a name like the rustle of a summer wind, had the terrible misfortune to awaken to a clear, sunny day. In the belly of the airplane rode "Little Boy," which was in fact an ugly snout of four-and-a-half tons. The American bomber soared high over the city and at nine fifteen by their watches the crew dropped the second of the bombs built on a lovely New Mexican mesa, half a world away.

Hours later, when America announced the atom bombing and the world reeled at the enormity of what had happened, a second ultimatum was issued to Japan—and Russia mobilized to jump into the war before it was over.

The knockout punch is always one-two, and, failing word from Tokyo, the United States hit Nagasaki with a "Fat Man" plutonium bomb on August 9. Japan surrendered the next day.

America exploded with delight and relief. Every woman with a man—son or husband or brother—in the Pacific gave thanks to the atom bombs and to the men who made them. As Washington released more and more details, incomprehensible to most people, a new kind of war hero took shape in the public mind—long-haired scientists in baggy pants who had toiled over this lethal substance called uranium in their secret laboratories, seeking no glory, dedicating themselves to produce the master stroke that would bring victory.

Their admirers were rather surprised and disappointed when they saw in the newspaper pictures how little their heroes looked like Einstein. The faces were frank and firm, the cut of them youngish, the hair cropped, the bank manager image. Not Robert Oppenheimer, however, with the thinness of him, the hungry quest of the eyes, stories that he was the guiding genius behind the atom could be believed.

The impulse to dance in the streets was short-lived at Los Alamos, for these men who did not have the serene, other-worldly appearance of Einstein were indeed men of the moment. By their deeds had the citizens of Hiroshima and Nagasaki been slaughtered. Their innocence was shattered and they felt guilty. In the days following Hiroshima they talked of nothing but redemption for themselves, for their beloved physics that had become now so sinister in the public mind, and for America.

Oppie's most comforting word came in a letter from a G.I. based somewhere in the Pacific. "Hey, Oppie," said the big, scrawling letters, "you're about the best loved man in these parts." The letter was signed Rossi Lomanitz.

The turmoil going on in their heads was all the more difficult to cope with because each one of them felt that what they had done was necessary. It was not a question of second-thinking the issue. They had just not been prepared for the personal remorse that would set in after the flush of victory.

Reaction to the first news of Hiroshima had been tremendous relief that "Little Boy" had worked. There was the same back-slapping that had gone on after Trinity. The nausea came when the casualty reports arrived, perhaps eighty thousand civilians dead, countless burned and maimed. Killing on this order with one bomb somehow went beyond the rules of even the most extreme civilized conduct. For the trained combatants on the delivery airplane *Enola Gay* it was a nightmare, for the intellectual scientists on the mesa it was absolute dismay.

"There are people who say they are not such very bad weapons," Oppie told an audience of scientists later. "Before the New Mexico test we sometimes said that too, writing down square miles and equivalent tonnages and looking at the pictures of ravaged Europe. After the test we did not say it any more.

"Some of you will have seen photographs of the Nagasaki strike, seen the great steel girders of factories twisted and wrecked; some of you may have noticed that these factories that were wrecked were miles apart. Some of you will have seen pictures of the people who were burned, or had a look at the wastes of Hiroshima. That bomb at Nagasaki would have taken out ten square miles, or a bit more, if there had been ten square miles to take out. . . .

"The pattern of the use of atomic weapons was set at Hiroshima. They are weapons of surprise, of terror. If they are ever used again it may well be by the thousands, or perhaps by the tens of thousands. . . ."

Oppenhemier turned away from this grim specter of the future and concentrated on the hope.

The tragedies of Hiroshima and Nagasaki must be used to trigger a warless, open world, the fraternity of international scientists must be reunited and purified. Most people on the mesa caught his spirit and endorsed his crusade.

But there was a shadow over any extravagant hope. Oppenheimer knew, they all knew, that a more powerful weapon than the fission bomb was possible. Edward Teller had been preoccupied with it for a long time, and he was confident it could be done. This was the thermonuclear bomb. Rough calculations showed that a fusion weapon, a hydrogen bomb, could wreak havoc to make "Fat Man" seem tame—it would be a hundred times more powerful.

After consulting with the other members of the wartime scientific panel, Fermi, Compton, and Lawrence, Oppie flew to Washington with a warning of this unconscionable weapon and a recommendation that all atomic weapon development be immediately brought under international control. Wartime secrecy must go, said the scientists. Oppenheimer did not get to see Secretary of State Byrnes personally, but he received a chilling memo from him. A world pact was "not practical" for the time being, said Byrnes. Los Alamos should go to work on the thermonuclear bomb.

Oppenheimer sought out Stimson, whom he greatly admired, and asked what Truman had said to Stalin in Potsdam about the bomb and postwar cooperation and what Stalin had replied. The replay of the incident was his second severe shock.

Aggrieved and perplexed, he returned to New Mexico, at a loss as to what to do next. Morale on the mesa was already low. Apart from the lack of American action to lift the secrecy on atomics, the younger scientists were in rebellion against a bill that had been hastily introduced into Congress to perpetuate military control over all atomic energy work.

Oppie remembered Lawrence's visit to Los Alamos a few days before, when Ernest had urged him to stick to science and leave the politics to politicians. Lawrence had said Oppie was a man of prestige now and should not get involved in the sort of leftist escapades that had so worried them all in the Berkeley administration before the war. He should crack the whip to get the mesa moving again, then return to his teaching at Berkeley. This was a regular plea with Lawrence. He had once collared Frank Oppenheimer, whom he liked very much, and asked him why he fooled around with "causes." As a scientist, Frank was a cut above people who just wanted to eat and sleep and make love, said Lawrence with elusive meaning.

Oppie could not recall much of his conversation with Lawrence, except that he had resisted his friend on every point and said something like, "To hell with Berkeley." The big man had slammed the door when he left. It still pained Oppie to incur anybody's displeasure, and he felt it wrong to condemn Ernest just because he was a snob. More than that, Ernest maybe had a point after all. He did have prestige and he should not dissipate it on alley fights.

In a letter of apology, Oppenheimer mentioned his "very mixed and sad" feelings about the earlier discussion. Certainly his team "would earnestly do whatever necessary in the national interest, no matter how desperate and disagreeable, but we felt reluctant to promise that much real good would come of continuing atom bomb work just like poison gases after the last war." Work on the mesa, said Oppie, had to be "based on a national policy which is intelligible in its broad outlines to the men who are doing the work."

Lawrence had been puzzled why the mesa scientists were upset by their creation and why Oppie sympathized with them.

"I think it would not have seemed so odd if you had lived through the history as we did," explained Oppie in his letter, "not so hard to understand if you remember how much more of an underdogger I have always been than you. That is part of me that is unlikely to change, for I am not ashamed of it; it is responsible for such differences as we have had in the past, I think. . . ."

As Enrico Fermi put it, America needed new generations of scientists as well as better weapons.

Answering this call the senior physicists and chemists started the exodus from Los Alamos, back to their universities. With a twofold mission of his own, Oppie was among them, turning over control of the laboratory to the Navy scientist Norris Bradbury, later confirmed as director.

Conant wanted Oppie to come to Harvard, and Columbia had offered him a generous deal, but the pull of the old Berkeley-Caltech days proved too strong in the end. "I would like to go back to California for the rest of my days," he wrote Conant. "I have sense of belonging there which I will probably not get over."

His first letters to Berkeley—to the University of California president, and to the indestructible old Professor Birge—were untypically clumsy. "As you can see," he said in his note to Birge, "I am worried about the wild oats of all kinds which I have sown in the past; nor am I quite willing in the future to be part of an institution which has any essential distrust or any essential lack of confidence in me."

He rejoined Caltech some months before Berkeley. With Caltech, Oppie put it on the line that he would continue to be active in doing what he could to influence national atom policy. In the meantime, he asked for a steady supply of graduate students to teach.

One of his last acts on the mesa was to make a speech of acceptance for a Presidential scroll praising the wartime contribution of the laboratory. It was the beginning of Oppie as the public man, the scientist-statesman.

He said the pride in the scroll must be tempered with concern, then he added: "If atomic bombs are to be added as new weapons to the arsenals of a warring world, or to the arsenals of nations preparing for war, then the time will come when mankind will curse the name of Los Alamos and of Hiroshima. The peoples of this world must unite or they will perish. This war, that has ravaged so much of the earth, has written these words. The atomic bomb has spelled them out for all men to understand. Other men have spoken them, in other times, of other wars, of other weapons. They have not prevailed. There are some, misled by a false sense of human history, who hold that they will not prevail today. It is not for us to believe that. By our works we are committed, committed to a world united, before this common peril, in law, and in humanity."

11

On the cab ride from Union Station to the State Department, Robert Oppenheimer poised himself in the corner of the seat puffing on a cigarette. His newspaper fans would have been startled to discover how much leaner and more angular he was in the flesh. His shirt collar gaped at the neck and the jacket of his brown tweed suit hung in folds. His knees and elbows poked at the cloth as he repeatedly shifted position. His face was wasted, though he did not look older than his forty-one years because of the tight jawline and the cropped black hair. A few strands of gray were showing, but only a few. The flourishes he made with the cigarette gave him an attitude of quickness even as he was sitting.

Two months had passed since Hiroshima and America's atom policy was hopelessly confused. Public opinion was astir.

A great number of people had had that delayed-reaction remorse; they were half-ashamed of the bomb and surely scared by it. An Arkansas preacher said the scientists had broken loose the forces of hell, which phrase, regardless of its accuracy, sounded right enough to those who saw pictures of Hiroshima.

Oppenheimer was worth watching closely that day.

The cab took him to the State Department. He had hoped to see Byrnes, but he was unavailable, and Oppenheimer's friend

Herbert Marks, a brilliant state legal aide, had arranged for him an interview with Under Secretary Dean Acheson. It was a good arrangement for Oppie. He knew Acheson had Truman's ear and he was told by friends that Acheson was as smart as his reputation. Oppie needed to know firsthand the sentiments of the people who mattered in the Administration. For his own peace of mind he had to be convinced that Truman was prepared to go all the way on international control of atomic energy. The President's statements in recent weeks had been alarmingly unspecific.

Almost as an act of ingratiation, Oppie had wired his support of the Administration-backed May-Johnson bill for continued military control of the atom laboratories. He saw this as stopgap legislation, which would be amended once atomics went under the management of a world body. The Chicago scientists, and many of his own people from Los Alamos, had felt betrayed by him on this and were even now spreading through Washington buttonholing sympathetic congressmen to resist the military pressure. They wanted a civilian commission to take over the entire atom establishment immediately. Only then, they felt, could planning begin for an international body. Oppie believed the exact reverse of this—first the world organization, then civilian management everywhere.

Somewhat reassuring to Oppie was Truman's regard for Henry Stimson and Stimson's last written message to the President before he left Washington for retirement. Oppie had sat on the bench in the Pentagon barber shop some days earlier while Stimson had his hair trimmed and told Oppie of his memo.

"Unless the Soviets are voluntarily invited into the (atom) partnership upon a basis of cooperation and trust," Stimson had written,

we are going to maintain the Anglo-Saxon bloc over and against the Soviet in the possession of this weapon. Such a condition will almost certainly stimulate feverish activity on the part of the Soviet towards the development of this bomb in what will in effect be a secret armaments race of a rather desperate character. . . . I consider the problem of our satisfactory relations with Russia as not merely connected with but as virtually dominated by the problem with the atom bomb. . . .

The chief lesson I have learned in a long life is that the only way you can make a man trustworthy is to trust him.

Stimson finished briefing Oppie, then reached for his cane to help lever himself out of the awkward barber chair. "Now, Dr. Oppenheimer," Stimson said, "it is in your hands."

It turned out that next to Oppie himself the man in Washington with the most arresting presence was Acheson. He came around his desk to meet the scientist like a cut from *Vanity Fair*. Gray suit, gray tie, graying temples, ruddy cheeks, immaculately trimmed moustache—he looked marvelous, and Oppie liked him on sight. How the impression went the other way was never quite clear, for Acheson's patience with the covey of lobbying scientists in Washington was wearing thin and, for all Oppie's distinction, he may have lumped him in with the others.

In Acheson's view, as near as it could be determined, the physicists had done their job and should retire back to their test tubes. All through the thirties they had labored in their laboratories, caring little about the outside world. Then they had made an invention that changed history; they had come from total lack of responsibility in human affairs into real contact with the world. Suddenly they were the universal conscience, each one an amateur politician, and frankly, Acheson had let it drop somewhere, they were a damn bore.

The Under Secretary was himself sympathetic to international control and had heard out Niels Bohr on this subject. That day he listened to the same words from Oppenheimer, though Oppie's presentation was obscured somewhat by literary parables which escaped Acheson.

They talked on for more than an hour, up to the time Acheson had an appointment with the President. He was about to break off with Oppenheimer when he had a sudden thought. "Come on, doctor," he said crisply, "we're going to see the President."

Suddenly there was the oval room and Harry Truman, his spectacles sparkling in the light, the polka dot tie arching jauntily. A strength about Truman seemed to fill the room. As he sat down, Oppenheimer took in the portrait of Franklin Roosevelt on the back wall and the many photographs on the desk, Truman's wife, daughter, and others Oppie did not recognize.

The interview accomplished nothing. While Oppie seemed to want Truman to say that he would fly off that night to talk with Stalin in Moscow about the atom bomb, all Truman could and would do was repeat his public statement to Congress that he was committed to finding some way to bring the atom under international control. He did not yet have a definite program about how to proceed, however.

To his surprise, Oppie discovered that the President's logic followed more closely that of the lobbying scientists than his own. Truman thought legislation on domestic control and management of atomic affairs had to precede any entry into a world authority.

Oppie's concern was that no progress was being made on anything. He sat there, a picture of dejection, and began to work the palms of his hands together.

"Mr. President," he said slowly, "I feel I have blood on my hands."

Truman craned forward, the corners of his mouth turning down. Stunned for a second he reached into a top pocket, removed the neatly folded handkerchief and proferred it. "Would you like to wipe them?" he said in a hollow voice.

Embarrassed by his dramatics and by the President's strange reaction, Oppie shifted about uneasily, allowing Truman to pick up the conversation. It was a relief when the President rose after a minute or two and held out his hand to signal the end of the talk. "Don't worry," he heard Truman saying, "we're going to work something out, and you're going to help us."

Truman remained standing in his office after Oppie had gone.

His lower lip was thrust forward. "Blood on his hands," he snapped. "Damnit, he hasn't half as much blood on his hands as I have. You just don't go around bellyaching about it."

In truth, Oppie was not too downhearted by his encounters with Truman and Acheson. They had seen him readily and listened to him patiently. He was still abysmally disappointed that Truman had not discussed the bomb with Stalin at Potsdam. There would never be another chance for such a clean, open beginning to atomic cooperation. Well, that day had gone, and Oppie's hope was that now his voice counted in Washington's top echelon he could hasten a new day.

The sooner the May-Johnson domestic bill was adopted by Congress the faster planning could begin on the international level. It irritated him that carloads of scientists from Chicago, Oak Ridge, and Los Alamos had hit town to fight the bill. The military control would be transitory, he told them. Once the world group took over, the secrecy and weaponry would end; he would not hear pessimism about international control. As his main argument, he told his younger colleagues that powerful congressional forces backed the May-Johnson legislation and to fight them was futile.

To the amazement of the scientists, Oppie actually campaigned for the bill. On the same day in New York, Oppie was downtown saying that any interim bill was better than nothing because the Manhattan district was floundering "without direction, without guidance, a burden to the people who are working on it," while uptown the Nobel laureate Harold Urey charged, "You can call it either a Communist bill or a Nazi bill, whichever you think is the worse."

In Washington, meanwhile, the newly formed Federation of Atomic Scientists was taking newspaper advertisements against the legislation, proclaiming, "To hell with politics—the question is: Are you pro- or anti-suicide?"

Among the dozens of scientists who said they could not figure Oppie on his stand—and they included his brother Frank—some said it must be because he had become corrupted by fame. Even such sensitive men as Phillip Morrison said later that Oppie had started to play God. Nobody went for the simplest explanation—the guru of the Berkeley physics students, the lord of the mesa, was acting true to character. It was a new scene, a new play, but Oppie still asked for the lead role. He wanted to do it his way again and be trusted until the final curtain.

A Manhattan district, run by and for the open world, was the goal and the steps toward it were not that important. By making bedlam outside the doors of Congress the scientists were simply creating diversion. Success, to Oppie's thinking, depended on communication between people in high places. Los Alamos had not cured the romantic sweep of Oppie's mind. The columnist Dorothy Thompson called him an "Elysian dreamer" and she was right. He was supremely more suited to those fabled fields than to the cold halls and rooms where practical atomic policy was being hammered out.

Out and about the country Oppie was followed by applause. His lectures on quantum theory at Caltech attracted such crowds that loudspeakers had to be set up for the people waiting outside. The gang remaining at Los Alamos observed the adventures of their leader with pride but secondary interest. What they really wanted to know, the scientists and their wives, was how Willie Higinbotham was faring in Washington.

Higinbotham, a young, short, thick-spectacled physicist who played the accordion for the wartime mesa barn dances, had gone to Washington in a bus with a few others to fight the May-Johnson bill. They had no money, no office, no staff, but they were making headway.

When Willie got his name in *Newsweek* the howl of delight on the mesa could be heard to Santa Fe. He was one of a very large and amateur lobby that found a champion in the staunch Connecticut Senator Brien McMahon. McMahon said the atom bomb was the biggest thing since the birth of Jesus and he was determined to stand against his seniors and take it out of the rough hands of the Army.

So Willie and the others kept pushing and Los Alamos kept rooting. Oppie, the man who called himself an "underdogger," was nowhere in sight. It had come to a few on the mesa that he was not so much for the downtrodden as for the heroic cause.

It developed that Harry Truman discarded the doomed May-Johnson bill before Oppie.

If his reputation was tarnished among American physicists, it was black in some quarters in Europe. There, he was denounced as a monster for ever making the bomb. German scientists said self-righteously that although the original fission experiment was performed in their country they had kept the gross implications from the Nazi war machine.

Nobody anywhere loved the atom bomb. The blame for it was treated like a hot brick. The atom scientists threw it to the public, the public tossed it back to the scientists, and at least a fragment of this group turned around and put it into Oppie's hands.

"We have made an evil thing," he told a National Academy of Sciences meeting on atomic energy. "And by so doing . . . we have raised again the question of whether science is good for man, or whether it is good to learn about the world, to try to understand it, to try to control it, to help give to the world of men increased insight, increased power. . . . Because we are scientists we must say an unalterable *yes* to these questions . . . knowledge is a good in itself, knowledge and such power as must come with it."

Oppie suggested the question of guilt more realistically hinged on the constructive or destructive use of that power. This was why there was such interdependence between science and society. While scientists should offer encouragement and advice in the present crisis, it was for statesmen to get the nations of the world to cooperate on peaceful atomic uses and to ban nuclear weapons. For people who heard Oppie talk there was no question that he saw himself as the bridge between science and statesmanship.

He granted newspaper interviews, shyly but readily, and made no attempt to quiet fears about the bomb peril facing the world. Reporters suggested that at a billion dollars apiece the bombs were too expensive for general military use. Oppie said a more accurate costing would be somewhere between a half million and five million dollars per bomb, which meant that for a small fraction of the national income America could have a stockpile of ten thousand atom bombs in little more than ten years. The inference was that so too could Russia.

Each day of inaction on the issue of international control would deepen Soviet mistrust and increase its resolve to make its own bombs, in Oppenheimer's view.

A breakthrough finally came in mid-November. Truman and the Prime Ministers of Britain and Canada announced in Washington their willingness to interchange fundamental scientific knowledge with any nation that would reciprocate. The concept was for establishment of a special United Nations commission to make proposals for international scientific exchange, confining use of atomic energy to peaceful purposes, elimination of atom weapons, and policing the world against abuses of agreed United Nations rules. Russia's initial reaction to the idea was to regard it as some kind of Anglo-American trick, but when the United Nations General Assembly convened in London in January, Russia voted with the world and the United Nations Atomic Energy Commission was born.

To formulate specific American policy, Secretary of State Byrnes appointed a special committee headed by Acheson and including Groves, Bush, Conant, and the War Department's John J. McCloy. This group in turn set up an advisory panel consisting of Tennessee Valley Authority boss David E. Lilienthal as chairman, nuclear chemist Charles Thomas, engineer Harry Winne, the wartime U.S.O. chief Chester Barnard—and Oppenheimer.

Herb Marks, the Acheson aide who was to assist the panel, introduced Lilienthal to Oppie in the Shoreham Hotel in Washington, and, as Lilienthal was to relate in his journals, "He [Oppie] walked back and forth making funny 'hugh' sounds between sentences and phrases . . . a mannerism quite strange, very strange. . . . I left liking him, greatly impressed with his flash of mind, but rather disturbed by the flow of words."

The next day, after Lilienthal had another session with Oppie in Acheson's office, he added to his diary that the scientist was "an extraordinary personage."

General Groves, who made an effort to think of as many arguments against international control as Oppenheimer could produce in favor, issued a few warnings about Oppie's persuasive tongue and kept saying darkly that Oppie had a fine brain but the man needed to be managed by a top executive like himself. To his dismay, Groves saw his alarums ignored.

"Everybody genuflected," he complained later. "Lilienthal got so bad he would consult Oppie on what tie to wear in the morning."

It was true that Lilienthal, an extremely able administrator and veteran handler of men, was infatuated by Oppenheimer. "He is worth living a lifetime just to know that mankind has been able to produce such a being," he was to tell Herb Marks. "We may have to wait another hundred years for the second one to come off the line."

Acheson had a little fun with his committee members, finding most of them prima donnas. Having Groves' assessment of Oppenheimer, he asked Oppie one day how a pompous fellow like the general could run such a successful show as the Manhattan district. "Oh," said Oppie, "he has a fatal weakness for good men."

As a lawyer, it was Acheson's boast that he could always learn enough about an issue to make a case for it. Atomic energy had him completely baffled, however, and he invited Oppie to be a houseguest at the Acheson home on P Street so that he could be tutored every night. John McCloy would come over after dinner and the three men would spend hours in the living room, with Oppenheimer filling a child's easel blackboard with equations and sketches.

"You two don't understand a thing," Oppie said after a week of it. "For Pete's sake, Dean, do you really think neutrons are little men without heads running around bumping into things?"

"Well, in a way, yes, Robert," replied Acheson, noticeably coloring. "Damn it, that is the way you explained it."

"Can't you understand the concept of energy?" Oppie persisted.

"My dear fellow," said Acheson, "I cannot even understand electricity."

Oppenheimer also lectured on nuclear physics to the members of the Lilienthal advisory panel, which met daily in a large loft room in a downtown office block. Although the group included a company president and two corporation senior vice-presidents, it was the atom expert who guided. After summarizing the technical background, Oppie spelled out his plan for a multi-nation agency to run all reactors, separate all uranium 235 and plutonium, monopolize all raw material—a worldwide Manhattan district without the bomb.

It was an appropriately revolutionary answer to the atomic terror facing the world, and the Acheson consultants warmed to it instantly. As the recommendation evolved in endless group discussions, the United States would favor an international corporation controlling all supplies of natural uranium. This was the key because without the basic uranium there could be no 235 or plutonium. The agency would thus have a check on whether any nation had sufficient materials for making secret bombs. For the benefit of mankind, the agency's reactors and separation plants and laboratories would go full steam in developing atomic power and the research and medical applications of radioactive isotopes. The plan would progress in stages with each nation proving good faith. In the beginning, every participating country would have to submit to a survey of uranium resources.

After much debate between the Lilienthal people and the policy group, Acheson endorsed the program as an imaginative starting point. Oppenheimer then wrote the final draft in his embroidered English.

He struggled particularly over one clause the panel wanted included to the effect that uranium could be released for commercial enterprise in crude "denatured" form, where the content of the fissionable 235 isotope would be so small that elaborate and therefore easily detected plants would be needed to bleed it out.

Among reporters in Washington the Acheson-Lilienthal report was eagerly sought. Inevitably something would leak. The Under Secretary had spread a few copies among the special Senate committee headed by Brien McMahon. Either from this source or the Acheson group itself the main points in the plan filtered to the newspapers. The ubiquitous Ed Condon, then doubling as National Bureau of Standards chief and as McMahon's technical adviser, had a call early one night from a *New York Times* reporter, who was worried because he had heard the *New York Herald Tribune* had the full text of the report. Condon got McMahon's copy and for two hours Condon and two *Times* reporters puzzled over the complex language of the long document. They could not even find a "lead" and finally, on deadline, one of the newsmen telephoned the *Herald Tribune* man and learned to his relief that the opposition did not have a copy at all.

"Let's leave it for now," said the reporter. "That stuff will take a day to understand. Who the devil wrote it?"

"That," said Condon, "is pure Oppenheimer."

Acheson called the game by officially releasing the report at the end of March. Most newspapers and public men were enthusiastic about the plan and the identification of Oppenheimer as the prime mind behind it won him fresh acclaim. It patched up some of the quarrel he had with scientists over the May-Johnson bill.

In looking for the dramatic points the newspaper rewrite men had seized on the word "denature" and the stories shouted that uranium could be deprived of its explosive forces before reaching the general market. The State Department's brief that the denaturing made the uranium less suitable for bombs and still effective for controlled energy release was ignored. People got the impression that uranium had an inbuilt firing pin which could easily be removed.

Enrico Fermi, who had moved back to Chicago by this time, telephoned Oppie and protested that the denaturing story was grossly misleading and falsely reassuring to the lay public. Oppie tried to explain that the report had been distorted on this, but Fermi would not listen to reason and rang off in anger. It was the one part of the report Oppie regretted and later amended.

Oppie's deeper worry, however, was the President's appointment of seventy-five-year-old elder statesman Bernard Baruch as his representative on the United Nations Atomic Energy Commission. Baruch, in turn, had recruited four associates, none of whom knew the first thing about nuclear energy. Lack of expertise did not prevent the old man demanding his right to put some of the old Baruch pepper into the Acheson-Lilienthal report before he presented it.

Almost every man in the Acheson group was annoyed at the selection of Baruch. With the future well-being of the world at stake, it was not felt the occasion for a sentimental appointment. Oppenheimer was so upset that he would not accept Baruch's personal invitation to join his staff as scientific adviser. By his resistance, and that of others, Oppie hoped the President would reconsider and put someone like Vannevar Bush at the head of the United Nations team.

Week after week the Baruch and Acheson camps bickered with each other. Assuming that the supreme management of the international atomic development authority would be the Security Council itself, Baruch insisted that the plan must eliminate the council veto provision in levying penalties for violation of the rules of the atom agreement. Baruch wanted immediate punishment for nations abusing the treaty. Oppenheimer said it was foolish to write this into the plan because the penalty for serious abuse would automatically be war. Oppie was also now against the emphasis in the plan of offering American atomic cooperation piecemeal—nations being forced to prove their honor before being allowed on to the next stage.

With the Atomic Energy Commission meeting only a few days

off, Baruch went to the Secretary of State with a virtual ultimatum: either Baruch presented a tough, specific plan or he would drop out and somebody else, maybe Acheson, could table the original report as a basis for discussion.

Byrnes took Baruch to see Truman and the President acceded to the hard approach, even to the extent of underlining the new penalty clause. Checking with the Joint Chiefs of Staff, Baruch found that both General Dwight D. Eisenhower and Admiral Chester W. Nimitz had misgivings about the practicality of retaliation against atomic transgressors, but he would not be dissuaded.

For Oppenheimer everything was going wrong. His conscience bothered him for not helping Baruch on the technical side, yet the old man's stubbornness frustrated him beyond endurance. Both he and Lilienthal agreed that the Security Council veto would have to be abandoned in atomic agency affairs, but they thought it disastrous to bring it up in the initial presentation of the plan.

Equally distressing was the American announcement of plans to stage two atomic bomb tests at the Bikini atoll in the Pacific. The Navy wanted to see the effect of an atom bomb dropped on a fleet. How totally inappropriate, Oppie wrote to Truman in a harsh memo, for the United States to conduct military bomb tests just when it was trying to eliminate atomics from national armaments. Oppie said the Bikini tests would cost more than one hundred million dollars. For less than one million, he said, the Navy could get more useful information in a simulated test with models. Scornfully he added his assessment of the effectiveness of an atom bomb against a ship: if the bomb were dropped close enough the ship would sink. This was exactly what happened at Bikini.

Two weeks before the highly publicized Bikini atom carnival, on the morning of June 14 in the hastily converted gymnasium of Hunter College in the Bronx, Baruch rose before the delegates of the United Nations Atomic Energy Commission and announced somberly, "We are here to make a choice between the quick and the dead. This is our business."

Oppenheimer sat with other scientists in the American section.

He was haggard and consumed with anxiety. In their account of this moment in the volume *The New World* the official historians were sensitive to what bothered Oppie.

"Six feet-four and lithe," they wrote,

> he [Baruch] presented an imposing appearance in his dark, double-breasted jacket and striped trousers. He seemed the embodiment of the elder statesman. Here was the almost legendary figure who had mobilized American resources in the First World War, the councellor of Presidents, the park-bench sage. Yet here too was a voice from another age. This son of a Confederate veteran had first seen the light of day in unreconstructed South Carolina. As a young man, he had known Diamond Jim Brady and seen John W. Gates bet a million dollars on a poker hand. On advance news of the Navy's victory at Santiago, he had hired a locomotive, rushed back to New York, and made a fortune. Now, forty-eight years later, he was at the center of the stage, wrestling with an issue that would set a pattern for the future.

Baruch promptly got to the central issue: once the international authority was in business, the world uranium deposits surveyed, the punishments for violations agreed on and the Security Council veto waived, then American manufacture of atom bombs would cease and all existing atom weapons would be dismantled.

Soviet representative Andrei Gromyko said the Russian plan called first for the destruction and outlawing of atom bombs, then consideration of world interchange of information on atomic matters. He added that any tampering with the council veto was unacceptable.

Impartial observers could see that both countries had dealt their first cards out of self-interest; it was time then to get down to compromise. But as Oppie warned, the veto clause gave the Russians the excuse to stall with apparent justification—and the veto was indeed the *sine qua non* of the United Nations as it was then constituted. But really the Russians were being underhanded from the beginning. They had not the slightest intention of giving up any national sovereignty to an international group, and they had the comfort of knowing that the American atom monopoly would soon be broken. Oppenheimer guessed their feelings on this, though he did not realize how fast the progress was. Klaus Fuchs, back in England, was still considered a loyal Briton and was still passing information.

Acheson was angry at Baruch's heavy-handed approach and privately accused him of making a "jackass" of himself. Oppie also reproached Baruch, but as the debate continued and he saw the inflexibility of the Russians he developed a fierceness towards them and realized that what Winston Churchill had just said about an "Iron Curtain" was justified. They would not open their closed society to any foreign influence for any reason.

Oppie saw his dream dying there in the Hunter College gymnasium, his redemption stillborn. His bomb was not yet going to be the bright dawn of lasting world peace.

"The jig is up," he told his scientific friends. They did not quite know what he meant and his elaborations were too obscure. His acceptance of the essential tragedy of human affairs was barely sustaining him.

At the airport in Washington one evening Lilienthal encountered his friend without makeup, without costume, without lines.

"I am ready to go anywhere and do anything," Oppie said, according to the Lilienthal journals. "But I am bankrupt of further ideas. And I find that physics and the teaching of physics, which is my life, now seems irrelevant."

12

Astride a little fast-racking sorrel named Mickey, Oppenheimer roamed the Sangre de Cristos for a week. He stayed in one of the cabins at the Katherine Page ranch, where he had been twenty years before, and while he continued to pace the floor at night, contemplating, lighting a cigarette from the coal in his pipe and then the pipe again from the cigarette, his days were active and reviving.

His companion was John Donne, for his sonnets were a comfort.

> If poisonous minerals, and if that tree,
> Whose fruit threw death on else immortal us,
> If lecherous goats, if serpents envious
> Cannot be damn'd; alas, why should I be?

Mickey took him to the high ridges where he searched for unusual wild flowers. When he saw one he gathered the plant, packed the roots in wet moss and carried it back to the ranch.

Most often he was alone, Donne excepted, but once he stopped by the neighboring Mountainview ranch managed by a man called LaMar Lamb and asked him to come along. Oppie patted his saddlebags and said he had lunch for two. Lamb was happy to join the ride and delighted when Oppie reined in after a few hours and produced the meal. Instead of salt beef, Lamb got Italian pepperoni loaf and Limburger cheese. Oppie lit a fire to prepare coffee—a heavy, dark Bulgarian brew.

Lamb tried to bring the luncheon conversation around to Los Alamos and atom bombs, complimenting Oppie on his accomplishment, but Oppenheimer just stared moodily into the fire. Preserving life, understanding life, and being a part of it, was the important thing, he said at length. That was why he liked the mountains and the people who lived there. They were close to the essence of life; they were innocent.

During his solitary nights Oppenheimer dwelt on his suspicions about the Soviet Union. At dinner one evening at Santa Fe's old La Fonda hotel, where he rejoined Kitty and Dorothy McKibbin, the woman who had acted as wartime den mother to the Los Alamos scientists, Oppie was interrupted by a telephone call from Washington. The caller reported Russia's latest mulish act at the United Nations. Oppie returned to the table and pushed his food away. "It's finished," he said. "Russia wants world conquest."

Back at Eagle Hill, he argued with Frank and Jacky about Russia's militant attitude and became impatient with their protests that Russia had grounds for apprehension too. His renewed friendship at Berkeley with Haakon Chevalier was lukewarm for the reason of his apparent growing conservatism.

Lawrence was enthusiastic about his friend's return to teaching, for he claimed Oppie as the best theoretician in the country and he enjoyed Oppie's liaison with the Radiation Laboratory. Unlike Los Alamos, Lawrence's domain had not faltered and, in fact, was stronger and more vigorous than ever.

Oppenheimer, however, seemed to have outgrown his professor's shoes. His mind was in Washington, fixing now on domestic atom policy. He had a group of graduate students, but the closeness of old was not there. "Sure we respect Oppenheimer," said one student, "but we don't idolize him."

Where Oppie's crusade had failed, that of the underdogs had

not. Belatedly he had joined them, but he felt guilty for not doing it much earlier.

Brien McMahon, backed by influential liberal spirits like Ed Condon and Harold Urey, had succeeded in getting a bill to establish a civilian Atomic Energy Commission accepted by the Senate. The commission, to comprise five presidental appointees, would take over the Manhattan complex from the Army and have sole responsibility for the production and custody of atom bombs as well as guiding development for peaceful atomic energy uses. The commission would be buttressed by a Military Liaison Committee, watching military interests, a General Advisory Committee of scientists, and a Joint Committee on Atomic Energy in Congress to safeguard the public interest.

Although a tough House fight was predicted, one of the most powerful opponents, Kentucky Congressman Andrew May, who had sponsored the original military bill, was muted because he was under investigation on wartime conflict of interest charges. The bill bounced out of his Military Affairs Committee and squeaked by the House Rules Committee despite the best efforts of New Jersey's J. Parnell Thomas, who said the legislation was a gift to Andrei Gromyko. But amendments tacked to the bill in the House debate were a sign of things to come in America.

One amendment made mandatory at least one military representative on the commission, another authorized the armed forces to produce atomic weapons, a third removed the commission's authority to establish international exchange if and when a world agency was created, a fourth added harsh penalties for security breaches and required the F.B.I. to investigate all commission employees.

The bill seemed on the verge of degenerating into a hopeless cripple and then dying when Californian congressman Jerry Voorhis took the floor and appealed to his colleagues for statesmanship. He finished with a ringing call to "raise our sights . . . to a vision of the stars themselves and the universe whence atomic energy has come." Chastened by Voorhis' speech, House members promptly voted and adopted the amendments and the bill.

At the subsequent Senate-House conference, the senators were able to get agreement on commission exchange with nations overseas of information relating to industrial use of atomic energy when the time was deemed appropriate, and they were able to win the fight on keeping a military man from commissioner status. The compromise bill, the Atomic Energy Act of 1946, was signed by the President on August 1, 1946.

Atomic energy was to be America's first state monopoly and Truman put weeks of thought into his choice of the five men to run it. His pick for chairman was Lilienthal and the four commissioners were the former Securities and Exchange Commission member Sumner T. Pike, the Wall Street banker and Herbert Hoover confidant Lewis L. Strauss, Iowa newspaper editor William W. Waymack, and physicist Robert F. Bacher.

Truman passed over Oppenheimer, possibly because of his glum memories of their first White House meeting, but Bacher, who had been head of the Los Alamos experimental physics division and a key member of the "Fat Man" design group, was widely respected in science. Strauss (pronounced Straws) was a poor Jewish boy from the south who had climbed the heights with a mixture of energy and charm. His most recent role, Ordnance Chief in the Navy Department, entitled him to the rank of Rear Admiral.

Because of the unrelenting bulldogging and manipulation of General Groves, the commission inherited a small empire. Groves had maintained production of uranium-235 and plutonium at Oak Ridge and Hanford, reorganized Los Alamos into a weapons research center under Norris Bradbury, and encouraged peacetime nuclear studies at a dozen universities and other institutions around the nation. It was all there, but, particularly at Los Alamos, morale was at a low ebb, and after noting this on a crosscountry tour the commission settled down in makeshift offices in the War Department Building to revitalize their secret world.

One of the first acts was to appoint the General Advisory Com-

mittee, and the commissioners quickly obtained presidential approval for a panel consisting of Oppenheimer, James Conant, I. I.
Rabi, Enrico Fermi, Glenn Seaborg, the new Caltech president
Lee DuBridge, Hanford engineer Hood Worthington, Los Alamos
group leader Cyril Smith, and a Bush associate, Hartley Rowe.

Oppie was elected chairman by his colleagues and although he
said that they as advisers must be careful not to intrude into policy
making, it was fairly obvious from the very beginning that Oppie's
team would be running the show. Apart from Bacher, the physicists' Manhattan comrade-in-arms, the commissioners knew very
little about atomics. Strauss did his homework and asked the
toughest questions. Lilienthal, however, could never quite get
the true concept of atomic energy and relied heavily on what
Oppie called "working papers giving certain comments and arguments that bear on questions."

Military influence on the commission was even less substantial
than Congress had allowed for. The Act was open to interpretation, and, to the lasting fury of Groves, the commission's young
general manager, Carroll Wilson, read it with civilian eyes.

First disappointment for the commissioners was that the smooth
flow of atomic power from reactors did not presage an entire net-
work of them across the country, running industry and lighting
cities. The General Advisory Committee said nuclear power could
not compete in price with conventional power and, except in
special circumstances, it could not see widespread use for at least
twenty-five years.

More promising in the immediate future, said the advisers, was
work with the radioactive isotopes of various elements—products
of the nuclear reactor—in both industry and medicine.

Radioisotopes mixed with normal materials provided the hidden eye inside metals and liquids, even inside plants and humans.
A radiation counter could find and read them at any time. At the
outset of 1947 the isotope studies were comparatively crude. Commission advisers said this work could prove to be the most fruitful
in the whole atomic business. Thus, the research was greatly en-

larged and it was not long before there was the reward of cobalt
40 isotope beam treatment for cancer, iodine for thyroids, and
phosphorus for leukemia.

Every man on the Oppenheimer panel was an expert and had
a point of view, and, as in the tiff about denaturing, Fermi was
poised for Oppie's mistakes. Yet he was such a grand expositor
that nearly all his ideas were adopted as committee ideas. Rabi
complained that his friend Robert was like a woman and always
wanted to have both the center of the stage and the last word.
Rabi went along because Oppie was right—or right enough.

Oppenheimer's influence came strongly to bear in two fields—
fundamental research and weaponry.

Following his earlier arguments, Oppie said the basic nuclear
knowledge gleaned in the thirties had been used up during the
war years and it had to be replaced. By basic he meant a return
to pure theory. At that moment he and Hans Bethe were interested in the problem of what he described as "radiation reaction
on the scattering of an electron in an external field," and when
he mentioned it to the commissioners they just went slack-jawed.
Oppie had given a lecture to the American Physical Society in
New York on mesons—the atomic nucleus "glue" particles—and
he pointed out that this was another elementary field that had to
be worked.

But of all the recommendations Oppie's group made to the
commission the most significant was to develop atomic weapons.
Apart from bombs both big and small, they envisaged nuclear
warheads for missiles and a wide range of nuclear rockets. What
they did not push, however, was the thermonuclear bomb. Its
main champion, Edward Teller, now teaching at the University
of Chicago, was somewhat angry and puzzled about why he was
not assigned to this project, but the Oppie panel simply put the
priority on having many weapons of wide variety and size than
on one super bomb.

Oppenheimer's later summary of the thinking on the weapons
issue was exquisitely characteristic of him. He said, "Without

debate—I suppose with some melancholy—we concluded that the principal job of the commission was to provide atomic weapons and good atomic weapons and many atomic weapons."

Consequently, the commission geared up for the suggested fundamental and applied research, planned more reactors, laboratories, and separation plants, and wrote uranium import contracts with a half dozen countries. Its capital investment alone was to grow quickly to five billion dollars, and it would soon be nothing to spend a billion and a half a year, yet the watchdog Joint Congressional Committee remained generous and trusting for some little time. The congressmen could not even see the minutes of the meetings of the Oppenheimer group or of the commissioners without making special application.

Security could not have been tighter. Under the Act, the Manhattan security files had been turned over to the F.B.I., which had the assignment of rechecking the loyalty of sixty thousand atom employees. It got through the lot, finding sixty doubtful cases, including Oppenheimer. This was in spite of a "clarifying" interview he had had with F.B.I. agents only a few months before he was appointed to the General Advisory Committee.

On this occasion Oppie confessed he had given Pash and Lansdale the wrong slant on the Chevalier incident during the war; Chevalier had in fact approached only one Manhattan scientist on behalf of George Eltenton and that was Oppenheimer. The affair had become vague in his mind and he had not remembered exactly to whom he had said what, or the real basis for his remarks at the very beginning to Pash, but he had been refreshed on it by Chevalier himself.

The French teacher was interviewed by the F.B.I. in June of 1946, before Oppie. Apparently, at the same time, though in different rooms, Eltenton was being quizzed on the same plot. Fortunately for them they had the same story—a remark by Eltenton to Chevalier about whether Oppie could be persuaded to give the Soviets information and this proposition being passed on to Oppie, who flatly refused.

Chevalier told Oppenheimer of his session with the F.B.I. soon afterwards in the garden at Eagle Hill, whereupon, according to Chevalier in his book *Oppenheimer: The Story of a Friendship,* Oppie became so disturbed he "let loose with a flood of foul language" when Kitty came to call them inside.

Shortly after Oppie was named adviser to the commission, F.B.I. director J. Edgar Hoover personally sent his fat file to Lilienthal. The chairman called in his four commissioners and they read the dossier together. They could see how Oppie hedged around with Pash and Lansdale in light of his later declaration, but to read the transcripts was to hear Oppie's familiar, reassuring voice. And Bacher could tell them that some of the names in the transcripts of suspected evil-minded communists were in reality invaluable men at Los Alamos—Serber and Morrison to mention two of them.

Lilienthal sought character references from the two senior scientists, Vannevar Bush and James Conant. In his note, Bush said, "I know him [Oppenheimer] very well indeed and I have personally great confidence in his judgment and integrity." Conant said there could be no doubt about Oppie's loyalty. "Furthermore," he added, "I can state categorically that in my opinion his attitude about the future causes of the United States Government in matters of high policy is in accordance with the soundest democratic tradition. . . . I base this statement on what I consider intimate knowledge of the workings of his mind."

Since the F.B.I. had made no attempt to evaluate Oppie's file —this was not the bureau's function—Lilienthal called Truman's aide Clark Clifford at the White House and suggested the best plan might be to set up a confidential board of jurists to look into the Oppenheimer matter. Lilienthal was obviously not enthusiastic and neither was Clifford. They let the matter drop and a memo was later put on file to the effect that the Atomic Energy Commission could see no reason why Oppenheimer's security clearance should not continue.

Returning the file to the F.B.I. Lilienthal probed Hoover for his opinion. Hoover seemed neutral and said his only reservation was Oppie's inconsistency in the Chevalier incident. As if to compensate for Robert's semi-respectability, the director volunteered the information that Frank Oppenheimer was of a different order, definitely undesirable.

It happened that Frank left Lawrence's Radiation Laboratory about this time to work on cosmic ray balloons and to teach at the University of Minnesota. Several physicists who sought to make Lawrence on ogre claimed that he had fired Frank after getting a telephone call from Hoover. In truth the two physicists parted on the best of terms, though this was not to last.

Robert Oppenheimer knew that his past "wild oats" were being raked over by the commissioners, and he was surprised when Lewis Strauss confirmed an earlier offer for Oppie to become director of the Institute for Advanced Study at Princeton, of which Strauss was a trustee. The admiral was known as an unbending anti-communist and the most security-minded commissioner of the five.

Undecided about how to react, Oppie said it might affect his eligibility for Strauss to know about derogatory information in his F.B.I. file. Strauss said he had examined the dossier and this did not make any difference. Like most others in first close contact with Oppie, the admiral had been overpowered. That this philosopher-physicist-poet could be a security risk was unthinkable. Strauss was not prepared then to believe that Oppie could be devious, that he could shuffle the facts a little as a legitimate means towards a worthwhile end.

Kitty and Robert paced around Eagle Hill for weeks trying to make up their minds about Princeton. The job paid eighteen thousand dollars a year, plus use of the rambling old residence, Olden Manor. He would watch over a group of distinguished professors in physics and mathematics and history, with their research assistants and guest intellectuals. The year at the institute dawdled from October to mid-December, from mid-January to April, and during that time nobody would complain if a single thesis failed to appear from this rustic den of thinkers. It happened, however, that much of value was accomplished in these depressurized conditions.

More than ten years earlier Oppie had visited the institute and written Frank about its "solipsistic luminaries," but now that he was older and half his life was lived in the east anyway, he was tempted. Driving across the bridge from San Francisco to Oakland one night in April, Oppie heard on the radio that he had been appointed the new director of the institute. "Well," he said to Kitty, "I guess that settles it."

His arrival in October that year was welcomed by most of the faculty members, though two had doubts—the odd duet who had been foundation members of the institute in 1933, aging humanitarian Albert Einstein and Hungarian mathematical genius Johnny von Neumann. They agreed the ideal director should be a man who knows how to keep out of sight and not disturb anyone. Oppie did not look the part.

When some of the faculty cooled towards Oppie later, one member was asked why he had not shared the prescience of von Neumann who called Oppie a storm center. "Hell," said the professor sourly, "this is a mecca for intellectuals and we were reading in the *New York Times* every day that Oppenheimer was the greatest intellectual in the world. Of course we wanted him—then."

13

In the fall of 1948, for the first time since that dim, coltish, pre-neutron era when Pauli had dubbed him the nim-nim-nim man, Robert Oppenheimer returned to Europe.

He had come through the field to take the reins of America's vast atomic enterprise and to win the directorship of a famous institute of international scholars, but the fatigue lines digging under the eyes and across the forehead and down the cheeks showed the ordeal of his responsibilities. As he moved about the physics centers of western Europe, with the people who maligned him about the bomb in private beaming at him face-to-face, he kept thinking of the rather trite little exchange he had had with his longtime friend Harold Cherniss, the sage of Greek philosophy now on his faculty, shortly before he left Princeton.

"The time has come, Robert," said Cherniss, "for you to give up the political life and return to physics."

And when he had hung at the door and not replied, Cherniss said, "Are you like the man who has a tiger by the tail?"

Robert had thought about that for a minute and then replied truthfully, "Yes."

Few outside the closed halls of the Atomic Energy Commission knew how tremendous Oppie's power was in America, how much his country's confrontation with Russia depended on his strategy, and how much that strategy was linked to eventual international ownership and control of atomic energy. He was ironbark tough still on the Kremlin attitude, but it had come to him, inevitably, that to renounce the only hope for a warless future was to fall into despair, and despair was insupportable.

Some months previously when General Frederick Osborn had taken over Baruch's role at the United Nations, Oppenheimer had followed him to his country place and spent the weekend imploring him to demand that Russia either lift the Iron Curtain or else the atom negotiations would cease. America was weakening on international ownership of the atom authority and talking of an inspection system for separate national atom works. This, in Oppie's view, would be useless. Osborn would not, could not, offer Oppie's ultimatum to force the Soviet hand and the debate drifted on.

In a recent talk to military and foreign service officers at the State Department in Washington, Oppie had attempted to present his reasoning on what he saw as the necessarily very long haul to international control. Successful dealing with the Russians presupposed a large measure of peaceful intention, of cooperation, of confidence, and of candor on both sides, he said. Russia did not bring any of this to the table because it had no intention of changing its present patterns of state power. Russia was increasingly secretive and distrustful. America's mistake was reacting in kind; it was souring its own soul.

While it was futile to expect an imminent change in the Russian policy, said Oppie, some day the United States would want to return to the Acheson-Lilienthal concept of a world atom authority because it had the seeds of a kind of security which was not obtainable in any other way. "And this means," he said, "that in our own operations, in the way we deal with atomic energy and its related problems in this country, in the way in which we deal with the Western European countries, one of the conditions . . . that needs to be kept in mind is that we conform to those plans which would make it most likely that in the long term the problem of atomic energy could not merely be borne with but could be solved, and that means internationalization. . . .

"If there is to be a solution along the lines of the United States proposals, not this year, not next year, but at some time in the future, then this area of work in atomic energy . . . must not be sewed up so tightly that it is not a part of the living culture and development of the country. . . . It means that the policy of sitting tight on our knowledge and on our stockpiles would neither be of use to keeping open the door to later internationalization, nor be an effective course for maintaining our technical superiority."

Oppie's point was that an exclusive policy of short-term security was folly; abiding strength lay in opening the vault on atomic energy and inviting the participation of all scientists in America and Europe and Japan. Meanwhile the Atomic Energy Commission was not so foolish as to gamble on international control. This was part of a balanced policy that also included maintenance of technical superiority and sure capabilities in atomic defense and retaliation.

While he had conceded in his talk that the pattern of civilized life in Europe had been worn thin, he mentioned that of the important postwar discoveries in physics, several had come from Europe.

He had gone off for his tour with the notion that he would be stimulated by the European spirit of vigorous intellectual inquiry. By the time he reached Brussels in late September he found a different story, and, in his peculiar switchback style of phrasing, he related it in a letter to Frank.

"The *Europa reise* is, as it was in the old days, a certain time for inventory," he wrote.

But all the tropisms are inverted. In science—all the love and also all the snobbishness—that would be apparent; yet it is even more true than I had thought. Even in the books it is largely true; along the river in Paris Steinbeck and Hemingway and Faulkner lie with

some Sartre more Gide and still more Stendahl. In physics the con-
ferences have been good, yet everywhere—Copenhagen, England,
Paris, even here, there is the phrase "you see, we are somewhat out
of things. . . ."

Above all I have the knowledge that it is in America largely that
it will be decided what manner of world we are all to live in. Here
there is benevolence surely, and sympathy and even a fairly high
level of informed debate, but no sense of issue, of struggle, or of
hope. I was not prepared to find it so, to recognize how little help
any of us could look for.

Oppenheimer's flow of words stopped there, as if he had been
trying to move up to his real worry with some ease and then lost
patience.

"The Hiss story," he wrote next, "seemed to me a menacing
portent."

For close on two months it had been the sensation of Washington. Whittaker Chambers, an ex-communist who was now a respectable magazine editor, had told the House Committee on
Un-American Activities that former State Department official Alger Hiss had been a communist spy during the thirties and had
passed on to him copies of confidential Government documents.
Hiss challenged his accuser before the same committee, denying
he had ever been a communist. The storm might have stayed in
the teacup, but, as the American correspondent for the *Manchester
Guardian,* Alistair Cooke, noted, "The United States was con-
vulsed, as at no time since the 1920's, with fear and hatred of the
Soviet Union," and Hiss had to stand against a political tide. The
House committee was out to show that Roosevelt's young New
Dealers had permitted communists to worm into the Washington
woodwork, where they were still eating away at the American
heart, now under the protection of Harry Truman. At the height
of the hysteria, the House committee allowed television cameras
into the hearing room, and millions of Americans watched and
applauded as the clean-cut young war veteran congressman from

California, Richard Nixon, made Hiss squirm under cross-examination.

With an angry mutter, the House committee had let Hiss go but he had restored himself in the newspapers—and precipitated calamity for himself—by suing Chambers for defamation. Oppenheimer found him there on the front pages as far away as Brussels.

The ruthlessness the House committee had shown in the Hiss case made Oppenheimer afraid—afraid for himself and Frank. If the un-American hearings remained in camera until evidence was properly and justly assessed it would not have been so fearful, but some committee members, J. Parnell Thomas in particular, had character assassination down to a science. They would allow names to be mentioned at the hearings in suspicious context and then watch public and victim reaction. Another ploy was to plant stories in sympathetic newspapers indicating that so-and-so might soon be subpoenaed to prove he was not a security risk.

Innuendo had already begun about Frank, and Haakon Chevalier had been a victim in a broadside that brought Robert's name under notice too.

Louis J. Russell, the former F.B.I. agent who worked as the House committee's investigator, mentioned in the course of a completely unrelated hearing one day that Chevalier had "approached" Robert Oppenheimer during the war for information to be given another "physicist" for relay to Russia. The other man was identified as George Eltenton. Eltenton, back in England, would make no comment. Chevalier, extremely upset to see his name trumpeted by the San Francisco newspapers, told reporters that all he had done was repeat to Oppie a conversation he had had with Eltenton. Nevertheless, California Senator Jack Tenney, who headed a local version of the House Un-American Activities Committee, subpoenaed Chevalier. It was a publicity play, for when Chevalier appeared before the Tenney committee it asked him a few inconsequential questions then let him go. For days on end, Chevalier waited for Oppie to make a public statement saying the so-called "approach" was totally innocent, but all his friend would do was withhold comment. Oppie was glad to see, for his part, that his old three-scientist story had been amended in the security files.

The episode with Frank dated back to March of 1947 when the Washington *Times-Herald,* a mouthpiece of sorts for the House committee, ran a story saying that Frank had been a communist and should be investigated. This was about the same time Hoover had told Lilienthal that Frank was an undesirable. Frank wrote a letter foolishly denying the truth of the story to the *Times-Herald,* which then unaccountably switched their attack to Ed Condon.

Condon was burly in spirit as well as body and when the attacks continued and J. Parnell Thomas wrote signed articles for magazines implying close Soviet connections with Condon, the physicist planned his counter attack. The battle was joined when Thomas got the House committee to call publicly for Condon's resignation from the Bureau of Standards on the grounds that he was "one of the weakest links in our atomic security." There was no evidence, just Thomas's malice against the man who had helped Brien Mc-Mahon get his bill through for civilian atomic energy management.

In rapid succession, Condon asked both the Department of Commerce and the Atomic Energy Commission to investigate him and, if he was clean, to confirm his security clearance. He was emphatically cleared. The American Physical Society, of which Oppenheimer was president, publicly backed Condon, and Harold Urey arranged a dinner of atomic scientists in New York to cheer on big Ed Condon. Oppie did not attend; it was the sort of noisy street crusade from which he held himself aloof.

Because of Frank's definite communist background, the Condon tactics would not work with him. In the letter from Brussels, Robert advised him, if the trouble deepened, to see commission counsel Herb Marks for "comfort and strength." And he added, more as a prayer than a conviction, "My own view (and it may be proven wrong before this reaches you) is that no need will arise."

The brothers did not have long to wait before they knew that nothing could keep them out of the accursed House committee. In June of 1949 both were subpoenaed to give evidence, Robert a week before Frank. Robert's was a secret session and obviously he would be asked for information on others; Frank's was semi-open and this meant public accusations. Distressed at the rough time facing his brother—and Frank, at thirty-seven, did still look delicately young—Robert urged him to see privately the committee's most responsible Democratic member, Francis E. Walter. "Talk things over with him, you'll be okay," said Robert.

This crazy idea was the only advice or help Robert offered. Frank's loyalty and affection for his brother did not permit him even to question why there was not more, but some family friends felt that Jacky was furious because Robert seemed to buckle at the very mention of the name of the committee.

The House committee had collared all the existing intelligence files about the Berkeley years and one by one it subpoenaed Frank, Joe Weinberg, then teaching at the University of Minnesota, David Bohm, of Princeton, Bernard Peters, of the University of Rochester, and Rossi Lomanitz, of Fisk University in Nashville. It was the same crew of hothead idealists that had left Oppenheimer's wing in the early years of the war to try to stay active in a leftist union and do secret war work at the same time. Oppie's reasoning with them had not been fruitful and he remembered telling Lansdale that they were near-Reds, though he was unsure about Weinberg.

That June the men could feel the net closing and Bohm and Lomanitz, at least, looked to Oppie to stand up for them, to vouch for their integrity and guide them out of trouble. When they saw him in Princeton, however, he gave them the impression of being more scared than they were. From his conduct they judged he could not be relied on for leadership. Weinberg, who was accused of actually passing documents to the Russians, had never gotten over his boyish adulation for Oppie and said he did not want to involve him in the shabby affair. The tough-fibered Peters, most

brilliant of the group, thought he could handle the committee
without help.

In his session with the committee, Robert Oppenheimer spent
much of the time listening to the wartime dialogues he had had
with Lansdale and the Los Alamos resident security man, Peer de
Silva. He saw no reason to change his statements. But what had
sounded reasonably safe during the war, when former communists
were not regarded as such bloodthirsty enemies, had a different
aspect in 1949. Oppie was slow to make allowance for this and just
agreeing with dated testimony without elaboration was his mistake.

The voices droned on in the caucus room:

"Doctor, do you recall making a statement to one of the security
officers on the Manhattan project to the effect that Dr. Peters was
a dangerous man and quite Red?"

"I made that statement to de Silva?"

"And also that his background was full of incidents that would
point towards direct action?"

"I would not have remembered it in such detail, but I recognize
it."

The old transcript contained more suppositions about the fugi-
tive from Nazism: Oppie agreed Bernard would have to show
guile to escape from a place like Dachau. Yes, Bernard was an activist all right, for when he came to California he was denouncing
the party in America as a do-nothing outfit.

Oppie gave no new information to the House committee that
day, but he missed the committee's plot. By reviewing the old
material and getting his confirmation, the hunters had made it all
fresh.

A week later Frank's wide-eyed, curly haired portrait was all
over the nation's newspapers. He and Jacky admitted to the committee that they had been communists, but they refused to discuss
or name their associates at the time. This was the practice followed
by the other young Berkeley scientists. "My wife and I," said

Left: Robert's parents, Julius and Ella Oppenheimer, circa 1905, the year after Robert was born. *(Courtesy of Frank Oppenheimer) Right:* Robert and Frank Oppenheimer. "Your guess as to age," says Frank, "is as good as ours." *(Courtesy of Frank Oppenheimer)*

From the family album . . . Robert Oppenheimer (aged 11) looks on while his father asks directions in a country town. The Oppenheimer car is pulled over against the curb. *(Courtesy of Frank Oppenheimer)*

Above: A nucleus of physicists. Robert Oppenheimer at Caltech in 1935 with Nobel laureates P.A.M. Dirac (left) and Robert Millikan. *(Associated Press) Below:* The pork pie hat was part of Oppie's wartime uniform. Here he is seen at the Alamogordo atomic bomb test site in 1945. *(Wide World Photos)*

General Leslie Groves and Robert Oppenheimer, the two men who did most to develop the world's first atomic bomb, inspect the twisted remains of the tower that had held "Fat Man," the test bomb exploded at Alamogordo. *(United Press International Photo)*

Ernest Lawrence (left), chief of the Berkeley Radiation Laboratory, called Oppie "my theoretician." Their friendship was to dissolve in the troubled years after this picture was taken, in 1946. *(Wide World Photos)*

Physics professor Raymond T. Birge, shown here in 1946, hired Oppie on to his Berkeley faculty in 1929. *(United Press International Photo)*

General Kenneth Nichols and Professor Henry Smyth listen to Oppenheimer's account of the Nagasaki atomic bomb explosion. Nichols was to brand Oppie a security risk; Smyth to vote for his exoneration. *(United Press International Photo)*

In 1947 Oppenheimer became director of the Institute for Advanced Study in Princeton. Shown here with Professor Oswald Veblen. *(Wide World Photos)*

Oppie returned to his old school, Harvard, in 1947 to receive an honorary degree. His fellow recipients are General George Marshall and General Omar Bradley. At right is Harvard president James Conant. *(United Press International Photo)*

Frank Oppenheimer's wife Jacky.
(Courtesy of Frank Oppenheimer)

Frank Oppenheimer admitted to
the House Un-American Activities
Committee in 1949 that he had been
a card-carrying Communist before
the war. *(United Press International
Photo)*

In the immediate post-war years Oppenheimer seemed to spend half his life in Washington. *(United Press International Photo)*

William L. Borden, formerly on the staff of the Joint Congressional Committee on Atomic Energy, wrote to FBI chief J. Edgar Hoover in November, 1953, that Oppenheimer was probably a Russian agent. *(United Press International Photo)*

Atomic Energy Commissioners voted four-to-one to deny Oppenheimer his security clearance in 1954. From left, Thomas Murray, Eugene Zuckert, Joseph Campbell and Chairman Lewis Strauss. The dissenting vote came from Henry Smyth (not shown). *(United Press International Photo)*

At a congressional hearing in 1949 Oppie first crossed swords with Admiral Lewis Strauss when he vigorously defended the free export of radio-active isotopes. *(United Press International Photo)*

Physicist Henry D. Smyth was the lone dissenting voice in the four-to-one vote of the Atomic Energy Commissioners denying Oppenheimer his security clearance in 1954. *(United Press International Photo)*

Atomic Energy Commission Chairman Lewis L. Strauss was one of the instigators of Oppenheimer's security trial in 1954. *(Wide World Photos)*

Above left: In the Matter of J. Robert Oppenheimer, the security hearing that startled the nation in 1954, was chaired by Gordon Gray, then president of the University of North Carolina. *(United Press International Photo) Right:* Thomas A. Morgan, former chairman of the Sperry Corporation, joined with Gordon Gray in the majority ruling of the special inquiry board which found Oppenheimer a security risk. *(United Press International Photo)*

Below left: Ward V. Evans, a distinguished professor of chemistry, was one of the three-man board of inquiry passing judgment on Oppenheimer's trustworthiness at the famous 1954 hearing. Evans wanted to restore Oppie's security clearance, but was outvoted. *(United Press International Photo) Right:* Roger Robb, a tough and able Washington lawyer, was the prosecuting attorney at Oppenheimer's security trial. Oppie's attorneys were no match for him. *(Wide World Photos)*

Edward R. Murrow interviewed Oppenheimer in his Princeton office for a memorable "See It Now" TV program in 1955. *(United Press International)*

With Albert Einstein in Princeton. *(Wide World Photos)*

Oppenheimer was visibly moved when newsmen informed him on his arrival in Seattle in April 1955, that Albert Einstein, a good friend and colleague, had died. *(Wide World Photos)*

At his study in Princeton in 1957. The security hearing three years earlier had noticeably aged him. *(Wide World Photos)*

April in Paris, 1958, and the Oppenheimers, Robert, Kitty and daughter Toni, head for the Sorbonne, where Oppie gave a series of lectures. *(Wide World Photos)*

Below left: Oppie on the grand tour. Athens, 1958. *(United Press International Photo)*

Right: On a two-day visit to Greece in 1958, Oppenheimer spent most of his time at the Acropolis. He is accompanied by wife Kitty and daughter Toni. *(Wide World Photos)*

Prime Minister David Ben Gurion and his wife, Paula, were Oppie's hosts on his visit to Israel in 1958. *(Wide World Photos)*

Oppenheimer led a distinguished roster of speakers at the conference of the Congress for Cultural Freedom, held in West Berlin in 1960. Next to him are Gaston Berger of France and Denis de Rougement of Switzerland. *(Wide World Photos)*

It was an emotional moment for Oppenheimer when he was called to the White House in 1963 to receive the coveted Enrico Fermi Award. He was flanked by his wife Kitty, son Peter and daughter Toni. *(United Press International Photo)*

On his first and only visit to Japan in 1960 the father of the atomic bomb faced a torrent of questions from newsmen in Tokyo. *(Wide World Photos)*

At the time Oppenheimer received an honorary degree from Princeton in 1966, he already showed the ravages of his last illness. *(Randall Hagadorn)*

Frank, "joined the Communist Party in 1937, seeking an answer to the problems of unemployment and want in the wealthiest and most productive country in the world. We did not find in the Communist Party the vehicle through which to accomplish the progressive changes we were interested in and so we left it about three and a half years later and never rejoined."

The next day the University of Minnesota announced it was accepting Frank's resignation because Frank had lied to the faculty, and to a newspaper, two years before about his communist membership. Many scientists, including Edward Teller, protested to the University, citing Frank's valuable work in cosmic rays. It was to no avail. Frank and Jacky put their young children, Judith and Michael, in the station wagon and headed up to Blanco Basin, a beautiful, remote section of southwestern Colorado, where Frank had first ridden with Robert. For many years to come he would be a rancher.

Frank's former boss, Ernest Lawrence, was not among the sympathetic. The Radiation Laboratory had been getting the reputation as a communist breeding ground in official quarters some time before the publicity. Lawrence had severed connections with the old leftist crew entirely and created a strong conservative image for the present-day laboratory. He would not allow Frank even to visit. Robert scolded Lawrence about this on a visit to Berkeley—the headline story about Frank had not even broken yet —but Lawrence was adamant. He was fed to the teeth with political scientists. According to Lawrence's official biographer, Herbert Childs, Oppie did not think his friend minded his rebuke, "but, as often was the case, my wife said something sharper, and I think maybe he minded that." Whatever it was Kitty said, and she could be rather fierce, the two men did not ever heal the breach and drew further and further apart.

Frank himself had to live with the feeling that he had failed everyone and his science as well. There was no self-pity at being a victim of lunatic times, just tremendous regret that he had disqualified himself from teaching and from continuing his research project on cosmic rays. It disturbed him also that he had brought a measure of trouble for his brother.

But it was the Bernard Peters' case that brought Robert down.

Peters followed Frank into the grim caucus room and was surprised when the committee dismissed him after a dozen nonincriminatory questions. Nobody referred to the newspaper smear that Peters was one of the members of the former communist "apparatus" at Berkeley. On his way back to Rochester he called into Princeton to see Oppie, who said the committee had just gone over a lot of old accusations with him and he had not said anything that was derogatory.

The visit irritated Oppenheimer because he did not particularly like Peters. This coolness was in such contrast to his admiration of the man when he first joined him as a student that one mutual friend, Sam Goudsmit, then trying to help Peters through the Federation of American Scientists, asked the reason.

"The man is no good," Oppie said. "Can't you tell that by looking at him."

Five years earlier Oppie would have been incapable of a statement like this, just as he was once reluctant to believe in the existence of evil. The bomb did not change him. It was the venality of Washington, the gross conduct of men like J. Parnell Thomas, soon to be jailed himself for payroll padding. The only thing that counted in Washington was influence, and the foulest men frequently had the most influence. After the comparatively modest halls of science, it was a bullying neighborhood to move into. Oppie's students of the thirties would have furiously rejected the idea that low-based human flaws could ever develop in their master. The fact remained, however, that Oppenheimer adopted some cunning to survive in Washington. Like everyone else he was a little corrupted. Thus, when Peters came to him he resented being faced with his calumny and took some justification for himself in passing off the fellow as a bad egg anyway.

Puzzled by the whole affair, Peters then wrote to the House committee demanding a chance to answer the charges against him.

There was no direct reply, but a few days later the direct quotes from Oppie's secret testimony about Peters being "dangerous" were published in the Rochester *Times-Union.*

America's community of atomic scientists, virtually a brotherhood after the shared wartime experiences at Los Alamos, was deeply wounded. To most of them Oppie was still the leader, notwithstanding his relapse over the May-Johnson bill, and to have him revealed as an informer to the despicable House Committee on Un-American Activities against one of their own kind was unbearable.

From the Massachusetts Institute of Technology, Victor Weisskopf, highly regarded everywhere and long close to Oppie, wrote to his friend that if Peters lost his job because of Oppie's statements then scientists would lose their confidence in him. "I beg you therefore Robert, set this record straight and do what is in your power to prevent Peters' dismissal, even if you have to pay for it by losing reputation somewhere else."

Weisskopf added, "I know he is not the first scientist who has been fired because of political hearings. He would be the first one, however, who is fired on the basis of information from another scientist, and, what is more, from you, whom so many of us regard as our representative in the best sense of the word."

Many of the physicists had been attending a conference at Idaho Springs when the Peters story broke. Its discussion took over the proceedings. Hans Bethe wrote Oppenheimer that he must have been quoted out of context. Even so, he said, Robert should write to the University of Rochester setting out his true opinion of Peters, whom he had always thought Robert liked.

Ed Condon censured Oppie's terrible deed, writing that one was tempted to feel that Oppie was so foolish as to think he could buy immunity for himself by turning informer. If Oppie's own dossier was made public, said Condon, it would cause a sensation.

Emilie Condon had a sizzling note from her husband, in which Condon talked of Oppie's very high state of nervous tension in the past few weeks. People from Princeton had said he seemed to be greatly strained for fear he himself would be attacked. By the tone of Condon's letter, he seemed to think Oppie might crack up completely, and if this happened, Condon wondered bleakly, how many others would be dragged down, too.

Now Condon was being reckless. He well knew his Washington telephone was tapped and that letters to and from his home would likely be intercepted. And on the day of Frank's hearing, the House committee's Richard Nixon had said that he was not finished yet with Condon. The scathing letter he wrote to Emilie was indeed stopped and copied before delivery, for a committee investigator showed it to Robert Oppenheimer in Princeton.

"You can see Condon is your enemy so why not come clean and help us get the goods on him," the agent coaxed.

"But there are no goods to get," Oppenheimer protested.

Later, Oppie told Condon of the exchange. The big man was mortified. Whatever did Robert think of him?

"It was not a comforting letter," Oppenheimer said flatly, yet the two men continued as uneasy friends.

Oppie did take the personal risk as Weisskopf suggested and amend his testimony. The Rochester *Times-Union* carried his letter shortly afterwards.

"I knew him [Peters] not only as a brilliant student but as a man of strong moral principles and of high ethical standards," he said.

> During those years his political views were radical. He expressed them freely and sometimes I thought without temperance. This seemed to me not unnatural in a man who had suffered as he had at Nazi hands. I have never known Dr. Peters to commit a dishonorable act nor a disloyal one. . . . From the published article one might conclude that Dr. Peters had advocated the violent overthrow of the constitutional government of the United States. He has given an eloquent denial of this in his published statement. I believe his statement.

Oppenheimer tried to explain that the House committee had based its release on his wartime conversations with the intelligence officers at Los Alamos. "I wish to make public my profound regret that anything said in that context should have been so misconstrued, and so abused, that it could damage Dr. Peters and threaten his distinguished future career as a scientist."

Towards the end of his letter, Oppie put down his thoughts on the harassment of scientists by the House committee. It was clear that he had Frank in mind more than Peters.

"Political opinion no matter how radical or freely expressed does not disqualify a scientist for a high career in science," he wrote.

> It does not disqualify him as a teacher of science. It does not impugn his integrity nor his honor. We have seen in other countries criteria of political orthodoxy applied to ruin scientists and to put an end to their work. This has brought with it the attrition of science. Even more, it has been part of the destruction of freedom of inquiry and political freedom itself. This is not the path to follow for a people determined to stay free.

Following this furore the young rebels scattered.

The University of Rochester, made of sterner stuff than the University of Minnesota, refused all the pressure to fire Peters and actually promoted him—with warm endorsement by Oppenheimer —before he went off in 1951 to work in India. Peters exchanged letters with Oppie about physics and the younger man decided he felt no bitterness towards Oppie, but was sorry that this man who needed people had driven away friends and become "isolated."

Weinberg fared the worst, though Oppie could not have done much here. Only after cruel courtroom trials that broke his health was Joe able to return to teaching physics. And when he did a *Time* magazine cover of Oppie was thumbtacked on his office wall.

Bohm went abroad contemplating the root causes for Oppie's "panic" but still with lingering affection for him. Oppie understandably turned aside a faculty suggestion to get Bohm into the Princeton institute, recommended him instead to a position in Brazil.

Lomanitz worked for years as a day laborer, and was located once living in a shack on the edge of a swamp in Oklahoma, before he too found his way back to physics and the lecture hall.

"I doubt that any of us who as young people looked on him [Oppie] almost as a god ever came to believe him malicious," Lomanitz was to write later.

> I think mostly we came to feel sad personally about the man's weaknesses, and also very sorry that he was not able to give any kind of leadership needed during very bad times. . . . I think that the same ego problems that led him to want to be in a god-like position in 1940 led him into disaster a bit later. And therein I think is a tragedy. For, otherwise, he and a whole generation of theoretical physicists could almost surely have come through the 1950's less scarred.

14

─────────

That old line about a man carrying within himself the seeds for his own destruction occurred often to the men who knew Oppenheimer and watched him perform. His physical habits were suicidal for a start. He coughed, as somebody said, fit to die right in front of you, yet he would not cut down on his smoking. Nor would he eat more regularly to add flesh, dispense with the jackhammer martini at night in deference to his tender stomach, or rest to ease his chronic lower back pains. But this catalogue of self-injury paled before the dangerous personal antagonism he was almost willfully building up for himself in Washington by acting the role of the supreme advocate in all matters atomic.

Running concurrently with the Bernard Peters affair was another *cause célèbre* in which Oppenheimer led the players—the affair of the isotopes.

It had started in May when he returned to Washington after a weekend in an old stone inn on the Hudson with Bethe, Weisskopf, Schwinger, Teller, Christy, and perhaps a dozen others of the top physicists in America. Oppie had organized informal meetings like this in previous years and it was the mark of a man's stature in the science as to whether he was invited or not. The assemblies were to stop for good when enough people objected to being left out and demanded a reason.

Anne Marks, Herb's new pretty young wife, who had been a secretary in Los Alamos during the war, gave Oppie a quick run-down on the basket of troubles that had been emptied on the Atomic Energy Commission.

On May 12, Republican congressman W. Sterling Cole, of the Joint Committee on Atomic Energy, introduced into the *Congressional Record* the script of a radio broadcast by arch conservative commentator Fulton Lewis, Jr., who revealed that an avowed communist had been studying for months at the University of North Carolina under a commission scholarship. Brien McMahon, chairman of the joint congressional committee, called an inquiry and Lilienthal defended the commission policy of not probing the political affiliation of those on the fellowship programs. On May 1 the story broke that uranium-235 was missing from the Argonne laboratories. Four days later Senator Bourke B. Hickenlooper, Republican of Iowa, a member of McMahon's committee, made public his open letter to President Truman demanding Lilienthal's resignation because of his "incredible mismanagement" of the commission. Hickenlooper, who had sniped at the former Tennessee Valley Authority boss for years, also claimed Lilienthal was too complacent on security and had allowed strategic radioactive isotopes to be sent overseas. Immediately then, Lilienthal, a cool man in a crisis, asked for a full and open investigation by the congressmen of Hickenlooper's charges.

Oppenheimer backed Lilienthal without qualification, which was about the same as supporting his own policies. The lost uranium was nonsense; ten ounces of uranium oxide containing a bare smidgen of 235 had been misplaced at Argonne. Now for the rest.

In a note to McMahon, that caused the newspaperman Commissioner Waymack to slap his sides with glee, Oppie defended the commission's policy of noninterference with the political views of research fellows by observing with studied cleverness that "it would be contrary to all experience to suppose that only those who throughout their lives had held conformist political views would make the great discoveries of the future."

Another notable commission adviser, Lee DuBridge, endorsed Oppie's letter with his own memo saying police state methods could not be tolerated. He suggested that to burn down the house because the dog had a few fleas was surely not justified.

This left the question of the export of isotopes, which was the basic issue all along, and the one that had set Lewis Strauss against the other four commissioners since the exports started two years earlier. Oppie had been the main champion of the program from the outset, for he saw it as "the beginning of an attempt to make available to wider circles some of the information of atomic energy." He had told a State Department audience some time before that the isotopes were "being made available for our own benefit, for the good will involved, for the knowledge we hope to obtain, and because this is a decent, consistent gesture, painting some slight stroke in the picture of the world as we would like to see it in the future."

There was an admission in this speech that the commission had gone far beyond the list of supposedly non-secret isotopes drawn up with congressional approval. To isotopes of value in biological research had been added some useful in industrial work.

Strauss had boiled up because one millicurie of iron-59 had been sent to the Defense Research Establishment of Norway for diffusion measurements in high temperature steel alloys. In Strauss' mind this was the first step to building warplane jet engines or new weapons. What he did not make clear was that the speck of isotope was equal in radioactivity to one-thousandth of a gram of radium. Hickenlooper had the impression at first that fissionable material was being shipped overseas.

On the first day of the congressional hearing Strauss insisted the commission had overstepped its authority in approving the shipment. He cited the Act: "There shall be no exchange of information with other nations with regard to the use of atomic energy

for industrial purposes . . . atomic energy shall be construed to
mean all forms of energy released in the course of, or as a result
of, nuclear fission or nuclear transformation."

Technically, taking the widest meaning of fission and transformation, Strauss was right. He backed his stand by quoting Dr.
William Shoupp, manager of Westinghouse's electronic and physics department, to the effect that the isotope would be helpful for
developing strategic alloys.

"My colleagues think they are right; I think they are wrong,"
said Strauss.

As the next day's witness in the caucus room at the Senate Office
Building, Oppie did not refute Strauss' testimony, he ridiculed it.

Radioactive isotopes emitted radiation so they were easy to detect
and therefore ideal as tracers in industrial and medical research, he
explained. As an example he told how Lawrence had used him as
a guinea pig ten years before. Ernest had put a Geiger counter in
his hand and then made him drink water containing salt spiked
with radioactive sodium. The sodium ion diffused from the mouth
and through the bloodstream to his hand, making the counter
clatter.

The General Advisory Committee, he said, had thought it appropriate to send abroad isotopes, made by neutron bombardment
of metals, for basic research purposes.

"No one can force me to say that you cannot use these isotopes
for atomic energy," he said, then added with a sigh, "but you can
use a shovel for atomic energy. In fact you do. You can use a bottle
of beer for atomic energy. In fact you do."

Oppie had the congressmen absorbed with his homespun anal-
ogies; it was like a Berkeley lecture hall in the thirties. He said
that under the Act definition coal was atomic energy and so was
oil, and so indeed were people. "Come now," he chided, "one
must do better if one is to have a sensible export policy."

In the benches, Strauss' face was thunderously dark and Hickenlooper tried to pick up the threads. "People certainly would not

be construed as coming under that definition of atomic energy,"
said the Senator impatiently.

"I would not wish to construe it that way," Oppie challenged
him, then insinuated that Hickenlooper regarded the shipment of
isotopes as tantamount to allowing a foreign nation to develop in
its backyard the makings of large numbers of atomic bombs, yet
the strategic value of isotopes was "somewhere between electronic
devices and vitamins."

Hickenlooper brought up Strauss' authority William Shoupp,
whom Oppie had never heard of before. He said he could not
make "head or tail" of the statement Strauss had attributed to
Shoupp and in any case he understood Shoupp now regretted that
his statement had been misinterpreted.

As far as Brien McMahon was concerned this finished the whole
farce and he allowed Oppie to leave. On the way out of the room
he stopped by the table of young Joe Volpe, one of the commission's lawyers.

"How did I do?" Oppie asked.

"You did too well for your own good," said Volpe, who had
been watching Strauss and grimacing at Oppie's piece of theatre.

Lilienthal also left the room with a sinking heart and told Oppie later he had been too offhand.

Strauss got Shoupp on the telephone within the hour and asked
him who was quoting him correctly, Strauss or Oppenheimer. The
Westinghouse man said he stood by his original statement, as presented by Strauss, and, in fact, Shoupp never amended his warning
then or later. The commissioner shot off a letter to McMahon,
with copies to Oppie, putting Shoupp on the record again and
insisting that if Oppenheimer prevailed the entire Act would be
jeopardized.

It was too late; Hickenlooper's case had collapsed. Strauss would
survive, mightily, to fight another day. For a long, long time he
smarted over Oppie's public scorn. He never gave up trying to
prove he was correct, and in his book, *Men and Decisions*, he could
not resist stating that the Norwegian official who had requested

the controversial isotope was "allowed to resign" because of his
Communist Party connections. In reply, the Norwegian Government chemists, who had been getting ready supplies of isotopes
from England all through 1949, said Strauss was wrong—the man
had not been dismissed or eased out.

On the issue of veracity the incident was a standoff between
Oppenheimer and Strauss; both had reshaped the facts to serve
their separate causes.

What Strauss could not forgive was Oppie's ingratitude after
getting him the most prestigious job for a scholar in the United
States. Only weeks previously Strauss had been a guest at Olden
Manor and it had been strictly a Robert-Lewis relationship. Oppenheimer's attitude was that Strauss was being stupid about the
isotopes and should have known better, and, whatever other kind-
nesses he had, Oppie had never in his life been polite to fools. He
further irked Strauss by getting the commission to issue a report
showing that radioisotopes were now used in twenty-one foreign
countries and nearly two thousand research papers had been published on them.

Practical philosophies were in contest over the isotope issue.
Strauss, the banker, believed in tight security. Oppenheimer the
scientist, believed in progress through sharing knowledge and
experience.

He had said, "The indispensable element in giving meaning to
the dignity of man, and in making possible the taking of decision
on the basis of honest conviction, is the openness of men's minds,
and the openness of whatever media there are for communion between men, free of restraint, free of repression, and free even of
that most pervasive of all restraints, that of status and of hier-
archy."

Strauss prided himself on his interest in science and his good
relations with many able practitioners, but he did not think like
a scientist. While he and others were inclined to talk of the great
American discoveries in atomic energy during the war, physicists

simply called it technology. They were returning now, in peace, to discovery.

Oppenheimer talked over and over about the concern of physicists in identifying and characterizing adequately the subatomic elementary particles, in studying the behavior of electrons within atomic systems, of understanding the forces that gave atomic nuclei their great stability and transmutations their great violence. It was total violation of scientific spirit to conduct fundamental research like this behind high walls. In fact, it could not be done. Yet repressive secrecy threatened continually in the United States and, as in the isotope issue, Oppenheimer felt he had to keep up a pitched battle.

A large number of congressmen and most in military and defense agreed with Strauss. Many developed a surly distaste for the arrogant Dr. Oppenheimer. His personality was much discussed by members of the Joint Committee on Atomic Energy, and the keenest listener was the popular and industrious young committee manager, William Borden.

A graduate of Yale, the slender Bill Borden had piloted a *B-24 Liberator* on thirty missions over Europe during the war. It was a lone wolf, black-painted, stripped-down airplane with the job of parachuting supplies and O.S.S. agents into Germany and occupied countries. Up there in the inky sky with the fear running up and down his back, both for himself and for the men going down below, Borden came to detest war. He dreamed up a good plan: find out how peace was maintained among dissimilar people on a national level and then try to extend this principal on a global basis.

After the war, because of the atom bomb and communist tyranny, he shifted his emphasis. In a book called *There Will Be No Time,* Borden said that while America should not give up its peaceful quest for a unified world, it must remember that other nations might try for the same result by conquering what was not already theirs. Therefore, America must be strong and mobilized on a war footing. Whatever the cost it must have massive bomb power.

Factors that undermined American preparedness should be eradi-
cated. In particular Borden worried about espionage and urged
an expanded F.B.I. and very careful screening of those charged
with research and weapons production. Although the book was
written in 1946 the author spoke of intercontinental rockets with
atomic warheads being flung at America from either Europe or
Asia.

Borden was a patriot and regarded his work for the Joint Committee on Atomic Energy as a duty. It annoyed him to see Oppenheimer toying with the committee; galled him that the physicist
was getting away at least partly with his open research ideas. Borden had no patience with the argument that scientists could not
work successfully under controls and secrecy. Mentioning Germany's wartime V-weapons as an example, Borden had made it
clear once that if muscle was needed to keep scientists in line then
muscle should be used in the greater interest of national security.

Borden's position obliged him to be nonpolitical, so, outside
his closest associates and friends, he remained silent on these sentiments. His dim view of Oppie, however, could not have been
helped by the newspaper headlines two days after the isotope hearing, "Atom Expert Admits He Was Red." Frank Oppenheimer
had just had his day before the un-American committee.

Events of the late forties seemed to justify the tight-lipped attitudes of men like Borden and Strauss, and to make Oppenheimer's
"open world" ideals, as markedly qualified as they were, appear
hopelessly unrealistic. Since Czechoslovakia had gone under to the
communists in February of 1948, the Cold War had worsened by
the month. By the summer of 1949, the situation was critical. The
Allies and Russia were involved in a perilous contest of wills in
the Berlin Airlift, while Mao Tse-tung's Red armies were on the
verge of proclaiming conquest of all China.

Oppenheimer returned from a brief vacation at Perro Caliente
with his family and tried to get some fresh guidance for himself
in an exchange of letters with the poet Archibald MacLeish.

An article by MacLeish in *Atlantic Monthly* had impressed

Oppie. The poet had asked what had happened to the American dream, American assertiveness, the revolution, the big future, the good old Yankee cock-suredness. America was reacting instead of acting, subordinating the realization of historic American purpose to the defeat of the Russian purpose. Instead of beginners and be-getters, changers and challengers, creators and accomplishers, Americans had become resisters and protectors and preservers, de-fending and not using freedom. America, said MacLeish, had reached a spiritual impasse. Too many had given up the pursuit of liberty for the safer assurance of discipline and peace. What was needed was affirmative recommitment to the revolution of the in-dividual. A world of individual men was wanted, each relating to each in freedom and thus creating a society in which a man could live as himself.

With the thesis on the negative and defensive attitude that had overtaken America, Oppenheimer agreed entirely. But he was not so sure that the way to resume the pursuit of the American dream was through the kind of free-swinging individualism MacLeish proposed. He wrote a note to the poet which was typical of his tendency to intellectualize a subject so thoroughly and present so many for and against questions that he finished virtually empty-handed.

"I think that what is needed is something far subtler than the emancipation of the individual from society," said Oppie.

> It involves, with an awareness that the past 150 years have rendered progressively more acute, the basic dependence of man on his fel-lows. . . . What is needed is to forge in the present situation an affirmation which is as surprising in its concreteness and its breadth as was Jefferson's. . . . It is because I think that there will be a real novelty and real creation in what we have now to say and think and do, that I take a more tolerant attitude towards the confusions and fumblings of the last years.

MacLeish's thoughts about the shriveling effect of a national policy based narrowly on checking Russian moves were vivid in

Oppie's mind all through September because he was assessing top secret Air Force pictures and samples and calculations that showed extraordinary radioactivity in the eastern atmosphere. Russia, the American people were told on September 23, had the atom bomb.

In the days preceding the announcement, Oppenheimer had consulted with Conant, Fermi, and others on his advisory committee about the Soviet test—they called it Joe 1—and late in the month he wrote to Lilienthal that the committee was ready to meet and advise "on call."

"We felt quite strongly," Oppie said in his letter, "that the real impact of the news of Operation Joe lay not in the fact itself but in the response of public opinion, public policy to the fact."

Public opinion manifested itself as a frightened gut reaction, "What now?" The extreme secrecy surrounding atomic energy had left Americans in total ignorance of their country's military strength. Brien McMahon, their key representative in the whole show, had said before the Joe 1 test that he did not know whether the United States possessed five atomic bombs or five hundred.

"How can congressmen who lack essential information make wise decisions regarding defense and taxes and foreign policy?" he asked. "Free and candid discussion of vexing problems is the bedrock of democracy and it may be our surest safeguard for peace."

Policy to answer the new snarl from the Russian bear therefore had to be shaped on the persuasions of congressmen who knew public responsibility but not atoms, scientists who knew atoms but not Russian will and strategy, and military men who thought simply in terms of superior strength. Most insistent of the military voices belonged to the Air Force, and particularly the Strategic Air Command, which tended to reject tactical planning on the premise of communist advances through little wars, and gamble on making Soviet Russia behave through the threat of pulverizing nuclear retaliation.

President Truman asked for advice from Secretary of State Dean Acheson, Secretary of Defense Louis Johnson, and David Lilienthal. The commission chairman, himself disturbed at the military turn his job had taken, asked Oppenheimer's committee for a report.

"The commission is, of course, asking itself afresh if the present and presently planned program constitutes everything that is reasonably possible for us to do for the common defense and security," Lilienthal wrote. He added that advice was sought on "as broad a base as possible."

Oppenheimer said he could get the committee together on October 29 and 30. Glenn Seaborg would be abroad, but he would get his views in writing and relate them to the meeting. The rest of the team was unchanged, except that New Jersey Bell Telephone chairman Oliver Buckley had replaced short-term member Hood Worthington. Oppie had been re-elected chairman that year on the motion of Hartley Rowe, who said frankly, "I am fully convinced that the country will best be served and the committee will operate best by following your direction and sage advice."

Nobody in the group had any doubts about their assignment. They were being asked for technical information and advice on how America could go Russia one better, and this meant beyond the production of bigger and better atom bombs and delivery systems. Already there was a huge stockpile of bombs for all purposes; weapons had always had the priority over civil development of atomic energy.

They were being asked now when and if America could make the "super" bomb, the thermonuclear weapon. Only minimum research had been done on it for the stated reasons that the scientists did not have the basic know-how nor the sufficient expandable stocks of fissionable material that would be needed for testing if they did. The unstated reason was that none of the Oppenheimer panel had the stomach for fathering a bomb capable of obliterating the world's biggest cities, of killing a million people.

The passage of time had lessened but not removed the moral concern many physicists felt over Hiroshima. Oppie had tried to spell out this anguish in a much-publicized address at the Massachusetts Institute of Technology. "The physicists felt a peculiarly intimate responsibility for suggesting, for supporting, and in the end, in large measure, for achieving the realization of atomic weapons," he said. "In some sort of crude sense which no vulgarity, no humor, nor overstatement can quite extinguish, the physicists have known sin; and this is a knowledge which they cannot lose."

While a majority of scientists said "amen" to Oppie's speech, several, led by Ernest Lawrence, took angry exception to it, claiming that their colleague was exaggerating their chicken-heartedness. It was clear that the Lawrence group would push for development of the thermonuclear bomb with all the congressional support it could muster. Oppenheimer himself felt that to oppose the program would be fruitless. Lawrence had a strong and familiar argument: if America did not do it, Russia might do it first. Oppie could see that once again Russia would, in effect, be making American policy, but perhaps even MacLeish could not suggest an alternative in this case.

It came as a surprise to him to find one of the most politically canny scientists, James Conant, firmly against the hydrogen bomb. Since the war, Conant had been the nearest thing to Oppie's mentor and now "Uncle Jim" was in his late fifties and thinking about one world war spent in chemical warfare and a second in atom bombs. He had had enough, and was determined to get Oppie's dominant voice on his side.

Conant wanted to force the issue right out into the public arena. He felt that an announced stand by the nation's most renowned physicists against building a super weapon of a hundredfold horror to the Hiroshima bomb would attract the immediate support of citizen groups and churches. And he would not be dissuaded.

While these two talked the subject back and forth, Lewis Strauss was campaigning within the commission for a crash program on the super bomb, Brien McMahon was doing the same within his committee in Congress, and Ernest Lawrence and Edward Teller led a small scientific lobby in favor of the fusion bomb. In this they were helped by the University of California chemistry dean, Wendell Latimer, and by one of Lawrence's top men, physicist

Luis Alvarez. Teller and Alvarez were the only two among all the scientists who had lived through the war at Los Alamos who were enthusiastic about the prospect of another Manhattan project, this time to develop the thermonuclear weapon. Latimer had produced chemists for the original Manhattan, but not been directly involved himself. For more than fifteen years he had harbored an intense dislike for Oppenheimer, and this colored his thinking on everything concerning him, and made him an ever-ready Oppenheimer combatant. His hatred of Oppie, said friends, began because Oppie was such a sparkler at the Berkeley parties and Latimer such a dullard.

Teller had been working off and on at Los Alamos on the thermonuclear device, and he had convinced himself that with a team of good men and enough tritium—the heavy hydrogen isotope—he could make the bomb. The Hanford pile was producing too little tritium even for experimental purposes; obviously there would have to be more reactors. Lawrence accepted Teller's confidence and agreed that more reactors could be built without problem. The plan was presented in Washington this way: an assuredly feasible project. Nothing was said about reapportionment of the atomic budget, changing priorities, the cost to the program of "conventional" nuclear weapons, nor about the grave doubts scientists held about Teller's fusion bomb blueprint. Teller was giving congressmen and the Air Force the cheering news they wanted to hear, and when he realized that he might win this battle his worries about whether his bomb would really work sent him off in some alarm to recruit Hans Bethe, the acknowledged master on atomic fusion.

Of the entire Los Alamos team, Teller saw Bethe as his best hope. He was heartened when his old colleague did not wince in horror at the thought, as most others did, and he agreed to go with Bethe to see Oppenheimer.

Only a week remained before the crucial committee meeting and Oppie, with his resolve not yet set on joining Conant in rejecting the super bomb, dared not give any indication of his think-

ing to either Bethe or Teller. Both men went away with the idea
that Oppenheimer was open-minded, although he had shown them
Conant's latest negative letter on the subject, probably to fore-
warn Teller that opinions were divided and passions were up.
Bethe was left undecided and sought out Weisskopf and other
friends before turning down Teller, at least for a time.

The same day as the visit from Teller and Bethe, Oppie had
seen the commission's research director, the Berkeley chemist, and
Latimer's friend, Kenneth Pitzer, who said that both he and the
commission's military director, General James McCormack, supported the urgent development of the hydrogen bomb. It was positive that McMahon would endorse a crash program, and, Oppenheimer reasoned, President Truman would have no political
choice but to order the work to proceed.

"Everyone wants to get back to the happy days of monopoly via
super," he told the resolute James Conant. "What does worry me
is that this thing appears to have caught the imagination, both of
the congressional and of military people, as the answer to the
problem posed by the Russian advance. It would be folly to oppose
the exploration of this weapon. We have always known it had to
be done; and it does have to be done, though it appears to be
singularly proof against any form of experimental approach. But
that we become committed to it as the way to save the country and
the peace appears to me full of dangers."

On the cold Friday morning of October 29, Oppenheimer welcomed his fellow committeemen to the round table in an unusual
state of mind. He was ready to be persuaded. Glenn Seaborg had
sent in his opinion by letter, but it was so hedged that it was apparent that like Oppie he was prepared to be convinced one way
or the other. After hearing a few witnesses on the diplomatic and
military angles, Oppie opened the meeting for discussion.

Conant said he was flatly and forever against the super weapon
and Hartley Rowe, a former technical adviser to General Eisenhower and consultant engineer at Los Alomas, agreed with him.

"We built one Frankenstein," said Rowe. "We don't want another."

When Oliver Buckley suggested there was no difference in the morality between building an atom bomb and a hydrogen bomb, Conant said there was a difference in degree and this was vital. The Harvard president added that the issue at hand was so shattering that the public should be informed of all necessary details for proper debate. Cyril Smith was firmly in favor of this. Rabi, who had been talking with Oppie previously, told his associates that they were spitting into the wind. The decision would be made to go ahead. The more pertinent question was: who would be willing to work on the project? Fermi was most negative on the technical side at first. He felt the talk of a crash program was premature in the absence of any real knowledge of how a thermonuclear bomb could be built. Exactly the same reservation had been expressed to some of these scientists by the Los Alamos chief Norris Bradbury.

Oppenheimer expressed his worry that a priority program on the thermonuclear weapon would take all their stocks of uranium-235 and plutonium and limit even more than now America's military flexibility. "About all we will be able to do is bomb Russia," he said.

All through Friday and Saturday and into Sunday morning the scientists debated and towards the end Oppie was leaning towards the position of Conant and Rowe. Perhaps there was a chance that public revulsion could head off the monstrous possibility of a thermonuclear arms race. Russian resources must already be stretched thin, he thought, and if they were convinced the United States would not proceed with the super bomb they would hold off themselves. It would be a way to buy time in which Soviet belligerence could well diminish and increase chances for a detente based on arms control and inspection. Until there was some evidence of Russian repugnance to the super bomb, Teller and the others at Los Alamos could continue their exploratory work. Meanwhile, the message to get to the Kremlin was that nobody yet knew how to

build such a bomb and it was better for both countries that nobody ever found out. Against this view, and the justified doubts
of Fermi, was the lesson of the war years; a program with the spirit
and money of the Manhattan project tapped such reserves of scientific ingenuity that thermonuclear theories might indeed be transformed into a practical bomb.

At the approach of noon on Sunday the scientists had figured
out a halfway happy compromise. Technically, they said in a report, they had to assume that "an imaginative and concerted attack on the problem has a better than even chance of producing
the weapon." It would be wrong, however, to commit to a crash
effort the development of the particular device proposed by Edward Teller. There was no confidence that this design would be
functional. Prior to the commencement of experimental and production stages there should be more calculations and theoretical
studies. At this stage the fusion bomb did not deserve a higher
priority. Fission bombs in the works offered to produce the explosive effect of a half million tons of T.N.T. and surely that was
enough.

Politically, the scientists wanted to go on record as opposing the
thermonuclear weapon. In an annex authored by Conant and
signed by Oppenheimer, DuBridge, Rowe, Buckley, and Smith,
they said:

> We all hope that by one means or another the development of
> these weapons can be avoided. We are all reluctant to see the
> United States take the initiative in precipitating this development.
> We are all agreed that it would be wrong at the present moment
> to commit ourselves to an all-out effort towards its development.
> In determining not to proceed to develop the super bomb we see a
> unique opportunity of providing by example some limitations on
> the totality of war and thus of eliminating the fear and arousing
> the hope of mankind.

A minority annex submitted by Rabi and Fermi took a slightly
different tack:

The fact that no limits exist to the destructiveness of this weapon makes its very existence and the knowledge of its construction a danger to humanity as a whole. It is necessarily an evil thing considered in any light. For these reasons we believe it important for the President of the United States to tell the American public and the world that we think it wrong on fundamental ethical principles to initiate the development of such a weapon.

Rabi and Fermi were not saying categorically, do not do it. Their report said it was wrong to do it and added that, backed by American public opinion, an agreement banning hydrogen bomb development and production should be sought with the Soviet Union. If that failed America would have no choice but to go ahead with a high priority thermonuclear program.

Oppenheimer recorded that the meeting broke up cheerfully and everybody thought they had done a fine job. However, when his confidential secretary Kay Russell came to type the reports, she was surprised to see the boss's signature on the stronger Conant annex. "This," she said, "will cause you a lot of trouble."

Oppie had thought to add Seaborg's letter as yet another annex, but he discussed it with some of the others, including Cyril Smith, and they decided that since it took no firm view one way or the other they would just keep it on file.

Despite the soul the team had put into the advisory memorandums to the commission, Oppie thought they had little chance of winning the debate. This was confirmed for him when he telephoned Dean Acheson with the results and the Secretary told him with an edge of impatience in his voice that he could not see how the President could survive a policy of not making the big bomb. Acheson duly reported to President Truman that the Oppenheimer panel had taken a "religious attitude" to the question, and the President's reaction was to indicate that he wanted practical advice not a lecture on morals.

As was its custom, the commission adopted the advisory committee report by a 4–1 vote, with Strauss vehemently objecting and writing his own separate letter to the President. Brien Mc-Mahon, who was disgusted by the result of the Oppenheimer meeting, also kept recommending a rush fusion bomb program to the President. The strength of the weaponeers built up day by day. Gordon Dean, who had been McMahon's law partner in Connecticut and had been appointed to replace Waymack on the commission, now changed his vote and supported Strauss. Edward Teller thundered into Washington to testify that the negative technical report was misleading. He gave the picture of a Los Alamos eager to go on with the super bomb, though Bradbury was still mystified about the exact direction such a program should take.

Advisory committee secretary John Manley, the Los Alamos associate director, served notice on the members that they must meet again on December 1 to clarify their report. Deftly, he suggested they could move the emphasis a little because "the major policy matter to which so much time was devoted at the last meeting will still be in a fluid state."

The consequent memorandum to the commission was straight to the point: the Oppenheimer people were not opposed to the plan to investigate the possibilities of a fusion bomb, just to an immediate and determined effort to build one.

During the first weeks of January, 1950, President Truman knew that Acheson and Louis Johnson would be urging a super bomb and Lilienthal would be suggesting preliminary research tagged to a review of weapon priorities.

Truman's reputation for quick, sure decisions would have suffered if the public had any inkling of the issue during that momentous January. The man who authorized the dropping of the atom bomb on Hiroshima was now asked to push the button for a race between the world's most powerful nations to arm with doomsday weapons. He was still holding back on January 27 when word came that Klaus Fuchs, then in a high executive position at England's Harwell atomic energy plant, had turned himself in to British authorities as a Russian spy. In the days that followed, Truman had the full story. Fuchs had been at Los Alamos and given Soviet scientists details on how to make a "Fat Man" bomb. Furthermore he had been present at wartime discussions among mesa scientists about the thermonuclear weapon—and in those days it had been thought a distinct possibility for the near future.

Acting on Fuchs' intelligence, the Russians probably had their own super bomb program in operation. Truman got the advice he expected from his three key advisers and announced publicly on January 31 that he had directed the Atomic Energy Commission "to continue its work on all forms of atomic weapons including the so-called hydrogen or super-bomb."

Truman had not used the phrase "crash program" but Teller had his authority—the same authority in connection with the super weapon Secretary Byrnes had given Oppenheimer four and a half years before—and Teller was not about to ignore it as Oppie did. The argument of Luis Alvarez and Lewis Strauss that if Russia alone had the big bomb it could blackmail the United States into surrender was Teller's spur. This turbulent Hungarian with the beetling brows had crusaded for a world government like so many others after the war. Then his patience with Russia had completely evaporated; he hated communists as he had hated the Nazis who persecuted his family.

Because so many of the nation's most eminent scientists started taking a public stand against the super bomb, Teller was in trouble at the beginning. The two key men at Los Alamos, Bradbury and Manley, held back total support because of conflicting priorities, and the entire mesa suffered from the confusion. "There seems to be little sanity left, lack of balance, reasonableness of judgment," Manley complained to Oppie at this time.

One cause of the problems was Teller's bomb design. Further checking into his calculations of nuclear action and reaction showed that the bomb would not work and even if it did it would be ridiculously large. By enlisting the help of two brilliant mathematicians, Stanislaw Ulam, of Los Alamos, and Johnny von Neumann, his countryman at Princeton, Teller did eventually get his bomb, but minimum assistance from the Oppenheimer group

forced him to seek help from the most warlike inner circle at the
Air Force, and Teller never forgave Oppie for this disaffection.

In the fierce hydrogen bomb debate that followed the President's announcement, the Teller supporters among top scientists
could be counted on one hand. Those who stood by the James
Conant argument, which was to become wrongly sourced to Oppenheimer, numbered in the dozens.

An old Oppenheimer antagonist, Harold Urey, said the President had made the right decision, and he attacked the "curious
prejudices" of the Government advisers who had said otherwise.
Urey said no such prejudices existed in Russia and because of the
delay America might already have lost the armaments race.

A group of twelve leading physicists, including Los Alamos veterans Victor Weisskopf, Hans Bethe, Sam Allison, Ken Bainbridge, Robert Brode, and Charles Lauritsen issued a document
stating that America did not have the right to use such a bomb no
matter how righteous its cause. "This bomb is no longer a weapon
of war but a means of extermination of whole populations," said
the manifesto. The scientists asked, but did not get, a declaration
from President Truman that America would never use the super
bomb first.

For all this the groundswell of public opinion condemning the
bomb did not develop into a political force as Conant had hoped.
The majority of people still did not understand a thing about
atom bombs and were not ready to grapple with the hydrogen
bomb. And the language of megatons and megadeaths had so much
the sound of hideous science fiction that the public mind, not being able to cope with it, turned off.

Robert Bacher, the former atomic commissioner, could see this
happening and one night he took the stage of the Los Angeles
Town Hall and told the audience more detail about nuclear
bombs than had ever been heard before. He deplored the decision
on the super weapon, he said, and asked why America needed a
super bomb if it had a thousand atom bombs. He seemed to regret
not speaking out previously, for the crazy super program was an

example "of what can happen in a democracy when a decision of far-reaching national significance is made without public scrutiny of pertinent information."

It was at this period of national doubt and fear that many, both inside and outside science, looked to the distinguished person of Robert Oppenheimer. He had indeed become the scientist-statesman, the successor to Vannevar Bush and James Conant, who, out of weariness as well as revulsion, wanted no part of the thermonuclear weapon.

Oppenheimer spoke his piece on Eleanor Roosevelt's nationwide radio program *Round Table* just twelve days after Truman's decision.

"The decision to seek or not to seek international control of the A-bomb, the decision to try to make or not to make the H-bomb, are issues, rooted in complex technical matters, that nevertheless touch the very basis of our morality," he said.

> There is grave danger for us in that these decisions have been taken on the basis of facts held secret. This is not because the men who must contribute to the decisions, or must make them, are lacking in wisdom; it is because wisdom itself cannot flourish, nor even truth be determined, without the give and take of debate or criticism. The relevant facts could be of little help to an enemy; yet they are indispensable for an understanding of questions of policy. If we are wholly guided by fear, we shall fail in this time of crisis. The answer to fear cannot always lie in the dissipation of the causes of fear; sometimes it lies in courage.

They were fine words, Oppie words, delivered in that sad and hesitant voice, but after the applause died two judgments were given—one that Oppenheimer's failure to remonstrate publicly against the bomb proved that he was being corrupted by politics, the other that he would not be sidetracked from continuing his crusade against the tightening fist of secrecy and suspicion in the United States.

It was said that Oppie did not condemn the bomb for fear of

jeopardizing his influence in Washington. The decision had been made and he felt it irreversible. Oppenheimer enjoyed influence for its own sake—this was undeniable—and he also wanted to use it to convince the policy makers that reliance on big bomb strategy was both perilous and foolish. America needed a varied arsenal— bombs, surely, but also tactical weapons for battlefield use, and defense weapons and systems for the protection of mainland America.

This judgment would not have been harsh on anyone but Oppenheimer. The man who had gone to Washington to internationalize atomic energy had apparently switched his mission to shoring up the national military strength and setting its strategy. The change was so dramatic, so inappropriate for a physicist, and it came so soon after the Bernard Peters affair, that a distrust of Oppenheimer's character took root in several quarters.

However, another school paid heed to the one certain consistency about Robert Oppenheimer: at every possible opportunity since the war he had attacked the proliferating strictures in American society, based on formal security and on fear. Oppie had done this without thought to consequences. As Bacher had said, the hydrogen bomb decision was an effect of withering secrecy. Oppenheimer was lunging at the causes not the effects.

Both assessments of the man were strongly grained with truth. He did not speak for himself, but after his *Round Table* talk he drove home to Princeton and began to prepare an address he would make soon to high school science students in Washington. He searched through some Thomas Jefferson volumes to find the text of a letter Jefferson had written in 1799 to a young man who had inquired of him as to the usefulness of his studies in science. This would be his theme.

The letter talked of the immense scientific discovery that awaited and of the despots who would deny this and say the human mind could progress no further. "But thank heaven," wrote Jefferson, "the American mind is already too much opened to listen to these impostures; and while the art of printing is left to us, science can never be retrograde; what is once acquired of real knowledge can never be lost.''

Oppie read on, committing the words to memory, until he came to the centerpiece he had known for a long time: "To preserve the freedom of the human mind then and the freedom of the press," said Jefferson, "every spirit should be ready to devote itself to martyrdom; for as long as we may think as we will, and speak as we think, the condition of man will proceed in improvement. . . .''

15

In the late winter and spring of 1950, Wisconsin Senator Joseph McCarthy was spreading a fanaticism over communist intrigue through the United States. He talked of a generation of treason in the highest offices of the country, of card-carrying communists even now walking the halls of the State Department. His accusations made the earlier efforts of the House committee seem like a bloodless preliminary for the purge to come.

Then up stepped Paul and Sylvia Crouch, former top officers of the American Communist Party, who had decided to turn informers for profit. First they railed against Harry Bridges, the San Francisco wharf boss, and then they denounced Robert Oppenheimer.

Sylvia Crouch told the Jack Tenny California Committee on Un-American Activities that Oppenheimer was present at a secret meeting of communists that she and her husband Paul attended in July, 1941, at the Oppenheimer house in Berkeley. Paul had then been the county organizer for the party, preceding Steve Nelson. His wife said she had seen Oppenheimer's picture in a recent issue of *Life* magazine and recognized him as the host for the cell meeting.

The story was a sensation and headlined in newspapers every-

where in the practice of the time to put the victim under the blaz-
ing national lights and make him prove his innocence.

After consulting Herb Marks, Oppenheimer had a statement
issued through the Atomic Energy Commission that he had never
been a Communist Party member and had never attended a party
meeting "in my home or anywhere else." A Californian committee
member described this as a weak, left-handed denial, and the im-
plied sinister past for the atom bomb creator was given further
substance when an ex-communist truck driver appeared and said
he had seen Oppenheimer at another cell meeting in Berkeley in
the 1941 summer.

The witness, identifying Oppie from current pictures, said that
he had changed little, yet in 1941 he had long black curly hair and
in 1950 his hair was graying and cropped. The committee did not
check this nor did they extend their investigation to finding that
during the summer in question Robert and Kitty Oppenheimer
were at their ranch in New Mexico—an eventful summer in which
Robert had badly twisted his knee and Kitty had crashed in the
car.

Herb Marks began collecting the evidence to disprove the
charges when rescue came from an unexpected source.

Richard Nixon, then campaigning for the United States Senate,
and nationally known because of his work, particularly in the Hiss
case, for the House committee in Washington, told an audience
in his home state of California that he had total confidence in
Oppenheimer. Nixon himself had frequently questioned him before the House committee.

"We found him, on all occasions, a cooperative witness," said
Nixon. "From these conversations and others I am convinced that
Dr. Oppenheimer has been and is a completely loyal American
and further, one to whom the people of the United States owe a
great debt of gratitude for his tireless and magnificent job in
atomic research."

Nixon's statement ended the public hounding of Oppie, but the
California committee prepared a dossier shot-full of wild supposi-

tions for the official F.B.I. files; that was the way it worked in America in 1950.

The document said:

> When Steve Nelson was sent to Berkeley in 1941 to replace Crouch, he lost little time in trying to obtain secret A-bomb information from Dr. Oppenheimer. Having met and befriended Mrs. Oppenheimer in Spain and having been associated with her former husband in the Abraham Lincoln Battalion, he had an ideal entree.
>
> Nelson was making progress reports at this time to a superior in the East who used the cover name "Al." The reports were sent to a mail drop in New York and one of them stated that both Dr. Oppenheimer and his wife were uncooperative and unsympathetic towards communism.
>
> In many counter-espionage cases the agents have assumed that their activities were under surveillance and that their reports were being intercepted. In such cases the messages were plainly written for the purpose of planting erroneous information or to divert suspicion from a valuable contact. . . .
>
> Whether Nelson employed such a stratagem is, of course, a matter of pure conjecture. The facts, however, are that his record was well known, his report concerning Dr. Oppenheimer's failure to cooperate was couched in simple and unmistakable terms, and Nelson *was* under surveillance and his reports *were* intercepted.
>
> In view of his Moscow training it is quite possible that Nelson's report was a deliberate ruse, and in light of later developments it should not be regarded too seriously. If he had wanted to protect himself he could have employed a code. . . .
>
> The facts are quite plain that [Russian agents] were unanimous in picking Dr. J. Robert Oppenheimer as the most suitable man to contact. They knew his record much better than our own security agencies, and they evaluated him as a "potential traitor."

The California committee further erroneously related that "Katherine [Kitty] married a man named Stewart-Harrison, whose political views were considerably left of center, as he not only enlisted in the International Brigade to fight in the Spanish Civil

War but was on intimate terms with the ubiquitous Steve Nelson."

Even without knowing of this damning document, Oppenheimer had been shaken by the publicity from California.

"I took it all very badly and feel now like a man slowly convalescing from a serious illness," he wrote to his friend Robert Bacher.

At Perro Caliente that summer, Oppenheimer tried to relax with his family but he sensed that the persecution was not over, that many more men would be held to account, vilified, and perhaps destroyed in 1950 for their passions of 1940.

The rapacious Senator McCarthy, supported by a strong clique of conservative midwestern congressmen, was after big game.

Oppie was target-sized for McCarthy and he was frightened of him. Ed Condon told Oppie there was no sin in this; everybody was. He joked that he had looked outside his hotel window in New York one day and seen Cardinal Spellman obsequiously escorting the frowning Senator to Mass.

One night at the ranch, after hours of tiddledywinks in front of the fire, Oppie accompanied his son Peter upstairs to bed. He tucked him in and sat on the side of the cot. It was not something he did habitually, and Peter was all ears.

"Pete," he said, "it may happen that we will be called communists. . . ."

The boy waited while his father fumbled about for words.

"Well, if it does happen I don't want you to worry about it, that's all," Oppie finished. He turned back the lamp to the barest glow and went wearily down the stairs.

His son lay awake repeating the conversation over and over in his head. He had relished the confidence. Another time his father had brought him to bed and in much the same way had said, "Pete, always be honest, no matter what, be honest in everything." And Peter remembered that, too, though he never could figure why his father said it.

Even through the eyes of a nine-year-old, that summer did not quite come off. Peter, a thin, handsome boy with large gray eyes, remembered the rented horses in the corral, the fast drives over rough mountain roads in their new station wagon, "Airlift," the Sunday poker—draw, stud, five or seven, often with deuces or one-eyed jacks wild. Kitty would sit by the hour with her watercolors trying to get the distant Santa Fe Baldy right. Robert drank beer on the porch with his neighbor, Art Windsor.

His parents were not whooping and hollering and jumping their horses as Peter had heard about in the old days. It seemed they had sought some of this lost gusto, wanted to share it with Peter and little Toni, but it was not there and they did not persist.

Oppenheimer's digestion and back were troubling him, and Kitty herself was unwell with the first of a series of chronic internal ailments.

Robert blamed himself for anything that caused Kitty suffering and tried to absorb her miseries into his own. She was his obsession. Instead of riding that year they walked the upper pastures searching for four-leaf clovers. Malformed four-leaf clovers they would have to eat, but the good ones would be exchanged, mounted on cardboard, and then autographed with love from one to the other. They continued this private ritual for many years and they took endless delight in it.

The feeling came to Peter that he was getting less of his beloved Pa than he should; indeed he had taken this same problem to the family maid once. She knelt at his side and explained that his Pa loved his mother very much and that they had had children late in life and therefore did not pay so much ne'ermind to children as younger parents. This did not mean their love was not as strong.

Confidences, father to son, therefore became all the more precious, as did the moments when Oppie would shed his grave manner and indulge in a bit of fun. His stoicism was his particular pride. Once when the sink was filled with boiling water from the stove to wash the dishes and the billowing steam made it obvious the water was too hot to touch, Oppie casually walked over and plunged in both hands. He busily scrubbed away for a while, then sneaked a look behind to see if anybody had noticed. When he saw

Kitty staring in disbelief, he turned back to the sink with a boyish grin all over his face.

The family fun flickered as suddenly as it flared.

Oppie, foremost, was a professional physicist and he had that preoccupation common to all dedicated scientists. Perhaps it was not as intense as it had been at Berkeley, for he had so many other intrusive interests, but it was still there. Private engrossment with mesons and electron fields accounted for some of Oppie's long brown study of the summer. He did not brood on the communist bogey, though it was ever-present like a distant whining wind.

For the first time in his life Oppie was aware he had enemies, not just disappointed scientific friends, but powerful enemies in Washington who would be seeking to cut him down—and Mc-Carthy might be their means.

16

THE QUALITY OF PERSONAL courage is not dominant with many, perhaps most, intellectuals, so it becomes a measure of Oppenheimer that knowing his vulnerability he took on Jefferson's challenge to speak his mind.

Outbreak of the Korean War in June, 1950, and communist China's entry into the battle in November, gave haste to his two-tongued crusade: to alter the exclusive city-massacre strategy and diversify American arms for the field, while at the same time taking a step towards a moderation of the massive terror of the big bombs. On the quest for the hydrogen bomb he remained an influential neutral.

Through the General Advisory Committee and also the Defense Department's Research and Development Board, of which he was a member, Oppenheimer had been urging the greater production of small, tactical nuclear weapons for use in limited wars. These would be for the Army and the Navy, as well as the Air Force. Always he and his supporters had been confounded by the air chiefs, who laid claim to all fissionable material. The Air Force, spoken for by such tough characters as General Hoyt Vandenberg and General Curtis LeMay, feuded with the other services over this question, but were accustomed to winning. They demanded bombs, as large as possible, as many as possible.

Oppenheimer pressed his campaign harder, presenting Korea as his case for an alternative strategy to big bomb power. Edward Teller's new approach to building a hydrogen bomb, discussed and approved by scientists in Princeton in June of 1951, seemed to give Oppie new urgency. He did not either encourage or discourage Teller's work. The Hungarian now had lavish support from the Air Force, which saw to it that he had his own personal bomb laboratory in the small Californian town of Livermore. Los Alamos, however, continued to do nearly all the work and it was from the mesa that America's first cumbersome, experimental thermonuclear device was shipped to Eniwetok in the Pacific and exploded towards the end of 1952. The force was measured in the range of several million tons of T.N.T.

From the 1951 spring there was no doubt in Oppenheimer's mind that Teller would perfect his hydrogen bomb, but he did question what use the bomb would be. The Strategic Air Command was anxious to get the super weapon, and Oppie thought about those giant bombers roaming the skies of the world with hydrogen bombs in their bellies. A panicky mistake, a foul-up in signals, and the world would be set on a course of self-destruction.

Others who saw the perils of this eventually sought Oppie's endorsement for disarmament negotiations between Russia and the United States before it was too late, but, against the background of Korea, he thought talks would be useless and perhaps even heighten the distrust. His notion was for America to start the return to sanity by example, but by example that would in fact increase the country's abilities to cope with any situation. The idea of Truman and Stalin agreeing to disarm struck Oppie as absurd.

"If Aesop were to produce a fable on this subject," he said, "it would be this: Two stags confronted each other across a pond in the mating season and agreed that combat was ridiculous. Each would, that night, retire to his own woods and remove his antlers.

In the morning the two met, only to discover that each had cut off one lower point in his antlers and burnished the others to needle sharpness."

Caltech president Lee DuBridge, who had been assigned by the Department of Defense to head a study program—Project Vista—on fresh strategies that would include tactical nuclear weapons, gave Oppie the forum he wanted to further his crusade. At DuBridge's invitation, Oppenheimer wrote most of the chapter on atomic defense in the European theater. As in Korea, Oppie said in his part of the report, there was a need for special atomic weapons that would be useful against troops deployed over large areas. Atom bombs were unlikely to be dropped in any situation short of total war. Russia had shown no taste for this. Limited wars were the danger and therefore limited atom weapons should be an integral part of military operations.

Project Vista scientists agreed that for balanced development of the right sort of weapons, fissionable materials should in future be split three ways among the services. The Army and Navy liked the report; the Air Force was apoplectic. Air Force secretary Thomas Finletter, the Philadelphia lawyer, took Oppie to lunch to try to talk him around, for nobody had any doubt who had written the offending chapter. The Air Force scientific adviser, the geophysicist David Griggs, also had an angry session with the unshakable man from Princeton.

Towards the end of 1951, Oppenheimer and other members of the Vista team turned up at the Paris headquarters of General Eisenhower to plead their case, finding him appreciative and enthusiastic but noncommittal. However, after suggestions for improvement by top Eisenhower aides, the Vista report was filed to all services for comment the following year.

The Strategic Air Command, fearing loss of its atom bomb monopoly, was working up a counter-argument based on the fact that the only way to hit a land power like Russia was from the air, when Oppenheimer delivered another slap at the Air Force. A new scientist study project, this one called Lincoln and conducted at the Massachusetts Institute of Technology, had inevitably summoned Oppie for help. He joined others in recommending a much more sophisticated defense system for the United States in case of atomic attack. One suggestion was for a Distant Early Warning line of electronic alarms across northern Canada. Oppie said money and materials must be allocated for defense as well as attack, and while there was no question the Strategic Air Command was needed it should be supplemented with a stronger defense arm. "I have never seen a first class prize fighter with a complete glass jaw," was Oppie's crack about the Strategic Air Command.

First public hint that Oppenheimer was incurring wrath in high places—and therefore making headway—was a story in the *Wall Street Journal* in the summer of 1952. The reporter had been talking to the Air Force; this much was clear despite the lack of detail.

The article, datelined Washington, said the battle of the "daring" scientists versus the "go slow" scientists was splitting the Administration. The good scientists wanting to double work on H-bombs and cut back on conventional weapons were identified as Kenneth Pitzer, Harold Urey, and Ernest Lawrence, and these men were backed by Secretary of Defense Robert Lovett and Air Secretary Finletter. The bad scientists were listed as Oppenheimer, Conant, and DuBridge.

Rumors of Oppie in trouble were fed because right at this time he and DuBridge both retired from the General Advisory Committee. They had had enough. DuBridge wanted to concentrate on Caltech, and Oppenheimer wished to continue his campaign without any halters. There was no thought of quitting his Government service, though he told friends that he was beset with fatigue, worry, and harassment, and, in a letter to Frank, he said it had been a long six years with the committee. "And now I find that physics is much too hard for me except as a spectator," he added.

In the final months of the Truman Administration, Oppenheimer was appointed chairman of a special State Department

Advisory Committee on Disarmament along with Vannevar Bush, Allen Dulles, and others. Their first suggestion, to postpone Teller's H-bomb test, was ignored. Bush and Oppie both thought it disgusting to set off the super bomb only a few days before the presidential election—the explosion was November 1.

"We were about to make a portentous change in the world and probably irreversible," complained Oppie, who said the decision to test should be taken by the new President because he would have to live with the bomb.

The main recommendation of the panel, submitted to President Eisenhower early in 1953, had Oppenheimer stamped all over it. Operation Candor was the name, and it involved a revelation to the nation by the President of the facts on the nuclear arms race, telling the public the type and quantity of weapons America had and the variety thought to be in Russian hands. The influence of an informed public was needed in the current debates over strategy and defense, said Oppie's team.

Even as this was being prepared for White House scrutiny, Oppenheimer delivered a lecture before the Council of Foreign Relations in New York that made some people, notably in the Air Force, believe that their bête noire had gone mad.

Indeed Oppie was disturbed, for Eisenhower's campaign promise to reduce defense expenditure had already pretty well killed the chances for the Project Vista and Project Lincoln concepts. Available money was poured into the thermonuclear program. Strategic air power was winning such devotees as the new Treasury Secretary George Humphrey, who said the United States had "no business getting into little wars."

In his address to the council, Oppenheimer scooped his own panel's report about the need for telling the American public the truth about nuclear arms race and then, publicly, lit into the Air Force.

As an example of the ignorance surrounding the atom, Oppie quoted "a high officer of the Air Defense Command" as saying that it was Air Force policy to attempt to protect its striking force, but not really to attempt to protect the country, for "that is so big a job that it would interfere with our retaliatory capabilities." Oppie finished the quote and commented that "such follies can only occur when the men who know the facts can find no one to talk to about them, when the facts are too secret for discussion, and thus for thought."

Having indicated that the Air Force was both brutish and stupid, Oppenheimer then pointed to an inefficiency admitted by its own Chief of Staff. Oppie said he did not believe defense systems constituted a permanent solution to the problem of the atom, but he considered that a better job could be done than at present. "Not long ago," he said with a touch of scorn, "General Vandenberg estimated that we might, with luck, intercept twenty or thirty percent of an enemy attack. That is not very reassuring when one looks at numbers and casualties, and what it takes to destroy the heart and life of our country."

The speech was noted widely, to the displeasure of the Air Force, for Oppie used in it an analogy that was to become famous. Predicting a long, tense Cold War ahead, Oppie said, "During this period the atomic clock ticks faster and faster; we may anticipate a state of affairs in which two Great Powers will each be in a position to put an end to the civilization and life of the other, though not without risking its own. We may be likened to two scorpions in a bottle, each capable of killing the other, but only at the risk of his own life."

In revenge, the top Air Force command told its side of the story to a friendly reporter and the article damning Oppenheimer was published in the May, 1953, issue of *Fortune* magazine. The subheading described it as "The Story of Dr. Oppenheimer's persistent campaign to reverse U.S. military strategy."

At contention, said the unsigned and highly colored article, was this issue: Should the Strategic Air Command discard or drastically modify its retaliatory-deterrent strategy in favor of a defensive strategy where the American atomic advantage would be confined to short-range tactical forces?

Obviously, the writer was going to answer with a firm negative, for he embarked then on an attack on Oppenheimer's attitude towards the H-bomb. Praising Lewis Strauss for exhorting the Atomic Energy Commission to reconsider the thermonuclear weapon in 1949, the article then said Oppie had persuaded the members of his General Advisory Committee to oppose the bomb. Only Fermi, said *Fortune*, "forthrightly" sided with Strauss. Then came the arrest of Fuchs, and Teller suddenly remembering the spy being present at an H-bomb seminar in 1945 when "he might have gleaned the correct solution." With the President's go-ahead, Teller proceeded on his bomb but had to switch laboratories to Livermore when Oppenheimer's influence stifled him at Los Alamos. Despite all these handicaps, continued the story, Teller triumphed.

Project Vista was Oppenheimer's next ignoble adventure, said the article. He and his two "disciples," DuBridge and Lauritsen, had collaborated on a report that contained a "veiled suggestion that Air Force doctrine was based on the slaughter of civilians." Oppenheimer proposed diverting Air Command atomic stockpiles to support for ground battle, and Finletter "read it as a brief for disarming the nation's strongest weapon while the Red Army and its tactical air forces otherwise still held the military balance of power in Europe."

Turning to Project Lincoln and the influence of a secret clan of scientists calling themselves ZORC—initials for physicists Jerrold Zacharias, Oppenheimer, Rabi, and Charles Lauritsen—the *Fortune* piece said that Oppenhemier had been the mastermind behind the plan for a defense system that was in concept an "electronically hedged Maginot Line," costing as much as $150 billion. The final verdict on Oppenheimer was that he had been guilty of impropriety and it was as well that he was losing and that "SAC, under General LeMay, retains its mighty mission."

This issue of *Fortune* circulated widely through the Government and the science community, and it was read as the final bell for Oppie. He had no powerful support in the Eisenhower Administration, in which Strauss had been given the inside role as atomic energy advisor. Long a servant of Democratic rule, Oppie had little magic for the Republicans. He was not alone. The McCarthy menace had persuaded Eisenhower to prescribe tough new regulations authorizing any Government department head to suspend an employee pending investigation "if he deems suspension necessary in the interests of public security." All over Washington the heads of Democrats were rolling.

Oppenheimer still had his top security "Q" clearance because he remained a member of the Defense Department's Research and Development Board and a consultant to the Atomic Energy Commission. The new Defense Secretary, Charles Wilson, took away one of Oppie's oars by disbanding the whole research board. Lewis Strauss, appointed chairman of the Atomic Energy Commission in July, removed the other oar by instructing the then commission general manager, Marion Boyer, to discourage all future attempts to consult Oppenheimer.

The Admiral made this stick a few months later by replacing Boyer with the old Groves' aide, General Kenneth Nichols, who had since been an assistant to General Vandenberg. Strauss was able to steer the commission as surely as the Lilienthal-Oppenheimer team had years before. Commissioner Thomas E. Murray, a Democrat and a New York millionaire, was a devout Catholic and violently anti-communist. He hated Strauss but had not yet come into open, bitter conflict with him. His colleagues were Eugene Zuckert, an agreeable Washington lawyer, Joseph Campbell, a New York associate of Strauss', and Professor Henry D. Smyth, the Princeton physics professor who had written the official handbook on atomic energy after the war. Smyth had voted with Lilienthal against a crash program on the hydrogen bomb, but he was not by any means considered a rebel. He knew Oppie but was not a particular friend. Even so he resented Strauss' order about not consulting Oppie because Smyth had to find out about it unofficially.

Secretary of State John Foster Dulles, confident that Teller would soon have a hydrogen bomb small enough to fit into an airplane, was preparing his doctrine of massive retaliation against any sign of Russian aggression when American radiation patrol aircraft returned in August with the evidence that Russia had already exploded a thermonuclear bomb.

The name of Oppenheimer became a curse among many in the Administration from that day, for he was seen as the rascal who had allowed the communists to get ahead while he went about his private evangelism. By unanimous vote he was elected scapegoat. Teller said he could not test his bomb for another six months, which turned out to be right, so meanwhile Eisenhower felt he had to assure the public that America was not in peril because it had so many more big atom bombs than Russia. He looked over Operation Candor again, but firmly rejected its blunt approach.

What evolved finally was the strange American "atoms for peace" proposal, in which the United Nations would establish an International Atomic Energy Agency charged with the development of atomic energy for peaceful purposes. Atomic power nations would be asked to donate fissionable materials to the agency, thus reducing the stockpiles available for weapons.

"Today," said Eisenhower, with ill-disguised purpose, in concluding his speech to the United Nations General Assembly, "the United States' stockpile of atomic weapons, which, of course, increases daily, exceeds by many times the explosive equivalent of the total of all bombs and all shells used in World War II." The President said America possessed atom bombs with twenty-five times the detructive power of the Hiroshima bomb.

The irony of the tailpiece matched an earlier statement before the United Nations by John Foster Dulles, which Oppenheimer's secretary clipped and preserved. Dulles said, "Governments which exert themselves without reserve to the creation of even more powerful means of mass destruction, which tolerate no delay and spare no expense in these matters, and which at the same time are dilatory, evasive and negative towards curing the situations which could bring these destructive forces into play—such governments cannot but stand morally condemned."

Throughout the uproar in the White House and the American defense establishment, one man had a degree of satisfaction: William Borden was at last confronted with the sort of proof he needed to explain and expose Oppenheimer.

The former executive director of the Joint Congressional Committee on Atomic Energy had thought from late 1949 that anything less than a crash program on the super bomb would be national suicide. When McMahon had showed him the report of the Oppenheimer panel, he had shared the Senator's dismay. As the months and years went by Borden puzzled over Oppenheimer's continued lack of enthusiasm for the H-bomb, his constant warring against the Strategic Air Command. It did not seem to him the way a loyal intelligent American should act. He asked for and was given the Oppenheimer security file, which included the cloak-and-dagger material from the California committee. Borden studied it over and over for months with one of his staff, Frank Cotter. Finally, Cotter concluded that there was nothing there to indicate disloyalty, but Borden had left the committee by this time and never did get Cotter's opinion. Borden himself remained doubtful until the Soviet hydrogen bomb explosion, then he felt he had the reason for Oppenheimer's "tireless" campaign to "retard" the American super weapon.

He decided that Oppie was a Russian spy.

For two months he sat on this stunning piece of information, wondering what to do with it. Unaware that the Administration had already put the squeeze on Oppenheimer, he doubted that he would be taken seriously. The man who built the atom bomb ranked close to being an untouchable. Borden rejected the idea of going to McCarthy, now chairman of the Senate Permanent Subcommittee on Investigations, because the Senator would use the information to attack Eisenhower as well as Truman. A better assault would be through Senator William Jenner, the Indiana Republican who chaired the Internal Security Subcommittee and who had been conducting hearings on what he called "interlocking subverion in Government departments." Jenner was ruthless, but a shade more respectable than McCarthy.

Whatever preliminary feelers Borden put out—and they never became record—he had no question in his mind about exactly how to proceed on the morning of November 7. For it was then the newspapers carried under splashy headlines the report of a speech Attorney General Herbert Brownell, Jr., had made in Chicago the previous day. Brownell opened a renewed Administration campaign against the Truman regime on the grounds of corruption and communism in government by claiming that Truman had actually promoted a suspected Russian spy in 1946. Despite F.B.I. reports that flashed the red light, Truman had elevated Harry Dexter White from his job as Assistant Secretary of the Treasury to Executive Director of the International Monetary Fund.

Brownell said the White case was "typical of the blindness" of the Truman team, and thus far, the new Administration had had to eject 1,456 persons from Government service because they were found to be security risks.

"Americans are more secure in their homes tonight because the security progam, under the rigorous leadership of President Eisenhower, is cleaning up the mess in Washington," added Brownell.

The same day as the incendiary speech was published, Borden wrote to J. Edgar Hoover, "The purpose of this letter is to state my own exhaustively considered opinion, based upon years of study of the available classified evidence, that more probably than not J. Robert Oppenheimer is an agent of the Soviet Union."

In his articles of accusation, Borden detailed Oppenheimer's prewar leftist activities and drew up a case to indicate that his vigorous support of A-bomb and H-bomb development ended with Hiroshima. Since then Oppenheimer had used his "potent influence" against every effort to expand the country's nuclear capability, more probably than not acting "under a Soviet directive in influencing United States military, atomic energy, intelligence and diplomatic policy."

On the evidence, and bearing in mind Borden's attitudes and the political climate, his conclusions were not so stunning. Peer de Silva had reached similar ones ten years earlier. Air Force General Roscoe Wilson had gone to his intelligence people only months before with his worries about the pattern of Oppenheimer's activities. And later, when scientist David Griggs heard of Borden's letter, he asked one of Oppenheimer's colleagues, "Say, are you sure Oppie is not giving information to the enemy?"

Hoover freshened up Oppenheimer's dossier, attached the Borden letter, and sent it all to Herbert Brownell, who took it immediately to President Eisenhower. Thunderstruck at what he read in this raw FBI material, Eisenhower called in Defense Secretary Wilson and other Cabinet members—though not, apparently, Vice-President Nixon, who had personal knowledge of the case—and they all sat around gloomily letting their minds run to the opportunities the dossier could give Senator McCarthy. It was too much. Oppie's brother, sister-in-law, wife, mistress—as Borden referred to Jean Tatlock—all former Reds. His friend Chevalier another Red and protected by Oppenheimer in defiance of intelligence officers. And this was the man who knew more about America's nuclear arsenal than anyone alive.

President Eisenhower, given the people's mandate to protect them from communism and bedeviled by McCarthy who found him as "soft" as Truman, got Lewis Strauss around to his office at the double.

Oppenheimer's record, the admiral had to admit, was familiar to the commission, which had reviewed it and cleared Oppie anew years earlier. Only the subject's position on the H-bomb and Borden's letter were fresh. Strauss had his chance then, as the one expert in the room, to say that none of this was suspicious because Oppie's stand on the H-bomb was no different than that of a hundred other good scientists, and that Bill Borden was overly sensitive about spies and something of a fanatic on having America mobilized for total war at all times. But he did not, by his own account, defend Oppenheimer in any way and his silence in the circumstances was damning. Brownell and Wilson were certainly in no mood to take a generous view.

The President ordered a "blank wall" placed between Oppenheimer and any further access to secret information until his security file was again reviewed. This could be done almost as routine under the terms of the recent executive order requiring a current check of all government employees to ensure that they were loyal, reliable, trustworthy, and of good conduct and character.

Brownell's job was to pass Oppenheimer's suspect status to the F.B.I., the Central Intelligence Agency, and the top officers in State, Defense, and the services. The wall was up within twenty-four hours. Agents, meanwhile, were assigned to find Oppenheimer and watch him.

Back at the commission, Strauss set about informing his colleagues of the crisis and, with the help of General Nichols, prepared a long letter which listed the charges against Oppie and suspended his clearance until he had answered them before a commission-appointed, three-man board of inquiry. He would either have to submit to this confidential hearing or resign from his positions as consultant with the commission and other government agencies.

Strauss then sat back and waited for Oppenheimer to return to Washington from an overseas tour that almost at that very moment had taken Robert and Kitty to Haakon Chevalier's tiny flat in Paris for a reunion dinner.

17

In the summer of 1953 Oppenheimer was aware that he had been badly strafed by the Air Force. Though he was far from admitting a complete rout, he decided to rest from politics and he accepted an invitation to deliver a series of lectures on physics before the National Research Council in Brazil.

His old charm before an informed audience, able to appreciate the style and animation he brought to the universe of the atom, made him a sensation. The unrestrained Latin applause was a tonic that refreshed him for a challenge he counted as one of the most important of his life—delivery of the annual Reith Lectures over the Home Service of the British Broadcasting Corporation in London in November and December.

Through the fall Kitty and his secretary put off most callers, and, in the large room he used as a study at Olden Manor, he labored with joy over his Reith theme: "To elucidate what there is new in atomic physics that is relevant, helpful and inspiriting for men to know."

Duly read in London with those pauses and inflections and little throat sounds, the lectures received rave reviews. But they were a triumph in the way a Dylan Thomas reading was a triumph, for, as one critic said, "His glittering rhetoric held his listeners in a web of absorption that was often less attentive than trancelike"; and another was to comment, "It is incantation, not exposition."

Oppenheimer himself said later, "For all my trouble, I was told I was impossibly obscure."

Yet there was here a vivid explanation for his F.B.I. "biographers" in Washington of where he had been in the twenties and thirties. It had been the heroic time of atomic discovery, he said, and he wanted to relate it in such terms as "men listen to accounts of soldiers returning from a campaign of unparalleled hardship and heroism, or of explorers from the high Himalayas, or of tales of deep illness, or of a mystic's communion with God."

He did this eloquently, though hardly simply for a layman because the language and concepts of physics are so alien to common experience; then he made a classic bridge from physics to the community of the sciences and the community of man. He said:

> For some moments during these lectures we have looked together into one of the rooms of the house called "science." This is a relatively quiet room that we know as quantum theory or atomic theory. The great girders which frame it, the lights and shadows and vast windows—these were the work of a generation our predecessor more than two decades ago.
>
> It is not wholly quiet.
>
> Young people visit it and study in it and pass on to other chambers; and from time to time someone rearranges a piece of the furniture to make the whole more harmonious; and many, as we have done, peer through its windows or walk through it as sightseers. It is not so old but that one can hear the sound of the new wings being built nearby, where men walk high in the air to erect new scaffoldings, not unconscious of how far they may fall. . . .
>
> It is a vast house indeed.
>
> It does not appear to have been built upon any plan but to have grown as a great city grows. There is no central chamber, no one corridor from which all others debouch. All about the periphery men are at work studying the vast reaches of space and the state of affairs billions of years ago; studying the intricate and subtle but

wonderfully meet mechanisms by which life proliferates, alters, and endures; studying the reach of the mind and its ways of learning; digging deep into the atoms and the atoms within atoms and their unfathomed order.

It is a house so vast that none of us knows it, and even the most fortunate have seen most rooms only from the outside or by a fleeting passage, as in a king's palace open to visitors. It is a house so vast that there is not and need not be complete concurrence on where its chambers stop and those of the neighboring mansions begin.

It is not arranged in a line nor a square nor a circle nor a pyramid, but with a wonderful randomness suggestive of unending growth and improvisation. Not many people live in the house, relatively speaking—perhaps if we count all its chambers and take residence requirements quite lightly, one tenth of one per cent of all the people in this world—probably, by any reasonable definition, far fewer.

And even those who live here live elsewhere also, live in houses where the rooms are not labeled atomic theory or genetics or the internal constitution of the stars, but quite different names like power and production and evil and beauty and history and children and the word of God.

We go in and out; even the most assiduous of us is not bound to this vast structure. One thing we find throughout the house: there are no locks; there are no shut doors; wherever we go there are the signs and usually the words of welcome.

Returning to his own quiet room of atomic physics, Oppenheimer said that what was new here, and not anticipated a half century ago, was the recognition of an indeterminateness and unpredictability in the physical world. Isaac Newton's notion of a giant programmed machine of a universe was upset. For there was more than one way to describe and more than one way to measure any happening in an atomic system; each was proper, none was definitive. Electrons, for instance, could be equally validly considered as waves, like those of the sea, or as particles, like the grains of sand on the beach. This was the complementarity of the new physics that had broadened and humanized the understanding of the natural world.

"And so it is with man's life," Oppenheimer told his B.B.C. audience.

> He may be any of a number of things; he will not be all of them. He may be well versed, he may be a poet, he may be a creator in one or more than one science; he will not be all kinds of man or all kinds of scientist; and he will be lucky if he has a bit of familiarity outside the room in which he works. . . .
>
> So it is in the antinomy between the individual and the community; man who is an end in himself and man whose tradition, whose culture, whose works, whose words have meaning in terms of other men and his relations to them. . . . We cannot in any sense be both the observers and the actors in any specific instance, or we shall fail properly to be either one or the other; yet we know that our life is built of these two modes, is part free and part inevitable, is part creation and part discipline, is part acceptance and part effort. . . .
>
> So much of what we think, our acts, our judgments of beauty and of right and wrong, come to us from our fellow men that what would be left were we to take all this away would be neither recognizable nor human. We are men because we are part of, but not because only part of, communities. . . . It is not merely that without them the individual is the poorer; without them a part of human life, not more nor less fundamental than the individual, is foreclosed.
>
> It is a cruel and humorless sort of pun that so powerful a present form of modern tyranny should call itself by the very name of a belief in community, by a word "communism" which in other times evoked memories of villages and village inns and of artisans concerting their skills, and of men of learning content with anonymity.
>
> But perhaps only a malignant end can follow the systematic belief that all communities are one community; that all truth is one truth; that all experience is compatible with all other; that total knowledge is possible; that all that is potential can exist as actual.
>
> This is not man's fate; this is not his path; to force him on it

makes him resemble not that divine image of the all-knowing and all-powerful but the helpless, iron-bound prisoner of a dying world. The open society, the unrestricted access to knowledge, the unplanned and uninhibited association of men for its furtherance—these are what may make a vast, complex, ever-growing, ever-changing, ever more specialized and expert technological world nevertheless a world of human community.

The lectures revealed three facts about Oppenheimer. First, he was a patriot of his quiet room of atomic physics. Second, by the widest measurement of human trickery, he could not be a communist. Third, he now recognized and acquiesced in the ingredients of wrong and evil, as well as right and virtue, in any human community. They were among the universal constant inconstants.

It was a tough yet hopeful view of the world Oppie had developed—melancholy, of course, and not without the personal bias of a man who had left his physics for the rumpus room of politics, however temporarily, and found himself not immune to the corruptions and conceits.

After the lectures, and after he was awarded an honorary doctorate by Oxford University, Oppenheimer took his wife to Paris to visit friends and do some shopping on their way to see Niels Bohr in Copenhagen.

About a year earlier, Chevalier, whose first marriage had finally ruptured, had taken another wife and written to the Oppenheimers with news of this and also of his new position with UNESCO in Paris. The Oppenheimers had sent back a carved wooden salad bowl as a wedding gift, and, when Chevalier had heard of their coming visit, he had written reminding them of the promise "to come and have a salad out of our fine salad bowl."

On their last night in Paris, Robert and Kitty kept this dinner date, which Chevalier was to record as a happy reunion.

Also in Paris, Oppie saw his old Corsican comrade, Jeffries Wyman, who was science attaché at the American Embassy. A short time afterwards, Wyman was down on a Roman holiday, contem-

plating his friend's fame, when two F.B.I. agents introduced themselves, offered him a cigarette, and said they would like to talk
about Robert Oppenheimer's visit to Paris.

The way Oppie's own timetable worked out, he was able to take
the cab along Constitution Avenue to answer Strauss' request for
an interview just four days before Christmas. Robert was not a
Christian, though he knew Matthew as well as he knew Job, and
he enjoyed the apple-cheeked glow and happy mood of a Washington Christmas. And the season always brought to mind the
custom of the families he knew in the Sangre de Cristos, who lit
pinewood fires in their living rooms on Christmas Eve as an invitation to the Christ child to come in and be warmed.

Admiral Strauss and General Nichols took Oppie to the board
room at the commission building and, after a few preliminaries,
he was told that his security clearance had been suspended pending another review of his file. A former Government official had
made charges to the F.B.I. and the F.B.I. had referred this matter
to the President, who personally gave the directive to put Oppenheimer before a fresh hearing.

Stunned, and ignoring the cigarette burning down through his
fingers, Oppie wordlessly took the indictment Nichols handed
him. The eyes of the admiral and the general peered at him
through steel-rimmed spectacles as he read. Stoicism sometimes
came hard even to Oppenheimer, but he held on.

Strauss was saying now that Oppie could either resign from
everything or else submit to an in-camera hearing before an independent three-man board. Both he and the commission would
be represented by counsel, both could call witnesses, both could
cross-examine. If the vote went against him he could appeal it to
the commission.

Details of that terrible afternoon remained forever hazy to Oppenheimer. He just wanted to get out of the ugly, jangling room
and walk and think. An hour later he was in front of the building
where Annie Marks worked. He found her and asked her to drive

him to her home in Georgetown; he had to have a drink and he had to see Herb.

The three of them paced the floor that night planning what to do. Oppie kept clenching his fists at his side and protesting, "They can't do this to me," like a cliché scene at the movies.

Marks explained what had been happening in Washington during Oppie's absence—the McCarthyist rampage, the Jenner committee witch-hunts, the incredible Brownell speech on Harry Dexter White that so roughly impugned a former President, and the impotence of Eisenhower in the whole intrigue. Only a few days before, Marks said, the President had been asked at a press conference if confidential Government personnel files were being released to McCarthy and Jenner, and Eisenhower admitted that he simply did not know.

While Oppie was thinking this over, Marks added quietly that he had a tip from an excellent source that Jenner had also been about to call Oppenheimer for investigation.

So there was no alternative: Oppie would have to fight his case before the commission panel, or take his chances with the merciless Jenner committee.

The next day Marks informed Nichols that Oppie would submit to a personnel security board hearing.

18

Even while Atomic Energy Commission agent Ed Brosnan was in Princeton, rather apologetically removing secret documents from Oppenheimer's office safe, Herb Marks was on the road seeking witnesses to appear for his friend. Conant, Bush, Fermi, DuBridge, Rabi, Lauritsen, and a dozen more of the nation's scientific elite were astounded at Oppie's suspension and unreservedly ready to vouch for him any time and any place. Lilienthal thought it despicable, but decided his old colleague was only temporarily set back because the case against him was so weak.

This was John Lansdale's first reaction, too, though he soon changed it. Now comfortably settled away in the oak-paneled reaches of a rich Cleveland law firm, the former Manhattan security boss had no personal reason to disturb his life for Oppenheimer's sake. Oppie had caused him much trouble over the Chevalier incident. But to condemn any man on the distortions and exaggerations of F.B.I. files was heinous, in Lansdale's opinion, and when Marks told him the story he put on his hat and coat and flew down to Washington to see Nichols.

"There must be some way to stop this, Ken," he appealed to the general. "Oppie's contract with the commission only has a short time to run, so why not just let it lapse and then not renew it."

"Jack, I'm sorry," said Nichols. "There is nothing I can do about it."

There was nothing anyone could do, for the affair had picked up its own momentum. Jenner and McCarthy both knew of the suspension, and McCarthy had rumbled that it was long overdue. He had been doing research on the delay in the H-bomb program and had already concluded the delay was deliberate, caused by traitors in Government. Nichols had no power, and no inclination, to ride into the political gale. Strauss took his lead from the Administration, from Brownell, who saw Oppenheimer as expendable.

When the time came to appoint an attorney to develop the commission case against Oppenheimer, and to cross-examine the defense witnesses, Strauss went straight to Brownell for a recommendation. The Attorney-General consulted with his assistant, William Rogers, and they selected one of the most conservative trial lawyers in Washington, Rogers's friend Roger Robb, known also as attorney for the pet journalist of the McCarthyist groups, Fulton Lewis, Jr.

A robust man, with a shovel jaw and an Arab nose, Roger Robb was hired on February 1 at a hundred dollars a day to prosecute a man about whom he knew virtually nothing. Granted a "Q" clearance, he requisitioned every available document pertaining to Oppenheimer—including many even the F.B.I. had never seen —and shut himself in his office for two months studying and making notes. He smoked boxes of huge Havana cigars and read so much he had to visit his optometrist for stronger lens in his glasses. At the end of it all he was confident he could show Oppenheimer a positive security risk.

The defendant, meanwhile, was putting his faith in Herb Marks and Lloyd Garrison, a distinguished though comparatively mild Washington lawyer with little trial experience. The selection worried Joe Volpe, the one-time commission counsel, who urged Oppie to get a good, tough Irish criminal lawyer to go against Robb. Volpe had acted for the commission in previous loyalty hearings, one of which involved a famous university president, but this time Strauss had changed the whole concept of what was prescribed as an inquiry into an adversary proceeding by bringing in an outside prosecutor of Robb's formidable reputation.

Where Volpe and Oppenheimer disagreed was on the difficulty of defending the record. In Volpe's view, Oppie was as loyal as J. Edgar Hoover, but the raw biography, without the pastels of motives and intellectual and historic context, would worry anyone unfamiliar with Oppie's personality.

Naïvely and with some conceit—and certainly without regard for Robb's fierce brilliance—Oppie felt a superficial explanation of his life and work might hasten exoneration. He and his secretary, Kay Russell, composed such a reply to the original list of charges.

This commission document, signed by Nichols, had put Oppenheimer's trustworthiness under "considerable question" on the basis of his past communistic associations and those of his family. Also injected were the Crouch accusations, the charge that he knowingly employed communists on the Manhattan project, his association with Lomanitz, his strange conduct over the Chevalier incident, and his failure to "cooperate fully" in the H-bomb program. "It was further reported," added the letter, "that you were instrumental in persuading other outstanding scientists not to work on the hydrogen bomb project and that the opposition to the hydrogen bomb, of which you are the most experienced, most powerful and most effective member, has definitely slowed down its development."

Most startling paragraph in the indictment was the accusation that Oppenheimer had opposed the super bomb in 1949 on moral grounds, by claiming it was not feasible, by claiming that there were insufficient facilities and scientific personnel to carry on the development, and that it was not politically desirable. This was true enough, but Oppie wondered when he read it if the other members of the 1949 General Advisory Committee would also be banned from Government service for their opinions. Similar thoughts had occurred to Roger Robb, who decided to concentrate his strategy on the fashionable communist issue, and particularly the Chevalier affair. He had the information that Oppie had visited Chevalier in Paris weeks before, and this seemed to be a clincher.

In his forty-three-page reply to Nichols, formally requesting a personnel security board hearing, Oppie told of his early life and how he had built up his physics school, even how he learned Sanskrit. He talked of his descent from the ivory tower in 1936, fired by "a continuing, smoldering fury about the treatment of Jews in Germany." He had relatives there, he said, and later helped in extricating them.

Because of the depression, and the inadequate jobs available to his students, he felt the need to participate more fully in the life of the community. "But," he said, "I had no framework of political conviction or experience to give me perspective in these matters." Jean Tatlock had introduced him to many fellow travelers and communists, though she was not the sole reason for his growing left-wing associations. He was interested in many humanitarian causes, often also supported by communists, and made many contributions. Oppie mentioned the quote attributed to him in the Nichols charges that he "had probably belonged to every communist-front organization on the West Coast," and said if he did make such a statement—and he did not recall doing so—it must have been in a half jocular way.

(He did not have the benefit of the tape of his long-forgotten talk with Lansdale in 1943 in which Lansdale had baited, "You've probably belonged to every front organization on the coast," and to which Oppie replied offhandedly, "Just about.")

The war in Spain, he continued, engaged most of his sympathies and he contributed to the Loyalist cause through the communists. And he added with extraordinary frankness, "I did not then regard communists as dangerous, and some of their declared objectives seemed to me desirable." In 1938, Weisskopf and Placzek had helped persuade him that Russia was a land of purge and terror. His Soviet sympathies died at the time of the Nazi-Soviet pact and were buried with the behavior of Russia in Poland and Finland. He had a new wife, a former party member who had come to hold communists in contempt, yet it was true that this did not mean an instant break with old leftist friends.

As the war proceeded and his duties in the atom bomb program increased, Oppie stated that his communistic associations evaporated and the only individual he knew at Los Alamos who was once a member of the Communist Party was his wife—and, later, his brother. Of the Chevalier conversation, he agreed he should have reported the incident immediately, though nothing in his long friendship with the man led him to believe he was actually seeking information. To this day he thought of Chevalier as a friend.

There was much in Oppenheimer's reply of the splendid spirit of Los Alamos and of the scientists' concern for the future of atomic energy afterwards. He himself had been deeply involved in the effort to get international control and then, when that failed, to adapt the atomic potential of America to meet the Soviet threat. Tracing the work of the General Advisory Committee through to the historic meeting on the thermonuclear proposal, Oppenheimer said the unanimous opinion had been that a crash program at that time might weaken rather than strengthen the position of the United States. The opposition ended, however, with the President's order to proceed on the development. Thereafter he and his panel "reported as faithfully as we could our evaluation of what was likely to fail and what was likely to work."

Oppenheimer conceded that he had emerged from the war as a "kind of public personage," widely regarded as a principal author or creator of the atom bomb, yet he did not dwell on what Borden had repeatedly called his "potent influence" in scientific and political circles. Thus he left untouched the real reason he was on trial at all.

His modest self-portrait as one of a team of backroom Government advisors—this part mostly ghost-written by Kay Russell—

made Strauss smile when Oppie delivered his manuscript early in March. Oppie's mistake had been his giant stride from the role of atom consultant to lobbyist and political in-fighter, which were games for men who had first smuggled the skeletons from the closet. Because of his distant left-wing record the rattle of the bones was always at Oppie's back. Now he had become a nuisance, he was the easiest target in America to knock over.

It was not necessary to prove Oppenheimer disloyal to deny his security clearance—Roger Robb and Strauss and Brownell realized there was no real evidence for this—but under Executive Order 10450 and the Atomic Energy Act, the clearance could be removed permanently simply by showing that the defendant had at some time had sympathetic association with the Communist Party or its front groups or contact with suspected espionage agents. Guilty in advance on these points, Oppie was also pre-condemned because he had shown disregard for security regulations in the Chevalier case and had, in fact, been devious.

The categories of presumed risk were so broad, and Robb was so expert in them, that the only doubt in the outcome of the hearing lay with the personalities of the three independent judges. Strauss selected careful men of unassailable integrity who would perform strictly according to the rules.

Chairman of the board was Gordon Gray, forty-five-year-old president of the University of North Carolina and Truman's former Secretary of the Army. Although busy with other Government work, Gray consented readily because he thought it would be a routine, speedy hearing. Oppenheimer, he thought, was sure to be cleared.

Gray was so ignorant of the venom beneath the surface of this case that he suggested to Strauss that Lilienthal would make a suitable associate on the board. The admiral rejected the idea out of hand and instead settled on a prominent Democrat, sixty-six-year-old Thomas Morgan, the board chairman of the Sperry Corporation, who was known to abhor arrogance in all forms; and a self-described, rock-ribbed Republican, seventy-one-year-old Dr.

Ward Evans. Evans was seen as a perfect choice because he was also a reasonably noted scientist, serving now as professor emeritus of chemistry at Chicago's Loyola University.

Oppenheimer had the right to challenge the board and it was pointless naming antagonistic men. As expected, Oppie had no fault to find. The board members, in turn, did not think to question the security criteria laid down for their judgment, at least not until it was too late.

The intrigue continued to unwind over the fading weeks of winter and then into the spring, yet despite the very large cast of characters being assembled, not a word had yet been printed in the newspapers. As far as the public was concerned, Robert Oppenheimer was still the Government's crack atom man. But secrecy was Strauss' weapon, not Oppie's. He was not about to be swept under the rug as a political sacrifice. If oppressive security regulations and the fever of McCarthyism were to drive him, Oppenheimer, from Government, he wanted the country to know about it.

James Reston, of *The New York Times,* had wind of the story as early as January and had persistently sought the facts from Oppenheimer. Days before the hearing was due to open, Reston insisted the story could not hold much longer, so Garrison turned over the full texts of the Nichols and Oppenheimer letters to the reporter.

Unaware of the imminent national uproar, Gordon Gray called the hearing to order on Monday, April 12. Assembled in a small upstairs room in the commission's temporary office building were the three-man board, Robb and his assistant Arthur Rollander, the Garrison team, and Oppenheimer. The defendant, provided with a leather couch behind the witness chair, faced his judges, and the lawyers were at either side of the room. Robb had the window, which was kept slightly open, mercifully tugging away the lawyer's heavy cigar smoke and the aromatic fumes of Walnut tobacco from Oppie's pipe.

Gray thought it a cheerless place for their business and he tried

to give it some warmth with an opening statement that the proceeding was an inquiry and not a trial, and, with a glance at Robb,
said, "We should approach our duties in that atmosphere and in
that spirit."

By the time the charge letter and Oppie's reply had been read,
and Garrison had made an address, it was the luncheon break.
During the afternoon, guided by Garrison, Oppenheimer talked
of his career, including a few humorous asides for the audience.
Easily and confidently, he went into the way he had authored the
Acheson-Lilienthal report, how Strauss had hired him for the Institute of Advanced Study, and much other detail that had Robb
marvelling at his style. Right up to the adjournment at five
o'clock, Oppie acted as if he were presiding over a friendly meeting.

The next morning the *Times* published Reston's story and it
was picked up by every agency, newspaper, and radio station across
the nation. It was a crazy story: the Atomic Energy Commission
had suspended as a possible security risk the man whose work
had done most to create the Atomic Energy Commission.

One name jumped to people's minds—McCarthy. Reporters
found the Senator in Phoenix, Arizona, and asked if he had had a
hand in nailing Oppenheimer. Regretfully, McCarthy said the
credit would have to go to Lewis Strauss.

Hundreds of citizens sat down that morning to write to Oppenheimer, and while many called him a "Commie rat," the majority
said he was the victim of shameful times. Most puzzled American
was Robert's cousin Alfred Stern, who considered Oppie a great
patriot. "It was you who transmitted to us the very positive experience of belonging to and love of this country when we first
arrived as strangers," he wrote. "It was you who furnished us with
the appreciation of this country's spiritual and material values."

In laboratories and lecture rooms around the country petitions
supporting Oppenheimer were started immediately. The Berkeley
campus was strangely quiet, however. A scientist at Lawrence's
Radiation Laboratory put off a reporter by saying, "What of value

can we contribute by sticking our necks out?" It was a spurious remark, for several of the Berkeley stars—Lawrence, Alvarez, Teller, Latimer—had agreed to be witnesses for Robb.

Sam Goudsmit, who was mobilizing members for the annual meeting of the American Physical Society, commented that it was deplorable but true that some scientists indeed thought Oppie's opposition to the super bomb was proof of his disloyalty—a reasoning, in Goudsmit's view, that could be made only by a mind dominated by fear or jealousy.

Flushed with rage at Reston's story, Strauss, the self-styled patron of American science, could sense the scientific community splitting apart at the seams with the most distinguished of them regarding him as the ogre. The plot had been shattered. Strauss was a casualty now as much as Oppenheimer of a frightened Administration. Too late, he realized the best tactic would have been simply to let all Oppenheimer's Government contracts expire.

Defense Secretary Wilson was smugly congratulating himself before reporters with the statement that he had abolished Oppie's board because although he had great sympathies for people who had made mistakes and reformed, "we don't think we ought to reform them in the military establishment."

Trapped right in the middle of the storm was Gordon Gray, who had expected a quick, polite, confidential inquiry and suddenly found himself painted as one of the devils out to get Oppenheimer. When the hearing resumed that morning he was angry and, mentioning the *Times* story, pointedly said, "I do not suggest that represents a violation of security." He added, however, that the Oppenheimer team had assured him only the day before that it was doing all it could to keep the story out of the press.

Right then, on the second day of what was to be an exhausting three-week inquiry during which Gray would age noticeably, the chairman had the first intimation that Oppenheimer made his own cavalier judgments on what was and was not correct procedure.

Tempers calmed as Dr. Mervin Kelly, president of the Bell Telephone Laboratory in New York, was sworn in as the initial witness and talked of his defense research work with Oppie and of Oppie's "accuracy of thought and cleanness of expression." Actually, Kelly had been squeezed in the middle of Oppenheimer's monologue, for the telephone man's convenience, and the defendant later resumed the stand and his so-called "spiel" on his connection with the United States Government.

His address extended into the third day, when he talked frankly of his brother and his fondness for him in the early years. Robert said his relationship with Frank was less intimate after Frank married Jacky in 1936, and perhaps "somewhat strained." It was Jacky who had interested Frank in politics, and together they joined the Communist Party. Robert observed that Frank had so many other interests at the time—physics, music, art, summers on the ranch—that "he couldn't have been a very hard-working communist." Frank had quit the party in 1941 and worked hard and effectively during the war. Robert rambled on for so long about Frank that Robb showed signs of impatience. He itched to start the cross-examination and chip away Oppie's maddening aplomb.

Late in the morning, Garrison finished leading and Gray nodded to his counsel. Robb drove in hard to the heart of the issue, asking Oppie how he would rate his influence in science.

Oppie fiddled with the question for a time, then agreed that he would be "one of the most influential" scientists in the atomic energy field. He further conceded that he had participated in some way in all the important decisions respecting the atomic weapons program from 1943 onwards. Having set him up, Robb proceeded to develop his case that Oppie was unsuitable by character and association to be an American policy-maker in the vital area of confronting the communist menace both at home and abroad.

Just the day before, Brownell had made a public statement that in America the communists had a "professional, skilled, highly organized and mobile cadre." It was a convenient stage-setting for Robb, who took the attitude that what was true in the early fifties was equally true in the early forties. And he drew from Oppenheimer the admission that while today he would say close association with the Communist Party would be inconsistent with work on secret projects, this was not necessarily his point of view ten years earlier. He tended to make his own individual assessments then. Although Frank had gone on to classified war work, Oppie had not told anyone his brother had been a party member and Frank had not disclosed it himself. Nor did he reveal Lomanitz as a possible security risk. Oppie was not ruffled by this, but Robb knew he had scored well.

After a luncheon adjournment, Robb fired straight into the Chevalier incident with results that remained vivid in his mind for years afterwards. His opponent was a brilliant man, and, for all his apparent glibness on the previous days, had not said a word he had not meant to say. Oppie, in short, had retained control of the hearing. Now Robb set out to shake the scientist with the toughest kind of criminal-trial grilling. He just hoped Gray would be sufficiently fascinated by the exercise to let him go.

Robb established that Oppie had recited the Chevalier incident so many times that it was pretty well fixed in his mind, then proceeded to tear down the story he had originally told Pash and Lansdale.

"Did Chevalier in that conversation say anything to you about the use of microfilm as a means of transmitting this information?" demanded Robb.

"No," replied Oppenheimer, with a snap that got Robb's adrenalin pumping.

"Did he say anything about the possibility that the information would be transmitted through a man at the Soviet consulate?"

"No," said Oppie, biting his tongue, "he did not."

"Did he tell you or indicate to you in any way that he had talked to anyone but you about this matter?"

"No."

"Did you learn from anybody else or hear that Chevalier had approached anybody but you about this matter?"

"No."

The negative was almost inaudible. All the color had drained

from Oppie's face and he had slumped a little in his chair. Robb
thought he would faint, and paused. The witness put his hands
between his knees and rubbed them, as if to keep his blood flow-
ing. For a while, there was a deathly silence. Gray said nothing.

Right into the sticky afternoon Robb attacked.

"Did you tell Pash the truth about this thing?"

"No."

"You lied to him?" Robb persisted.

"Yes."

The sparring, informal conversation of an age ago between a
football coach turned Red hunter and a young scientist preoccupied with the terrible mission of building an atom bomb was now
inflated into perjury.

"So that we may be clear," Robb was saying, "did you discuss
with or disclose to Pash the identity of Chevalier?"

"No."

"Let us refer, then, for the time being, to Chevalier as X."

"All right," said Oppie, not caring.

"Did you tell Pash that X had approached three persons on the
project?"

"I am not clear," Oppie muttered, "whether I said there were
three Xs or that X approached three people."

Robb had felt for the past hour that he had broken the case and
now he was sure, but he had to have his kill.

"Didn't you say that X had approached three people?"

"Probably."

"Why did you do that, Doctor?" Robb asked.

"Because," said Oppenheimer, dropping his voice, "I was an
idiot."

From there on in that day Oppie agreed to every suggestion
Robb put up—that he had impeded the security investigation, that
he had not told one lie to Pash but a whole tissue of lies. Chevalier
continued as his friend, Oppie said, and he had seen him on his
last trip to Europe. Jean Tatlock? No, their relationship had not

been casual. Even between 1939 and 1944 he had seen her about ten times. She had still been in love with him, he said.

Robb's ammunition came from a table stacked with tape recordings, classified documents, old security diaries. There was no escape for the defendant. In the context of the cross-examination, Oppie was annihilated. To thrust the knife further, Robb quoted from a random report on the surveillance of the atom bomb chief during the war.

The date was March 16, 1944; the place was San Francisco . . . 6:05 P.M. subject and Frank Oppenheimer left hotel. Met David Bohm on Telegraph Avenue. 6:30 P.M. subject and Frank entered car, license 53692, with subject's luggage and drove to Fisherman's Wharf.

None of this meant a thing in fact, but Robb had constructed such a web of communist plotting and underhand behavior that even quoting the license number of the car brought the three judges forward in their chairs.

At the end of the day Robb watched Oppie's scrawny figure retreat from the room and he figured he had won.

Much to his surprise, his prey strode back next morning with all his old vigor intact. After a standoff session with General Groves, who seemed most concerned with getting in a few licks against his arch enemies Condon and Lilienthal, Robb got Oppie back on the stand and paraded a whole list of names of suspected communist friends from the past.

Robert Serber interested Robb, particularly, and he wanted to know if Serber had access to classified material.

"Indeed he did," said Oppie keenly. "He created it."

For all his hammering that day, Robb made little progress and he was still trying to pursue the Serber issue at the fifth session.

"Do you see them [the Serbers] frequently?" asked Robb.

"Very infrequently, to my regret," replied Oppie.

When Robb got on to the defendant's opposition to the hydrogen bomb, Oppie was at least even in the contest. Robb suggested the witness had "qualms" about the bomb, and Oppie said drily that he did not know of anyone who did not have qualms about it. Shifting tack, Robb scored once more off Oppie's bad memory, again putting his veracity in doubt. The lawyer said Oppie had once told the Joint Congressional Committee on Atomic Energy that Glenn Seaborg—absent from the 1949 meeting—had not expressed himself on the thermonuclear crash program. In fact, said Robb, Seaborg had written a letter on the issue before the meeting.

Oppie had forgotten that he had shown the letter around, and that since it boiled down to a non-opinion, he felt justified in presenting the committee's viewpoint as unanimous against the crash program.

The way Robb presented it the scientist's oversight sounded like a definite evasion.

Oppie's lawyers made mild protests about the developing Robb technique to quote from unseen, classified documents, for Robb would not submit the documents he was quoting. When Gray failed to act on this alleged sharp practice, the defendant himself complained, still without result.

After the session that day, Garrison and Oppenheimer called in the rugged Joe Volpe for advice. "I think you ought to tell the board and the prosecutor that either you get access to this material or you will walk out," said Volpe.

The Oppenheimer team, however, refused to take the tough line, and as the hearing went on, day after day, and sometimes until eight o'clock at night, most of the aggression was left to Robb.

John Lansdale was a refreshing change of pace because he calmly told the prosecutor and the board that their hearing was linked to an extremely dangerous hysteria of the times over communism. "I think," he said, in direct attack on a main plank of Robb's case, "that the fact that associations in 1940 are regarded with the same seriousness that similar associations would be regarded today is a manifestation of hysteria."

Just before Lansdale left after his defense of Oppie's loyalty, Robb engaged in a brief professional exchange that proved beyond doubt that Robb was functioning as a trial lawyer, not as a mere counsel to help the board. Lansdale had said that although Oppie had lied to them once, his general veracity was good. Reminding his fellow lawyer of the maxim, *"falsus in uno, falsus in omnibus,"* Robb asked if Lansdale would argue to a jury that a witness' evidence should be disregarded once he had been demonstrated a liar.

"It depends on circumstances, usually I do," said Lansdale.

"Sure," said Robb. "Any lawyer worth his salt would."

The succession of famous scientists who appeared to heap extravagant praise on Oppenheimer impressed the board, and specifically Ward Evans, who liked to question them on their opinions of scientists as a charmingly eccentric species. Yet even the most articulate of them unwittingly played into Robb's hands.

Hans Bethe, for instance, talked of Oppenheimer as the unifying force at Los Alamos, the man who was recognized by everyone as "superior in judgment and superior in knowledge to all of us." And when the great super bomb issue came up, and Teller asked Bethe to help him, Bethe had sought the guidance of Oppenheimer's wisdom.

To Robb, Bethe emerged as an Oppenheimer disciple and he could not resist a broad swipe before he left.

"Doctor, how many divisions were there at Los Alamos?" asked Robb.

"It changed somewhat in the course of time," said Bethe. "As far as I could count the other day, there were seven, but that may have been eight or nine at some time."

"Which division was Klaus Fuchs in?"

"He was in my division," said Bethe.

"Thank you," said Robb. "That is all."

Fatigue of mind and body set in during the second week as the questioning bounced haphazardly from communism in 1938 to Los Alamos to the hydrogen bomb, with much complicated detail about atomic energy and Soviet diplomacy in between. The embroidery fell away from the dominant personality traits of the leading characters—Robb's pugnaciousness, Gray's gravity, and Oppie's smartness.

Oppenheimer was a few minutes late after one luncheon adjournment and when he appeared, Gray observed unnecessarily, "You are back now, Dr. Oppenheimer."

"This," replied the defendant, "is one of the few things I am really sure of."

When Garrison asked Robb to name the board witnesses so that he could prepare for them, Robb refused brusquely. "I will let Mr. Garrison in on a little trade secret," he said. "In the case of almost all the witnesses, my only advance preparation for cross-examination was a thorough knowledge of this case."

The enmity between Robb and the defense team made it a bitter hearing. During a short recess once Robb and Oppie were out in the anteroom when Oppie had a coughing fit. Robb had suffered tuberculosis as a youngster and thought the cough sounded tubercular. "I'd watch that, if I were you," he said, not unkindly. Oppie spun around, his blue eyes glinting, and snapped out a remark Robb did not understand. The prosecutor walked away.

Oppie stayed at a private home in Georgetown during the trial, spending weekends in Princeton. His friends there admired his composure and attention to physics and institute business. Yet they saw the erosion of his gusty self-confidence and the collapse of that voluptuous melancholy. None of the evidence had appeared in the newspapers, and Oppenheimer did not comment directly, but he obviously knew he was licked. It was more than that; he was trapped.

Gray himself had all but stated at the hearing that everyone was trapped by the criteria of the recent presidential executive order and of the Atomic Energy Act of 1946. He read several of the items to a witness, Harry Winne, who had been closely associated with Oppie on the Acheson-Lilienthal report.

Among the grounds justifying a security ban, he said, was a reasonable belief that the individual or his spouse had "held membership in or joined any organization which has been declared by

the Attorney General to be totalitarian, Fascist, Communist, subversive . . . or, prior to the declaration by the Attorney General,
participated in the activities of such an organization in a capacity
where he should reasonably have had knowledge as to the subversive aims or purposes of the organization." Gray read two
other pertinent articles, establishing a man as a security risk if he
"committed or attempted to commit, or aided or abetted another
who committed or attempted to commit, any act of sabotage, espionage, treason, or sedition," or "violated or disregarded security
regulations to a degree which would endanger the common defense or security."

Winne, an Oppenheimer ally, had to concede that there was
proof that Oppie had supported to some extent organizations later
listed as subversive. Gray said the trouble was that his criteria did
not confine this activity to actual membership. And furthermore,
the inclusion of the word spouse gummed things up. Yes, agreed
Winne, for Oppie admitted his wife had been a member of the
Communist Party.

"So taking the strictly legal interpretation perhaps you have no
alternative then," said Winne, adding that none of this changed
his opinion that his friend was loyal and an asset to the whole
atomic and hydrogen weapons project.

"You may," continued Winne, "because of the wording of the
law, be forced to make an adverse decision. I hope you will not,
but you may be forced to."

Under the Act, the board still had instructions to exercise its
judgment, and Morgan later put it privately to Gray that the inquiry was really a challenge to them to find a way to get Oppie
off despite the criteria. This course became primarily an assessment of the defendant's character and method of action over the
years. Here again prospects were bleak, for right from the beginning Gray had sensed that Morgan and Evans were unsympathetic
to Oppenheimer. And, by his own account, Gray had a notion that
Evans' mind was already made up to vote Oppie down. In a restaurant one night he hushed Evans for commenting that every time

a subversive name came up it seemed to be Jewish. Yet Gray himself, by letting Robb run, indicated a dislike for Oppenheimer.

The straight disloyalty claim, at least, was untenable. They had cooled also on the suspicion that Oppie put loyalty to the individual above loyalty to the country. So how was he dangerous? Gray thought it might lie in the recurring theme of the defendant's "arrogance of judgment," his tendency on occasion after occasion to take his own approach on vital issues over those whose duty it was to make the decisions.

"Let's watch for this from now on," he told his colleagues before the hearing resumed one morning.

Gray might have just as well asked his associates to check the color of Oppie's eyes; if they were blue he was a peril to the country. Oppie's closest friends could not deny his air of superiority. They could argue that they had learned to understand this arrogance, and usually accept it, because Oppie was nearly always right, but this approach would not be acceptable. What did worry the board were the number of illustrious men who said Oppie had perhaps the most dazzling mind in the country and to throw him overboard for this would be a monstrous injustice.

Particularly painful to Gray was Rabi's little speech one day about the shabby treatment received by Oppie. "He is a consultant and if you don't want to consult the guy you don't consult him, period," said Rabi. "There is a real positive record. . . . We have an A-bomb and a whole series of it . . . and what more do you want, mermaids? This is just a tremendous achievement. If the end of that road is this kind of hearing, which can't help but be humiliating, I thought it was a pretty bad show."

Vannevar Bush came on then to drive the board further into distress. "Here is a man who is being pilloried because he had strong opinions and had the temerity to express them," said Bush, scarcely controlling his outrage.

Gray nodded and commented, "Whatever the outcome, this board is going to be severely criticized."

The chairman sought out Robb later and asked if there was a

procedure for not proceeding further with the hearing. Negative, said Robb.

They all hung in there, detesting room 2022 of the commission building, until May 6, with Robb the only one rattling along. The witnesses kept coming and going, unaware of the losing battle. Charles Lauritsen said he trusted Oppie as he would his own son, whereupon Robb extracted from him very crisply that Lauritsen had not even known that Frank Oppenheimer was a former communist. Oliver Buckley said he had voted against a crash program on the super bomb, then had to tell Robb he was not a nuclear physicist and naturally gave great weight to Oppie's opinion. Robert Bacher, a brilliant man and strong for the defendant, had to concede that it was he who hired Phillip Morrison, once a suspected communist, on to the Manhattan project.

As the grotesque inquisition neared its conclusion, Robb produced some of Oppie's Berkeley enemies, leading off with the chemistry professor, Wendell Latimer, who said he would find it difficult to trust Oppenheimer in matters of security.

Latimer was not a competent witness because he had never been involved in close counsels with Oppenheimer; his value was in peppering up the board's suspicions. "It is just astounding the influence he has upon a group," he said. "He is a man of tremendous sincerity and his ability to convince people depends so much upon this sincerity. . . . A whole series of events involved the things that started happening immediately after he left Los Alamos. Many of our boys came back from it pacifists. I judged that was due very largely to his influence, this tremendous influence he had over those young men."

The star witnesses for the prosecution were to have been Lawrence and Teller, but Lawrence got only halfway across the country before he became ill and had to return home. That left Teller, who had told Robb weeks earlier that he would appear, but would make his statements only in front of Oppenheimer. If Oppie expressed strong opinions without temerity, so did Teller—and Teller was the man whose cleverness and bull-dogging had given his nation the hydrogen bomb it had asked for.

Wisely, Robb did not try to play coy with the physicist; he put the question within three minutes: "Do you or do you not believe that Dr. Oppenheimer is a security risk?"

"In a great number of cases I have seen Dr. Oppenheimer act . . . in a way which for me was exceedingly hard to understand," said Teller. "I thoroughly disagreed with him in numerous issues and his actions frankly appeared to me confused and complicated. To this extent I feel that I would like to see the vital interests of this country in hands which I understand better, and therefore trust more. . . . In this very limited sense I would like to express a feeling that I would feel personally more secure if public matters would rest in other hands."

Teller went on to say that Oppenheimer's work on the postwar atom committees was more a hindrance than a help to the people actively laboring in the atomic and thermonuclear field, and he had not lifted a finger, though he was desperately needed, to assist the super bomb project.

As he left, Teller paused at Oppie's couch and reached out his hand. "I'm sorry," he said.

"After what you've just said," said Oppie, taking Teller's hand, "I don't understand what you mean."

What Teller meant, and Lawrence had agreed, was that Oppie had gotten too big for his breeches and was due for a squashing. Teller was sorry, but it had to be done, and he was elected. This was a good part of the Government case, and it was expressed a shade more squarely later by the British novelist E. M. Forster, who had a healthy disregard for power. "Owing to the political needs of the moment," said Forster, "the scientist occupies an abnormal position which he tends to forget. He is subsidized by the terrified governments who need his aid, pampered and sheltered as long as he is obedient and prosecuted under Official Secrets Acts when he has been naughty."

Forster's British cool was nowhere evident when the hearing

finished and the board members went home for ten days to consider and judge. The first thing Gray did was to dictate a memorandum for history, in which he said the proceedings had been as fair as circumstances permitted. He was uneasy over Robb's surprise tactics with his secret documents, but no damage had been done because everything pertinent had entered the record. Robb's cross-examinations had been vigorous, but since Oppenheimer's veracity was at issue this was necessary, too.

After the long break, Gray and Morgan met at the Raleigh-Durham airport and flew back to Washington together. Neither of them could find a basis for offering a security clearance; not according to rules under which they were operating. They felt this would make it unanimous, and were amazed when they found Evans in the commission workroom making notes for what he said would be a recommendation to restore Oppie's "Q" rating. They suspected that Evans had been "got at" back home in Chicago, long known for its liberal scientific community, but he furiously denied this.

Gray was to recall that Evans kept asking for the new issue of the *Bulletin of the Atomic Scientists,* the magazine of nuclear physicist opinion. Three days later the issue came out carrying a special sixteen-page supplement dealing with the Oppenheimer case. Forty leading scientists charged the Government with breach of faith and actions "contrary to decency and common sense." A note from Einstein said, "The systematic, widespread attempt to destroy mutual trust and confidence constitutes the severest possible blow against society."

There was no way to sway the chemistry professor after this, and Robb helped him write his lone dissenting notice. Evans found Oppie's judgment bad in some cases, excellent in others, but despite his proven mistakes of the past, "to damn him now and ruin his career and service, I cannot do it." He added that failure to clear Oppie would be "a black mark on the escutcheon of our country. His witnesses are a considerable segment of the scientific backbone of our nation and they endorse him. I am worried about the effect an improper decision may have on the scientific development in our country. . . ."

Evans' document was less of a minority report than a personal dropout. He left the dirty business to Gray and Morgan, who said they would have preferred recommending that Oppenheimer "simply not be used as a consultant," but this was not their assignment. They found him loyal, beyond question, yet found that some of his attitudes *did affect* the security interests of the United States. His candor about his position on the hydrogen bomb left much to be desired in his discussions with the board, said Gray and Morgan. They did not argue with his opinions, rather with his departure from his advisory role to one of persuasive influence that was "not necessarily related to the protection of the strongest offensive military interests of the country." On his attitude towards the security system in general, Gray and Morgan found he had "repeatedly exercised an arrogance of his own judgment with respect to the loyalty and reliability of other citizens to an extent which has frustrated and at times impeded the workings of the system." Furthermore, the two men could not accept his continuing association with Chevalier as consistent with security. In short, they recommended against restoring Oppenheimer's clearance because he considered himself his own law, was not above guile, even falsehood, and was devilishly influential.

Two weeks later, General Nichols passed on to the commissioners this Gray board condemnation, together with his own unfavorable conclusion. It was the general's assertion that Oppenheimer's original story on the Chevalier incident was the factual one; the revised version the lie.

Through the running transcript the commissioners had followed the hearings closely, and Harry Smyth, the physicist, had assigned two commission aides to prepare a special summary for him. It was a fine precis, but when Smyth offered it around only Eugene Zuckert accepted a copy. He took it with him to study in the train on the way to a weekend in New Haven, Connecticut, discovering to his horror the next morning that he had misplaced the confidential document. He thought he had left it on the train and began telephoning railroad lost and found offices. Meanwhile, he called Strauss in Washington with the grim news.

The admiral ordered a special meeting of the available commissioners on Saturday and said the summary of the transcript had been stolen by *The New York Times,* or perhaps by a communist agent. There was only one resort: to print the entire transcript and give it to the press.

Smyth and Murray protested that witnesses would be seriously embarrassed because they had testified in confidence, so Strauss said he would get the transcript printed but not published. Smyth got the clear impression that Strauss was out for revenge, as Oppenheimer's lawyers had leaked some details of the hearing, all aimed to show that their client was being crucified. By his reading of the proceedings, Strauss saw a vivid damnation of his enemy. That night Zuckert's missing document was located in the Boston lost property office, but Strauss still went ahead with the printing.

"Harry is almost sick tonight about Lewis Strauss," Smyth's wife noted in her diary. Smyth knew that Strauss would publish, and he did exactly that four days later, after a marathon session on the telephone by Nichols. The general called every witness and won consent, however grudging.

The strategy misfired, for some of the most widely read reporters in the nation, the Alsop brothers and Walter Lippmann among them, thought the hearing closer to a kangaroo court than an inquiry. One famous columnist telephoned Gordon Gray and said he had cancelled out every other service he had ever performed for his country by his decision against Oppenheimer.

Alfred Friendly, of the *Washington Post,* commented deftly: "As in Shakespearean drama, even after the play ends, the audience can argue endlessly about just what the motives were of everyone concerned, the witnesses and the judges as much as the judged. . . ."

Caltech president Lee DuBridge, not a man to dillydally, shot off a note to Strauss saying it was important that Oppenheimer's

"Q" clearance be restored as soon as possible because he needed Oppie's help and advice on the Science Advisory Committee of the Office of Defense Mobilization, of which DuBridge was chairman.

A week after all this, Strauss, Campbell, Zuckert, and Murray concurred that Oppenheimer should be denied access to secret data—Murray on the grounds of the scientist's disloyalty, and the others because Oppenheimer had fundamental defects in his character (he was a liar) and because of his associations (Chevalier). Smyth, the last man in, had known what Strauss and his friend Campbell would do and had the notion that Murray would count anyone who violated the speed limit as a security risk, but he was surprised at the genial, reasonable Gene Zuckert. Smyth's vote was a formality, he could not change the majority decision, but he was determined to be heard and he worked until dawn on the deadline composing his dissent.

After Evans' disappointingly personal stand, Smyth's vote for Oppie—a man he found somewhat high-handed in private life— was intelligently simple and objective.

> The only question being determined by the Atomic Energy Commission is whether there is a possibility that Dr. Oppenheimer will intentionally or unintentionally reveal secret information to persons who should not have it. To me, that is what is meant within our security system by the term security risk. . . . In my opinion the most important evidence in this regard is the fact that there is no indication in the entire record that Dr. Oppenheimer has ever divulged any secret information. . . . For much of the last eleven years he has been under actual surveillance . . . supplemented by enthusiastic help from powerful personal enemies.

There was much more, but the point was made, and Oppenheimer used Smyth's statement as his own comment. Later, in Princeton, Oppie thanked the physics professor for his vote, which he realized, in the political climate of the times, was a courageous one and had written at least a temporary end to Smyth's Government service.

"I must admit I find it hard to get over the whole thing," Smyth told Oppie.

Oppie put on one of his downward half-smiles. "I never expect to get over it," he said.

19

There is a warp in the American pattern which Raymond Chandler called the meanness of the streets. In the raw analysis, Robert Oppenheimer's tussle with the Eisenhower Administration was a street fight, and a very mean one. They could not cope with him; the town bullies said he was a communist; so they drove him out.

The enigma of the affair was Thomas Morgan, who scarcely spoke during the three-week inquiry. Often remarked as an underdog, an old pretense of Oppie's, he was ruthless in his verdict. "The question," he said, "is whether you are going to have one security system for the scientist who built a bomb and another for the chauffeur who drives a congressman around Washington."

Oppie's immense achievements apparently counted not at all with Morgan, who did not like the scientist's grip on the minds of his contemporaries. Without this, however, Oppie would never have been so successful in building up the physics school that helped move America to the forefront of science, nor been such an inspiration at Los Alamos. Criticism of Oppie's unconventionality came from the oddest quarters.

Why, asked the students at Amherst College not long afterwards, had not he helped his case by showing more repentence for his past associations? And Oppie had replied, "It may not be the obligation of a man in a position of responsibility to conform his actions . . . to what the public desires; but if he wishes to play an effective part in politics, it is clear that he must either conform himself to what the public desires, or persuade the public to accept what he is."

Oppie could not persuade the public, and the irony was that Joseph McCarthy could not either. The scientist and the Senator were both cast aside in the year 1954. Yet while McCarthy just ran down like a spent pinwheel firecracker and then died, Oppenheimer was to assume a new fame.

Teller remarked to one of his friends, who passed it on, that Oppie had a martyr complex. The fact was that the ingredients were rich in Oppie's case history for the construction of a legend, a mystique, and the man had the dramatic reserve to adapt to the role.

Nevertheless he was for a number of years privately shrunken by his censure, and it was much later before he could say with conviction that the hearing was not a tragedy but a farce, and that what had meant most to him had never emerged at the inquiry.

The immediate reminders of his rejection from the mainstream were sharp. F.B.I agents followed him on several journeys around the United States, and questioned his hosts after a vacation in the Virgin Islands. When the Alsop brothers wrote a strong defense of him, coupled with an attack on Strauss, in their book *We Accuse,* the commission replied in its press digest that Strauss had been the man noble enough to strike out the charge of adultery (Jean Tatlock) in the original indictment.

Chevalier wrote in shocked sentences of his friend's duplicity, claiming that finally he knew what had "played untold havoc with my career and life."

An invitation to chair a session in high energy physics at the University of Washington, in Seattle, was cancelled. An army private, also a physicist, was promptly dispatched overseas when he innocently asked Oppenheimer to address a service group of science graduates at the Army Chemical Center in Maryland.

Roughest cut of all, though offered as a kindness, was the visit one day from a Mr. Lal of the Indian Consulate in New York, who brought a personal message from Nehru that Oppenheimer was welcome to live with honor and continue his physics in India as long as he wished.

Nehru misunderstood Oppie's love of America and his real sense of failure, rather than defiance, at his censure. His brother felt that Robert came out of it with the sore realization that he had been too high-flown during the Washington years and had isolated himself from the journeymen of science. Frank's comfort was that his brother's quality had not been completely corrupted, otherwise he would not have been thrown out.

So it was that Oppie returned to his warm, quiet room of physics, where his closest friends had insisted he belonged, and from this retreat set his mind to work on the lessons of his adventure. His ego and his evangelism for the beauty of the intellect, and for the arts and sciences, would not permit him to withdraw from the public stage, and he prepared enthusiastically for his talk at the bicentennial celebrations at Columbia University late in the year.

His address, broadcast nationally, was a lament over the widening gulf between the mass of society and the sensitive brotherhood of scientists and artists, wherein, he seemed to be saying, lay the redemption for mankind. Even within science itself, thrusting far and quickly on a variety of frontiers, there was a dismaying fragmentation.

Speaking as poet and scientist, Oppenheimer remarked on the artist's sense of great loneliness, his attempt to communicate with a community which was largely not there, but dissolved in a changing world. And complementary to this was the terrible barrenness in the lives of men, "deprived of the illumination, the light and tenderness and insight of an intelligible interpretation, in contemporary terms, of the sorrows and wonders and gaieties and follies of man's life."

His theme established, Oppie went rapidly to a diagnosis of the human ailment that had indeed shown its first symptoms in some excessive reactions, of which he saw himself a victim, but was not to break out into galloping sickness for another decade. He said,

> In an important sense, this world of ours is a new world, in which the unity of knowledge, the nature of human communities, the order of society, the order of ideas, the very notions of society and culture have changed and will not return to what they have been in the past.
>
> What is new is new not because it has never been there before, but because it has changed in quality. One thing that is new is the prevalence of newness, the changing scale and scope of change itself, so that the world alters as we walk in it, so that the years of a man's life measure not some small growth or rearrangement or moderation of what he learned in childhood, but a great upheaval. . . .
>
> The techniques, among which and by which we live, multiply and ramify, so that the whole world is bound together by communication, blocked here and there by the immense synapses of political tyranny. The global quality of the world is new: our knowledge of and sympathy with remote and diverse peoples, our involvement with them in practical terms, and our commitment to them in terms of brotherhood.
>
> What is new in the world is the massive character of the dissolution and corruption of authority, in belief, in ritual, and in temporal order.
>
> Yet this is the world that we have come to live in. . . .
>
> This is a world in which each of us, knowing his limitations, knowing the evils of superficiality and the terrors of fatigue, will have to cling to what is close to him, to what he knows, to what he can do, to his friends and his tradition and his love, lest he be dissolved in a universal confusion and know nothing and love nothing. It is at the same time a world in which none of us can find hieratic prescription or general sanction for any ignorance, any insensitivity, any indifference. . . .

Oppenheimer was not of a mind, nor of a mood, to extend much comfort for men seeking to strike an easy balance between the in-

finitely open and the intimate. He talked of the separate villages
of mankind, the need to make gardens in the villages and to construct paths to connect one to the other. It would be a rugged assignment keeping the gardens flourishing and the paths free in a
great, open, windy world.

"But this, as I see it," he said, "is the condition of man; and in
this condition we can help, because we can love, one another."

What was also new was the humble public Oppie—a man not
yet fused with the private Oppie. A magazine writer of the time
listened to a few of his select pronouncements and talked of his
tranquillity, a word that brought affectionate guffaws from Vannevar Bush. And when, soon after the radio talk, Oppie appeared
in a long, reflective interview on Edward R. Murrow's television
show, See It Now, Dean Acheson was entranced with his friend's
sense of theatre.

Publicly, Oppenheimer was suggesting that perhaps some in the
nation "overestimated the nobility and perfection of our society,"
while privately he called it a "sickly scurrying." While he exuded
an extraordinary forebearance out among the people, he could be
ruthless in more intimate conversations. Liberals who sought his
signature on documents urging the Government not to go to war
over Formosa in 1955 were briskly turned away. He made it clear
the war might be necessary, even the use of atom bombs.

The contrary views on Oppie within his own institute were
scarcely believable. For a start, of course, there was Strauss, the
trustee, who found that however much he wanted to be rid of the
man, Oppie was the country's leading intellectual and he could
not do without him. Six months after the hearing, smiling and
slicked, the admiral came into Oppie's outer office and had himself announced. Oppie emerged immediately with his hand out-
stretched. "Lewis. . . ." Strauss, hardly crediting his luck, beamed,
"Robert. . . ." A visitor who happened to be in the room thought
that if a match were lit the whole place would explode.

Irritated by Oppie's martyrdom was one of the world's distinguished mathematicians, Deane Montgomery, who had been at

the institute for some years. He had fought Oppie continually over
selection of men as one-year members of the mathematics department, claiming that while he held out for excellence in the one
field, Oppie wanted rounded, colorful scholars. Many of the mathematicians, von Neumann included, sided with Montgomery, but
after the hearings the faculty chiefs thought it somehow unfair to
keep opposing Oppie.

The passage of time wore away this charity and Montgomery
was once more at Oppie's door, insisting they needed more scientific talent at the institute and less philosophers. Shouting matches
between the two, both lean, emotional men were frequent.

"I want the best men in the world," Montgomery snapped.

"I understand this, but we must consider how they will fit in
here harmoniously," resisted Oppie.

"Nonsense," yelled Montgomery.

"You," said Oppenheimer, raising his voice, "are the most arrogant, bull-headed son-of-a-bitch I have ever met."

And so it went on, a pair of the country's greatest intellects, getting more vicious by the moment. Montgomery nastily called
Olden Manor, where Oppie lived and often entertained at cocktail
parties, "Bourbon Manor." Oppie said Montgomery was a gossip
and a braggard.

The squabbling reached a childish low one day when Montgomery happened to remark that as a young man in Cambridge,
England, he had attended some seminars conducted by the British
philosopher, G. E. Moore. Oppie, triumphant, said Montgomery
could not have done that because Moore died in the 1880s. The
mathematician fetched a book of biographies to prove Oppie
wrong.

The director constantly went home growling about the mathematicians, who doubtless had some legitimate complaint because
while they were keen to make their department an international
mecca, Oppie was weighted on the side of physics. He had brought
a strong team of his graduates when he first came from California
and had subsequently built up the crew with such notables as the

young Chinese team, Lee and Yang, who won a Nobel Prize in 1957 for their work in quantum mechanics. Oppie took delight in just watching Lee and Yang walk the grounds of the institute. When they cabled him once in the Virgin Islands that they were on the threshhold of a breakthrough in their theory, he wired back an Oppenheimerism that pushed them forward. "Walk through," Oppie ordered.

Not every physicist who attended the institute loved the director. His old critical faculty was undiminished and many resented his coolness towards some of their ideas. A young Turkish professor disconsolately plopped into his chair after a visit with Oppie. And Dirac, the master physicist, who was there, knew the trouble instantly. "He was skeptical, eh?"

The thing was that many physics faculty heads at universities across the country would first check the credentials of applicant professors or researchers with Oppie before hiring. His power over the careers of these men was used scrupulously, but it was there nonetheless.

Now moving through his fifties, just a step behind the progression of the Twentieth Century, Oppie accepted that he himself could no longer be an expert practitioner in nuclear physics.

"Atomic physics, especially theoretical atomic physics, is a young man's game," he said. "The imagination and the vigor that contribute to the advances come most to men who are just completing or have just completed their formal education. It is a rapidly changing field; to be expert in it one must work at it without remission."

Now a life pattern of Oppie's had been to set extremely high standards for himself and then feel deflated, frustrated, when he fell short. Actual stupidity was so far away from his base that he could not brook it at all. That was why Robb had driven him close to nausea when the lawyer played back Oppie's muddle-headedness in the Chevalier incident. It was the reason that some people, despite his courtly manners, thought him overbearing and intolerant, and a few friends found it a strain to be in his presence for extended periods.

Long before, in Corsica, he had glimpsed the beauty though imbedded tragedy of life, and this view had slowly grown to the focus on man's inevitable fallibility and inconsistency as presented in the Reith Lectures, and the difficult task beleaguered man faced in welding any kind of lasting brotherhood as presented in the Columbia address. Gradually, thereafter, what had been a wisp of condescension, or at least a poet's commentary, changed to an acquiescence and he himself showed signs of retreat from Eagle Hill. The public and private individual came nearer together. It was not to be a bolt down the slopes, for even in the matter of leaving the physics frontier to the young, Oppie could not resist the hint of a comparison with Isaac Newton. After Newton's discoveries and his winning of renown, said Oppie, he had grown fat and driven around in a coach with servants and done very little.

His desire to be admired slowed his descent, for it was repeatedly gratified. After the Edward R. Murrow show, invitations to speak at colleges, at dinners, at clubs, and in foreign countries came at the rate of fifty a week, then one hundred a week. Even the University of Washington apologized for the ostracism of 1954 and asked him there for the International Congress of Theoretical Physics. Just by walking into a meeting of the American Physical Society he won a standing ovation. The French awarded him the Legion of Honor. Marlene Dietrich volunteered that Robert Oppenheimer was an outstanding man of his time.

"This is not only for his scientific achievement," she said, "but as a human being. He has character and modesty and the willingness to take what comes along without being dragged down into the mud."

Veronica Wedgwood, the British historian, wrote Oppie a note after a term at the institute and said his "transcendent intellect is of the vitalizing kind which brings out the full potential of lesser minds in contact with it." George Kennan, the former American Ambassador to Moscow, came to the institute, despite some opposition from the mathematicians, and praised his director for creating a place "where the work of the mind can proceed in its highest form."

This was salutory stuff for a man awakening to humility, and it did not diminish. Senator Clinton Anderson of New Mexico wrote saying that Oppie had been "had" by the Strauss team and asked if he could reopen the inquiry and get the scientist's clearance restored. Wisely, Oppie's lawyers first wanted to see the evidence that would bring a reversal.

Sweetest happening on the whole roster was the Senate's rejection in 1959 of Lewis Strauss as Eisenhower's Secretary of Commerce. Scientists, virtually en masse, said Strauss was unacceptable to them and their voice was strong enough to sway the Senate. The main charge leveled at the admiral was that he had misused the personnel security system of the Atomic Energy Commission.

None of this, however, could make up for the sobering sadness that approached misery in Oppie's life. Part of it was obvious. He missed his power in Government, his place at the center of scientific action, the telephone calls from secretaries of state and four-star generals. The other part was worse—Kitty's terrible and debilitating agony from a diseased pancreas that would only ease with drugs, and Robert's own enfeebling pains of back and abdomen. His weight was down to 115 pounds and the more insistently Kitty and Toni tried to make him eat more, the more stubbornly he resisted. He was hungry, he said, but could not eat comfortably.

Oppie was greatly impressed with bravery, a quality he saw in Kitty and was repeatedly and sometimes foolishly proving in himself. The family had acquired a cottage on St. Thomas in the Virgin Islands and went south every summer. On one of these trips, Robert had promised to visit Pablo Casals in Puerto Rico and stop in San Juan to address a physics seminar. Two days before the trip he caught intestinal influenza, but refused to put off his appointment. He flew to San Juan and lectured with a temperature of 103 and then returned to St. John in a state of collapse. The luxury of the talk with Casals was all he would postpone. Kitty helped him on to the sailboat that would take them across to St. Thomas. A few minutes out on the open water, Oppie took the tiller from a tanned and muscular charter skipper, who watched in admiration as the pale, gaunt physicist gunned the yacht forward, a half-point off the wind.

The following year tested him again. He was preparing dinner for friends at the cottage, and emptying kerosene from a can into a jug to fill the lamp. A wasp stung the hand holding the jug and he dropped it with a cry of pain. The jug shattered on the floor, driving a shard into his right foot. When Oppie limped down to the sea to wash the blood away, he found he could not move his big toe. A small sailboat was rigged and riding at the beach, so he commandeered this and whipped across the sound to a little hospital.

An examination of the bloody foot revealed that the shard from the jug had sliced the tendon and this had curled up his leg like a broken violin string. The surgeon muttered as he worked, "out of your mind . . . sailing across the bay . . . lucky you won't lose the whole foot. . . ." Catching the tendon, the doctor pulled it taut, attached it, sewed the wound and put the foot in a cast. "The cast," said the physician, "stays on until I say otherwise."

For those who loved Oppenheimer, the limitless woes that seemed to beset the flesh-and-blood man behind the public legend of visionary were distressing. No man loved him more than his son Peter, who resented everyone and everything that interfered with his Pa's enjoyment of the ordinary little pleasures of life.

Too frequently, and unjustly, in Peter's view, was his Pa reminded of his banishment from Government. He hated his mother's sickness because he felt it caused his Pa suffering. Happiness to Peter, through his middle teenage, was seeing his father at the wheel of the 1951 Cadillac convertible for which he had searched the country, or watching his Pa's delight in playing with the German shepherd Buddy, or having a stimulating conversation at parties. The Sunday poker games with the family were a joy. He liked it when his father wasted time watching Perry Mason on television, or, coming home tired from work, sneaking a shot of vodka in the pantry. He was pleased when Harold Cherniss or Francis Fergusson came to visit because he knew his father enjoyed their company.

Oppie had sent Peter to the Quakers' George School, in Bucks County, Pennsylvania, on the grounds that Quakers were honorable. The boy did only fairly, missing Princeton, and in the spring of 1958 Oppie made a decision that caused both himself and his son a deep hurt that lasted for years. Because Peter was not doing so well at school, his father refused to take him along when the family went to Paris for two months. Oppenheimer, his wife and daughter, packed off in April for Oppie to fulfil his assignment as exchange professor in physics at the Sorbonne, and later to give lectures in Israel, Greece, and Belgium. The trip turned into the grand tour, ending with a house visit to the Belgian Royal Family.

Before term's end, Peter returned from George, vowing to Oppie's current secretary, Verna Hobson, that he would never go back. Shortly after this the boy took off west, coming to Frank's ranch in Colorado when he needed to talk. Subsequently, father and son saw less of each other, to their mutual pain, although Oppie cut short a couple of vacations in the Virgin Islands because, as he wrote Verna Hobson, he was homesick for Peter. As in many families there was a conflict between mother and son, and there was only one choice, one side, a man could take.

Increasingly, Oppie was on the road, lecturing and traveling. In the fall of 1960 he accepted an invitation from the Japan Committee for Intellectual Interchange, defying the advice of some who said he would be badly received. He walked from the airliner to a combative clutch of Japanese reporters at Tokyo airport. They bore in quickly on the bomb. Was he sorry now he made it?

"I do not regret," he said, "that I had something to do with the technical success of the atomic bomb." He looked at the antagonistic reporters and made one of those nim-nim-nim sounds. He was their match; he really was anybody's match in a fair fight. "It isn't that I don't feel bad," he added softly, "it is that I don't feel worse tonight than I did last night."

He said he would not be visiting Hiroshima; it was not the wish of his Japanese hosts, though he himself would have liked to make the trip.

It was the following year, after the election of John F. Kennedy, that Oppie began to be accepted back into the good graces of his own Government. He was sponsored by the Organization of American States as a visiting professor to Latin America, a glorious tour that made him page-one news from Mexico to Brazil. The captions under the world familiar face, not unlike some shots of Bertrand Russell, made the identity he would never shake, *"El Padre de la Bomba Atomica."*

And the next spring he was invited to the White House, a spectacular guest even among the forty-nine Nobel Prize laureates who shared the evening with him.

John Mason Brown, the author, visited him in Princeton about this time and captured the ageing Oppie vividly in his book, *Through These Men.* Brown found him thin and small and frail to the point of transparency, yet singularly impressive.

> The power of his personality is the stronger because of the fragility of his person. When he speaks he seems to grow, since the eagerness of his mind so affirms itself that the smallness of his body is forgotten. His tiny hands and fingers are birdlike and as he talks, when not gesturing with his horn-rimmed glasses, he emphasizes his leanness by being apt to encircle his right elbow or forearm with his left hand, or stroke his scrawny gobbler neck with it.

Brown put it to him that his security hearing had been like a dry crucifixion, and Oppie replied, "You know, it wasn't so very dry. I can still feel the warm blood on my hands."

The torment of his eight-year exile by the Republican Administration showed in Oppie's every wasted inch, but in his recent lectures and papers it was apparent that his intellect and vision were stronger, surer, more constructive than ever, and it was not surprising that the Kennedy Administration began a graduated exoneration of him.

The new crew at the oars, men like Arthur Schlesinger, Jr., McGeorge Bundy, Dean Rusk, were aware that Oppenheimer's critical mind, tempered by all the hells of the Twentieth Century, was a rare resource. All had learned from him. For some years, in fact, he had been their champion.

They had heard him out on the injurious simplifications of Government attitude on the new and complex external and internal issues, and "why we, in this country, should be better able to take thought, and to make available in the pressing problems of policy and strategy the intellectual resources now so sorely lacking."

Kennedy speech writers had studied Oppenheimer, then seemingly prepared somewhat denatured versions of the raw material.

"What we here need," he said,

is a vastly greater intellectual vigor and discipline; a more habitual and widespread openmindedness; and a kind of indefatigability, which is not inconsistent with fatigue but is inconsistent with surrender. It is not that our land is poor in curiosity, in true learning, in the habit of smelling out one's own self-delusion, in the dedication and search for order and law among novelty, variety and contingency. There is respect for learning, and for expertness, and a proper recognition of the role of ignorance, and of our limits, both as men and as man; but none of these is there enough, either among us, or in the value with which they are held by us, if indeed government by the people is not to perish.

Oppenheimer's warning was that the human reluctance to learn and to change must be overcome on Kennedy's New Frontier, and nothing less than this. The dire alternative was that American organs of intelligence and perception would become coded, much as man's sense organs were, by prior commitments, and this to the extent that there would not even be awareness of error.

A revolution in education was needed, and one prime purpose would be to illuminate man's condition of ignorance as measured against the total fabric of knowledge. This was the import of his message to newspapermen once, to clarify the extent to which people did not understand each other. The way to this perspective, as he enlarged it before a Canadian audience, was a dedication on the part of men to adopt the habit of lifelong study and communication. He said:

> We have, on the one hand, to keep with utmost reverence and devotion and dedication our specialty, our own way, our own life, our own loves. If we do not do that we have no anchor at all in honesty . . . but we have also, with an equal importance but in a wholly different style, to be responsive to what others have to tell us, to be open to novelty and otherness, to have a sympathy which makes the understanding between men possible. . . . I can think of no greater ideal for the generations whom we in our schools and institutes and universities hope to encourage than to set them an example of people who are trying again to talk to one another, and who are trying again really to listen.

It was Oppie's idea to show how relevant an unremitting lifelong intellectual vigor was to practical daily life. "I think," he told a group of architects, "that we may come to see education not as a way of preparing people to take off and live, but as a way of preparing people to live and love and know and continue to learn. . . ."

And he posed to a gathering of publishers the question of St. Matthew, "Which of you by taking thought can add one cubit unto his stature?"

"By taking thought of our often grim responsibility," he suggested, "by knowing something of our profound and omnipresent imperfection, we may help our children's children to a world less cruel, perhaps less unjust, less likely to end in catastrophe beyond words. We may even find our way to put an end to the orgy, the killing, the brutality that is war."

One of Oppie's closest associates could never explain what made his friend tick, or say with any certainty why he did what he did, and he was doubtful sometimes whether Oppie knew himself. The mixture of intellectualism, sensitivity, and emotionalism was confounding. This changed in the early sixties. Under the stimulus of his desire to speak out with integrity, freshness, and plausibility, Oppie finally began to examine himself searchingly. He forced himself to do so, thanking Freud for his lesson that evil in man was a part of nature and could be treated without contempt or hatred.

"When we are blind to the evil in ourselves," Oppie said in 1963, "we dehumanize ourselves, and we deprive ourselves not only of our destiny, but of any possibility of dealing with the evil in others."

Those around him saw the arrogance of his earlier years dissolve, to be replaced by a healthy irony about himself, a humility, a compassion, a gentleness. Verna Hobson saw him mellow in what she felt a most extraordinary way. His son saw a new kindness, and noticed that his father no longer upstaged anybody in conversation.

He came to admit his reliance on others. A friend, posted to Switzerland, offered to take Toni with her so that she might attend a good finishing school. Oppie said he would have to reject the offer, though he realized how much Toni would enjoy it, because he and Kitty were both in ill health and they needed their daughter at home.

The gall of previous years had vanished. Two young physicists at the institute entered a physics essay contest and won first prize of a thousand dollars with a brilliant hoax paper called "Anti-Gravity." Quivering with anger when he heard about it, Oppie ordered the two men to confess their trick and return the money or leave the institute.

Playfulness entered his life, too—not much, but perhaps more and of lighter quality than his old stunt of plunging his hands in hot water. A female book editor who talked too much was forever calling him. Oppie usually suffered the conversations, but one time Verna Hobson took it on herself to intercept a call and say Oppie was out. A few minutes later the boss passed her desk and the secretary confessed. Oppie's face creased in a grin. He gave a little jump into the air and clicked his heels.

20

In OPPENHEIMER'S VIEW, a key source of the liberal spirit was hope and a key method was reevaluation. He found the Kennedy Administration adhering more surely to both articles as the months went by, and a letter he received in early April, 1963, moved him into the vicinity of actual optimism. Glenn Seaborg, then chairman of the Atomic Energy Commission, informed his friend that he was to be awarded that year's Enrico Fermi Award for his contributions to the national atomic strength.

The award, which included fifty thousand dollars in tax-free money, was basically a scientific one—Teller had received it the previous year—but Oppie realized the political overtones in his case. To give the Fermi plaque to a man still regarded as *persona non grata* in the nation's secret councils was an act of political courage, certain to be condemned by the conservative voices in Congress. True to form, Senator Bourke Hickenlooper led the chorus with his shout of "disgusting!" when the award was made public.

Oppie's gratitude to President Kennedy and to the White House academics he knew must have pushed his case, was boundless. He issued an immediate statement that showed these men what their kindness meant to him. "Most of us look to the good opinion of our colleagues, and to the goodwill and the confidence of our Government," he said. "I am no exception."

Reporters who pressed him to say more were resisted. "Look," Oppie told one of them frankly, "this isn't a day for me to go shooting my mouth off. I don't want to hurt the guys who worked on this."

While President Kennedy laid plans to make the honor complete by personally handing the award to Oppie in the White House late in the year, the man himself was busy with the greatest avalanche of mail since 1954. Most of it was congratulatory, some of it delectably so.

"In Victor Hugo's tale," wrote Adolf A. Berle, "they first decorated the hero, and then shot him. Happily in your case, the order is reversed."

"I thought this was a good day to tell you that I still feel what I said long ago . . . not only 'still' but more and more," wrote Marlene Dietrich.

Then came Edward Teller:

I have just heard on the radio that you are getting the Fermi award of 1963. This makes me happy for many reasons. One is the memory of our work in Berkeley in 1942. The other is your proposal which had become known as the Baruch plan and which is the only honest and effective suggestion in this field that was ever made. I have been often tempted to say something to you. This is the one time I can do so with full conviction and knowing that I am doing the right thing. I enjoyed getting the Fermi prize last year. If you had gotten it first it might have been perhaps better. But I am glad that the announcement was made early so you have more time for the pleasure. With sincere wishes for good luck—which we all need. . . .

The award ceremony was set for December 2, and, after a rapid year of lectures and travel, Oppie worked on his acceptance speech one Friday late in November. After some preamble, he wrote: "I think it is just possible, Mr. President, that it has taken some charity and some courage and some humor for you to make this award today. That would seem to me a good augury for all our futures. . . ."

He was reading this over and over when Peter walked into his office, his face ashen, and said in a sobbing voice that he had just heard on his car radio that President Kennedy had been assassinated in Dallas.

Oppenheimer was stricken, and he sat there for moments without the slightest movement. He stirred then and hoarsely asked Peter if he would like a drink. The boy nodded his head and his Pa walked to the cupboard where he kept the liquor. He opened it and stood there staring at the bottles. Minutes later, Peter said, "Well, never mind then."

Father and son walked out to the reception room where Verna Hobson was making arrangements to close the institute for the day. She looked up at Oppie and saw his grief. Their eyes met for a second and Oppie said in a distant voice, "Now things are going to come apart very fast."

On the Monday he was told that President Johnson would make the Fermi award as planned, so he retrieved his notes of the Friday, crossed out the three words "and some humor" and had them typed up. The next week he spoke them at the formal, though impossibly emotional ceremony at the White House. At the end he added quietly to Johnson, "These words I wrote down almost a fortnight ago. In a somber time I gratefully and gladly speak them to you."

Oppie's first visit to the White House had been the occasion of his unhappy interview with Harry Truman, in which he said he had the feeling of blood on his hands. Now the entire nation had the feeling, and, returning to Princeton, Oppenheimer wondered if there really could be a formula devised to lessen the violence on earth. His mind ran over the idea of gathering together notable world intellectuals, perhaps in a country inn, to engage in a dialogue aimed at seeking the human, ethical, cultural preconditions for a more peaceful civilization.

Agnes Meyer, widow of the former owner of the *Washington Post,* was enthusiastic when she heard of Oppie's musing, for she had the notion of bequeathing her home, Seven Springs Farm, at Mt. Kisco, New York, for just such a purpose. In the summer of 1964 the two arranged the first Mt. Kisco meeting, inviting Dr. and Mrs. Julian Boyd, he the renowned Thomas Jefferson scholar; Dr. Morris Carstairs, the Scottish anthropologist; Mr. and Mrs. Wallace Harrison, he the architect; Miss Jeanne Hersch, the Swiss philosopher; George Kennan; Dr. and Mrs. George Kistiakowsky; poet Robert Lowell; the ballet's Nicholas Nabokov; and the English philosopher Stuart Hampshire.

"We should try to look toward our future without flinching, without lying and without despair," Oppie told them at the first session.

He led the discussion with his thoughts on the complementarity he had first learned from Niels Bohr and had enlarged on in his Reith Lectures. "The truth is," he said, "that we never know enough about ourselves to answer properly such things as choice between right and wrong, beautiful and ugly."

The challenge was direct: the group in the sunny drawing room at Seven Springs must have perspective on themselves as individuals and should discuss themselves frankly, before they could move on to judge society generally. Oppie, the scientist, wanted the measuring device defined.

He did a brave thing then for a man who so coveted his privacy, who, in all his writings, and even at his inquisition, had kept back his inner self. He revealed himself to the heart. He said gently,

Up to now, and even more in the days of my almost infinitely prolonged adolescence, I hardly took an action, hardly did anything, or failed to do anything, whether it was a paper on physics, or a lecture, or how I read a book, how I talked to a friend, how I loved, that did not arouse in me a very great sense of revulsion and of wrong.

It turned out to be impossible . . . for me to live with anybody else, without understanding that what I saw was only one part of the truth . . . and in an attempt to break out and be a reasonable man, I had to realize that my own worries about what I did were valid and were important, but that they were not the whole story, that there must be a complementary way of looking at them, because other people did not see them as I did. And I needed what they saw, needed them.

For several days the gathered men and women of learning catalogued the world's ills, the elements of smugness, the falsity, self-satisfaction, and unction, but could not arrive at any foundation for establishing peace and a new unanimity. They came inevitably to simple protest, or as Oppie put it, the age-old impatience of the poet, the artist, and the young with the self-serving lies of the time.

"We have been crying the old cry," he said. "The king has no clothes."

Nevertheless the dialogue had been so stimulating that similar meetings were held in following years, keynoted again by Oppenheimer. His theme was strong now. "We most of all should try to be experts on the worst among ourselves," he said at one gathering.

> We should not be astonished to find some evil there, that we find so readily abroad and in all others; nor should we, as Rousseau tried to, comfort ourselves that it is the responsibility and the fault of others, that we are just naturally good; nor should we let Calvin persuade us that despite our obvious duty we are without power, however small and limited, to deal with what we find of evil in ourselves. In this knowledge, of ourselves, of our profession, of our country—our often beloved country—of our civilization itself, there is scope for what we most need: self-knowledge, courage, humor, and some charity.

Encouragement for Oppie to continue adding his voice to the whispering of reason around the world came from a man, once dear to him, but long silent—Max Born. The professor wrote to his old student that it was indeed his responsibility to challenge the cynicism of politicians, the indifference of the masses, the scientists' evasion of the troublesome issues.

Heartened by the letter, Oppie confessed in reply, "I have felt a certain disapproval on your part for much that I have done . . . a sentiment I share."

Although only just past sixty years of age, Oppie's health was failing badly. A long session with pneumonia weakened him further, and he sensed he had a short time left.

His doctors advised against tiresome travel, but there was one invitation he refused to give up—to return to Los Alamos and give a memorial address for Neils Bohr, who had died in 1962. The auditorium was jammed to the doors when Norris Bradbury, troubled by his friend's appearance, introduced Oppie as "Mr. Los Alamos." Bradbury held out his hands for quiet while he finished the introduction, saying that Oppie had built Los Alamos by the sheer force of personality and character. Then he could add no more, for the applause rippled from the front row and gathered in a deafening roar, until the hall was on its feet in the most moving outpouring of affection Oppie had ever experienced.

Never had Oppie disappointed an audience and that night at Los Alamos, as he traced Bohr's career as a scientist and humanitarian, the townspeople were transported to other times and other places, feeling the drama of the past that had catapulted this thin, beloved man at the microphone to glory and then to calumny. Oppie made Bohr the lone giant of the times and all others, including himself, the little men who scurried.

But at the finish, when he stepped away from the rostrum, the ovation exploded again and would not stop this time. Oppie's voice, so even during his talk, was husky when he spoke again. "I can say no more," he said, "except to encourage you to leave."

They did not see him again in Los Alamos, for the exhaustion of his life was overcoming him. He had to retire as institute director in 1965, accepting in its stead Einstein's old job as senior professor of theoretical physics. That, too, he had to give up early in

1966 because his physicians had diagnosed a new ailment for him, cancer of the throat.

Radiation treatment was started on the small lump in his throat and continued for months. He had to give up smoking, of course, but was forced into the new habit of sucking sugary throat lozenges, partly to soothe his irritated throat tissues and partly to make up for the malfunction of the salivary glands. The lozenges caused new agony, for his dentist, Warren Dodson, found rampant decay in practically every tooth.

After the radiation therapy sessions in New York, Oppie visited his dentist for repairs, even though he found it painful to open his mouth wide enough for Dodson's instruments. The dentist was amazed when Oppie refused an anaesthetic and marveled at his courage.

In the late spring he attended the commencement ceremonies at Princeton University to receive an honorary doctorate of science. He had pinched a nerve in his leg, using a cane to walk, and the sight of him on stage at Nassau Hall, hunched over the cane, his face etched with pain but his eyes clear, was memorable. As the moderator read the citation, "physicist and sailor, philosopher and horseman, linguist and cook, lover of fine wine and better poetry," it could have been that Oppie's mind went back to his own Fire Island commencement day, running the inlet in *Trimethy*, his first entrancement with Neils Bohr, the rides across the Sangre de Cristos with Frank, the Rhine wine in the saddlebag, the sessions with Donne.

He had a phrase, homesickness for time, and he had shared many times with Donne. The Englishman had written three and a half centuries ago, in an era of tumult, and Oppie found his poetry profoundly pertinent to the Twentieth Century. Shortly before his throat seizure, he had returned to Donne in an address at the Smithsonian, in Washington.

> And new Philosophy calls all in doubt,
> The Element of fire is quite put out;

The Sun is lost, and th'earth, and no man's wit
Can well direct him where to looke for it.
And freely men confesse that this world's spent,
When in the Planets, and the Firmament
They seeke so many new; then see that this
Is crumbled out againe to his Atomies.
'Tis all in peeces, all cohaerence gone;
All just supply, and all Relation.

Approaching the end, Oppenheimer seemed to retreat once more into his privacy. Donne had said it, and he had said it, but society was chronically foolish, and deaf to the early trumpets of revolution. He had campaigned well, and he took pride in this. "I have to die some year, and mine has been a pretty good life," he remarked to a friend.

There was brief reprieve in the summer when doctors found the knot in his throat had shrunk and was now quite soft, but soon afterwards the malignancy was discovered in the left palate and the corner of his tongue. He spoke with difficulty, he barely ate at all.

More tooth decay sent him back to his dentist, who nearly wept to see Oppenheimer come through his door at a totter, his mouth twisted, waving away the proferred assistance of the nurse.

Julian Schwinger, the physicist, who said he avoided Oppie's advice because it was too persuasive, sent the old master a paper to criticize, and picked it up in person one piteous day. "I could not read it myself," Oppie whispered, "but I gave it to an associate and he finds it excellent."

In reply to friends who wrote asking after him, he was coolly and tragically clinical. In October, 1966, it was that "my cancer is spreading rapidly; thus I am being radiated further, this time with electrons from a betatron." And in November, "I am much less able to speak and eat now." And in mid-February of 1967, "I am in some pain . . . my hearing and my speech are very poor."

And after February 18, there was no word at all because Oppenheimer, aged sixty-two, was dead.

Six hundred attended the memorial services at Princeton and listened to the eulogies from Kennan, Bethe, and Smyth. The Juilliard String Quartet performed the adagio and allegro movements of Beethoven's Quartet 14 in C-sharp Minor, after which Kitty and Frank received guests in the institute library. Then Oppie's ashes were flown to the Virgin Islands and scattered in the smooth blue sea.

But by this time Oppie himself had long gone, off with Donne:

> Death be not proud, though some have called thee
> Mighty and dreadful, for thou art not so.

BIBLIOGRAPHY AND
ACKNOWLEDGMENTS

Bibliography and Acknowledgments

In addition to the substantial primary material gathered for this biography, I relied heavily on *The New York Times*, gleaned valuable information from the Luce magazines, *Time, Life* and *Fortune*, and picked up data here and there from *Physics Today*, the *Washington Post, Bulletin of the Atomic Scientists, Atlantic Monthly, New Republic, Wall Street Journal, Saturday Review, Newsweek, Look, Science* and *Colliers*.

Because I was following Oppenheimer's path through life, I referred to the works which had influenced him, the Hindu classics and volumes by Proust, Shakespeare and Flaubert, but the books listed below were consulted more than others.

As remarked in the text, I quoted from several of these books. My special thanks to Norma Millay Ellis for permission to use the passage from Edna St. Vincent Millay's "Preface" to *Flowers of Evil* (Millay-Dillon translation of Baudelaire's *Les Fleurs du Mal*), Harper & Row. Copyright 1936, 1963 by Edna St. Vincent Millay and Norma Millay Ellis.

Allen, Frederick Lewis. *Since Yesterday.* New York: Harper & Brothers, 1940.

Alsop, Joseph & Stewart. *We Accuse.* New York: Simon & Schuster, Inc., 1954.

Birge, Raymond T. *History of the Physics Department.* Berkeley: University of California.

Borden, William. *There Will Be No Time.* Farmersville, California: Pacific Book Supply Company, 1946.

Brown, John Mason. *Through These Men.* New York: Harper & Brothers, 1956.

Chevalier, Haakon. *Oppenheimer: The Story of a Friendship.* New York: George Braziller, Inc., 1965.

Childs, Herbert. *An American Genius.* New York: E. P. Dutton & Co., Inc., 1968.

Compton, Arthur Holly. *Atomic Quest.* New York: Oxford University Press, Inc., 1956.

Cooke, Alistair. *A Generation on Trial.* New York: Alfred A. Knopf, Inc., 1952.

Davis, Nuel Pharr. *Lawrence and Oppenheimer.* New York: Simon & Schuster, Inc., 1968.

Dillon, George, and Millay, Edna St. Vincent, eds. *Flowers of Evil.* Charles Baudelaire. New York: Washington Square Press, 1962.

Donne, John. *The Selected Poetry of Donne,* ed. by Marius Bewley. New York: New American Library, 1966.

Eliot, T. S. *The Waste Land.* New York: Harcourt, Brace & World, Inc., 1934.

Fermi, Laura. *Atoms in the Family.* Chicago: University of Chicago Press, 1954.

———. *Illustrious Immigrants.* Chicago: University of Chicago Press, 1968.

Gilpin, Robert. *American Scientists and Nuclear Weapons Policy.* Princeton: Princeton University Press, 1962.

Government Printing Office. *In the Matter of J. Robert Oppenheimer;* manuscript of the hearings. Washington, D.C., 1954.

Groueff, Stephane. *Manhattan Project.* Boston: Little, Brown and Co., 1967.

Groves, Leslie R. *Now It Can Be Told.* New York: Harper & Brothers, 1952.

Hewlett, Richard G. and Anderson, Oscar E. *The New World 1939-1946.* University Park: Pennsylvania State University Press, 1952.

Jungk, Robert. *Brighter Than a Thousand Suns.* New York: Harcourt, Brace & World, Inc., 1958.

Lamont, Lansing. *Day of Trinity.* New York: Atheneum Publishers, 1965.

Lapp, Ralph. *Atoms and People.* New York: Harper & Brothers, 1956.

Lilienthal, David. *The Journals of David Lilienthal,* Volume II. New York: Harper & Row, 1964.

Oppenheimer, J. Robert. *The Open Mind.* New York: Simon & Schuster, Inc., 1955.

———. *Science and the Common Understanding.* New York: Simon & Schuster, Inc., 1954.

Smyth, Henry De Wolf. *Atomic Energy for Military Purposes.* Princeton: Princeton University Press, 1945.

Strauss, Lewis L. *Men and Decisions.* New York: Doubleday & Company, Inc., 1962.

Strout, Cushing. *Conscience, Science and Security: The Case of J. Robert Oppenheimer.* Chicago: Rand McNally & Co., 1963.

On the subject of books, *The Christian Century* once asked Oppenheimer which books had done the most to shape his vocational attitude and philosophy of life. Over breakfast in Princeton one morning in his later years, he prepared this list:

Baudelaire, Charles. *Les Fleurs du Mal.*

Bhartrihari. *The Three Centuries.*

Dante Alighieri. *The Divine Comedy.*

Eliot, T. S. *The Waste Land.*

Faraday, Michael. *The Notebooks of Michael Faraday.*

Flaubert, Gustave. *L'Éducation sentimentale.*

Plato. *Theaetetus.*

Reiman, Bernhard. *The Bhagavad-Gita,* collected works.

Shakespeare, William. *Hamlet.*

INDEX

Index

Abraham Lincoln Battalion, 182
Acheson, Dean, 119-122, 125-130, 132, 144, 173, 235
Acheson-Lilienthal report, 128-129, 213, 221
Adler, Felix, 6-7
Air Defense Command, 190-191
Alamogordo range, 103, 107, 108, 112
Alberg, Aarvo, 61
Allison, Sam, 109-110, 176
Alsop brothers, 228, 232
Alvarez, Luis, 168, 175, 214
American Physical Society, 138, 148, 214, 238
Amherst College, 231
Anderson, Carl, 32
Anderson, Clinton, 238
Anti-semitism, 6, 47
Argonne laboratories, 158
Army Chemical Center, 233
Army Corps of Engineers, 76
Atlantic Monthly, 164
Atom, 38, 42, 51, 59, 199
  nucleus of, 55, 163
Atom bomb, 89, 105-107, 168, 171, 174, 176, 177, 182, 188, 190, 193, 195, 196, 210, 223, 235, 241
  beginnings of, 67-72
  destruction caused by, 114
  dropped on Hiroshima and Nagasaki, 112
  first Soviet test of, 166
  first U.S. test of, 108-111
  Great Britain participation in, 98
  problems with, 75
  proposals for international control, 115, 119-121, 124-128, 144-145

raw materials for, 86
reaction to dropping of, 113
secrets passed to Soviet Union, 98, 104, 112, 175
security at Los Alamos, 80-83, 90-94
selections of assembly site, 77
tested at Bikini atoll, 130
Atomic energy, 136, 144, 159-161, 193, 194, 210, 220
Atomic Energy Act of 1946, 136-137, 139, 159-160, 211, 221-222
Atomic Energy Commission, 125, 129, 130, 135, 140, 143, 145, 148, 158, 175, 181, 192, 193, 206, 213, 229, 239, 247
  beginnings of, 125
Atoms and People (Lapp), 102

Bach, Johann Sebastian, 24
Bacher, Robert, 78, 136, 140, 176, 178, 183, 224
Bainbridge, Ken, 79, 109, 111, 176
Barnard, Chester, 125
Baruch, Bernard, 129-132, 144
Baruch Plan, 248
Batdorf, Sam, 51
Baudelaire, Charles Pierre, 43-44
Beethoven, Ludwig van, 24, 52-53, 255
Bell Telephone Laboratory, 214
Bergen, Edgar, 52
Berle, Adolf A., 248
Berlin Airlift, 164
Bethe, Hans, 74, 78, 98, 138, 153, 157, 169-170, 176, 220, 255
Bhagavad-Gita, 39, 110
Bhartrihari, 43, 107
Bikini atoll, 130
Birge, Raymond, 30-31, 39, 75, 117

Black, Hugo, 64
Bloch, Felix, 74
Bohm, David, 91, 149, 155-156, 218
Bohr, Niels, 17, 25, 26, 44, 67, 79, 100,
    102, 105, 120, 203, 250, 252-253
Bond, Julian, 250
Bond, Mrs. Julian, 250
Borden, William, 163, 195-197
Born, Max, 19, 23, 42-43, 251
Boyd, William, 15
Boyer, Marion, 193
Bradbury, Norris, 116, 136, 171, 174,
    175, 252
Braddock, Jim, 52
Brady, Diamond Jim, 131
Breit, Gregory, 71
Bridges, Harry, 46, 180
Bridgman, Percy, 12, 13
British Broadcasting Corporation, 199
Brode, Robert, 40, 79, 176
Brode, Mrs. Robert, 40
Brosnan, Ed, 206
Brown, John Mason, 242
Brownell, Herbert, Jr., 196-198, 205,
    207, 211, 215
Bryan, William Jennings, 3
B-24 Liberator, 163
Buckley, Oliver, 167, 171, 172, 224
Bulletin of the Atomic Scientist, 226
Bundy, McGeorge, 243
Bush, Vannevar, 68, 69, 76, 97-98, 100,
    105, 106, 107-108, 111, 125, 129, 140,
    177, 190, 206, 223, 235
Byrnes, James F., 105, 115, 118, 125, 130,
    175

California Institute of Technology, 25,
    29, 30, 32, 37, 40, 60, 116-117, 123,
    188, 189, 228
Calvin, John, 251
Cambridge University, 15, 16, 17, 21,
    38, 57
Camp, Glen, 36-37
Campbell, Joseph, 193, 229
Cancer, 138
Carlson, Frank, 36, 38
Carstairs, Morris, 250
Casals, Pablo, 239
Cavendish Laboratory, 16
Central Intelligence Agency, 198
Chadwick, Sir James, 38
Chambers, Whittaker, 146-147
Chandler, Raymond, 231
Chekhov, Anton, 9
Cherniss, Harold, 143, 241

Chevalier, Haakon, 80-82, 92-93, 95-97,
    134, 139-140, 141, 147, 197-198, 203,
    206, 208-211, 216-217, 227, 229
Childs, Herbert, 151
Christy, Bob, 57, 157
Churchill, Sir Winston, 98, 100, 103,
    108-109, 132
Clifford, Clark, 140
Cobalt 40 isotopes, 138
Cole, W. Sterling, 158
Columbia University, 67, 116, 233
Communism, 43, 57
    at campus level, 46
Communist Party, 46-48, 61-62, 81-82,
    94, 95, 151, 162, 180-182, 210-211,
    215-216, 222
Compton, Arthur, 68, 71-72, 74-78, 115
Conant, James, 68, 69, 97-98, 100, 105,
    106, 111, 116, 125, 137, 140, 166,
    168-173, 176, 177, 189, 206
Condon, Ed, 20-21, 79-80, 128, 135, 148,
    153-154, 183, 218
Condon, Mrs. Ed, 21, 153-154
Cooke, Alistair, 146
Corben, Bert, 53, 55-56, 67
Cornell University, 57
Cosmic rays, 42
Cotter, Frank, 195
Council of Foreign Relations, 190
Croker, Dick, 2
Crouch, Paul, 180, 182, 208
Crouch, Mrs. Paul, 180, 208
Commings, 27
Cyclotron, 68
Czechoslovakia, 164

Daily Worker, 61
Dallet, Joe, 61-62, 64
Dante, Alighieri, 21
Dean, Gordon, 174
Defense Research Establishment of Nor-
    way, 159
Descartes, René, 63
Deutrons, 45
Dietrich, Marlene, 238, 248
Dirac, Paul, 16-17, 21, 31, 43-44, 237
Distant Early Warning system, 189
Dodson, Warren, 253
Donne, John, 43, 103, 133, 253-255
Dostoyevsky, Fëdor, 17, 18
DuBridge, Lee, 137, 159, 172, 188, 189,
    192, 206, 228
Dudley, Colonel, 77
Dulles, Allen, 190
Dulles, John-Foster, 193-194

DuMond, Adele, 40
DuMond, Jesse, 40

Edison, Thomas Alva, 2
Edsall, John, 14, 17
Ehrenfest, Paul, 26, 28, 31-33, 37
Einstein, Albert, 26, 42, 55, 67, 100, 113, 142, 226, 252
Eisenhower, Dwight D., 130, 170, 188, 190, 194-197, 204-205, 239
Eisenhower Administration, 192-196, 207, 231, 242
Electrons, 38, 42, 138, 163, 185, 201, 254
Eliot, T. S., 9, 16
Eltenton, George, 80-82, 92-97, 139, 147
Eltenton, Mrs. George, 81
Eniwetok, 187
Enola Gay (airplane), 114
Enormous Room, The (Cummings), 27
Enrico Fermi Award, 247-249
Ethical Culture, 74
Ethical Culture School, 6, 10, 24
Evas, Ward, 212, 220, 222, 226-227, 229
Executive Order 10450, 211

"Fat Man" (bomb), 103-104, 108-110, 111, 112, 115, 136, 175
Faulkner, William, 145
Federal Bureau of Investigation, 82, 135, 139-141, 164, 182, 196-198, 200, 205, 206-207, 232
Federation of American Scientists, 152
Federation of Architects, Engineers, Chemists and Technicians, The, 70, 91
Federation of Atomic Scientists, 122
Fergusson, Francis, 8, 13, 27, 241
Fermi, Enrico, 42, 67, 71, 77, 87, 102, 105, 110, 115, 129, 138, 166, 171-173, 192, 206
Finletter, Thomas, 188, 189, 192
Fisk University, 149
Fleurs du Mal, Les (Baudelaire), 43
Formosa, 235
Forster, E. M., 225
Fortune, 191-192
Franck, James, 19, 20, 22, 23, 100
Franco, Francisco, 47, 49
Frankel, Stan, 68-69
Freud, Sigmund, 9, 245
Friedman, Ella, see Oppenheimer, Mrs. Julius
Friendly, Alfred, 228
Frisch, Otto, 67

Fuchs, Klaus, 98, 104, 112, 132, 174, 175, 192, 220
Furry, Wendell, 34-38, 57
Furry, Mrs. Wendell, 35-37

Gadfly, The, 15
Galilei, Galileo, 54
Garrison, Lloyd, 207, 212-213, 215, 219, 221
Gates, John W., 61, 131
General Advisory Committee, 135-137, 139, 160, 169-174, 186, 192, 208, 210
Germany, 42, 58, 99, 210
    capitulation of, 104
    invasion of Poland, 59
Gide, Andre, 22, 145
Goudsmit, Sam, 24, 152, 214
Grange, Red, 9-10
Gray, Gordon, 211-212, 214-217, 219, 221-223, 226-228
Great Britain, 98
Griggs, David, 188, 197
Grimm brothers, 2
Gromyko, Andrei, 131, 135
Groves, Leslie, 76-80, 83, 86-87, 90-91, 97, 99, 102-105, 109, 111, 125-126, 136-137, 193, 218

Hahn, Otto, 67
Hampshire, Stuart, 250
Hanford (village), 87, 98, 99, 101, 103, 136
Harrison, Wallace, 250
Harrison, Mrs. Wallace, 250
Harvard Lampoon, 15
Harvard University, 10, 11, 12-15, 24, 25, 45
Harwell atomic energy plant, 174
Hemingway, Ernest, 145
Herman, Colonel, 83
Hersch, Jeanne, 250
Hickenlooper, Bourke B., 158, 160, 161, 247
Higinbotham, Willie, 123-124
Hiroshima, 112-114, 117-118, 167, 168, 174, 194, 196, 242
Hiss, Alger, 104, 146-147, 181
Hitler, Adolf, 42
Hobson, Verna, 241, 245-246, 249
Hoover, Herbert, 136
Hoover, J. Edgar, 140-141, 148, 196, 208
Horgan, Paul, 8, 9, 13-14, 22
Horgan, Rosemary, 22
House Committee on Un-American Activities, 146-155, 164, 180-181

House Rules Committee, 135
Houtermans, Fritz, 21, 22-23
Howard University, 171
Humphrey, George, 190
Hugo, Victor, 248
Hunter College, 130, 132
Hydrogen, 75
Hydrogen bomb, 186, 190, 192, 196-197, 207, 208, 218, 220, 225, 227
  beginnings of, 114, 167
  debates on building of, 168-178
  early design for, 175
  first Soviet testing of, 194
  first U.S. testing of, 187, 190
  See also Thermonuclear bomb
Hydrogen isotope, 169

Ibsen, Henrik, 1
Institute for Advanced Study (Princeton), 42, 45, 141-142, 156, 213, 235-236
Institute of Technology (Zurich), 26, 57
Internal Security Subcommittee, 195
International Atomic Energy Agency, 194
International Brigade, 62, 182
International Congress of Theoretical Physics, 238
International Educational Board, 26
International Monetary Fund, 196
Iodine, 138
Iron-59, 159
Isotopes, 159-160, 162
  export of, 159

Jack Tenny California Committee on Un-American Activities, 180-182
Japan, 100, 104, 105, 108, 110, 112, 145
  Oppenheimer lectures in, 241-242
Japan Committee for Intellectual Interchange, 241
Jeans, Sir James Hopwood, 15
Jenner, William, 195, 205, 207
Jefferson, Thomas, 165, 178-179, 186, 250
Jews, 6, 47
Joe 1 test, 166
Johns Hopkins University, 32
Johnson, Louis, 174
Johnson, Lyall, 91, 92, 94
Johnson, Lyndon B., 249
Joint Congressional Committee on Atomic Energy, 135, 139, 163-164, 195, 219
Jornada del Muerto Valley, 103

Journal of the Cambridge Philosophical Society, 19
Journal Club, 41
Juilliard String Quartet, 255

Kennan, George, 238, 250, 255
Kennedy, Joe, 78
Kennedy, John F., 242, 247-249
Kennedy Administration, 243-244, 247
Kinetic Theory of Gases (Jeans), 15
Kistiakowsky, George, 109-110, 250
Kistiakowsky, Mrs. George, 250
Klock, Augustus, 7
Korean War, 186-187
Kramers, 34-35
Ku Klux Klan, 64
Kusaka, Hanuko, 84
Kusaka, Shuichi, 83-84

Lal, Mr., 233
Lamb, LaMar, 133-134
Lansdale, John, 69-71, 80, 82, 90-91, 94-96, 139-140, 149-150, 206-207, 209, 216, 219-220
Lapp, Ralph, 102
Latimer, Wendell, 168-169, 214, 224
Lauritsen, Charles, 60, 63, 176, 192, 206, 224
Lauritsen, Tommy, 40-41
Lawrence, Ernest, 29, 35, 39, 41-42, 53, 66, 68-71, 75-78, 86, 91, 93, 95, 105, 106, 115-116, 134, 141, 160, 168, 189, 213, 214, 224-225
League of Nations, 47
Lee, 237
Legion of Honor, 238
LeMay, Curtis, 186, 192
Lenin, Nikolai, 14, 48
Leukemia, 138
Lewis, Fulton, Jr., 158, 207
Leyden University, 26
Life, 180
Lilienthal, David E., 125-128, 130, 132, 136-137, 140, 144, 148, 158, 161, 166, 174, 193, 211, 218
Lippmann, Walter, 228
"Little Boy" (bomb), 103-104, 108, 111
Livermore laboratory, 187, 192
Lomanitz, Rossi, 91, 93-96, 113, 149, 156, 208, 216
Los Alamos, 77-83, 87-88, 90, 93, 94, 98, 99, 101-104, 106-107, 111, 115, 117, 119, 122-124, 134, 136-137, 140, 150, 153, 155, 158, 169-171, 174-176, 187, 192, 210, 220, 224, 231, 252
  security at, 80-83, 90-94

Louis, Joe, 52
Lovett, Robert, 189
Lowell, Robert, 250
Loyola University, 210

McCarthy, Joseph, 180, 183, 185, 193, 195-197, 205, 207, 213, 232
McCloy, John J., 125-126
McCormack, James, 170
McKibbin, Dorothy, 134
MacLeish, Archibald, 164-165, 168
McMahon, Brien, 123-124, 128, 135, 148, 158, 161, 166, 168, 170, 174, 195
McMillan, Edwin, 77
Manchester Guardian, 146
Manhattan Engineer District, 76, 81, 82, 86, 94, 97, 100, 104, 122-123, 126-127, 135, 139, 150, 169, 172, 208-209, 224
Manley, John, 72-73, 79, 174, 175
Manley, Kathy, 73
Mansfield, Katherine, 9
Mao Tse-tung, 164
Marks, Herbert, 119, 125-126, 148, 181, 205-207
Marks, Mrs. Herbert, 158, 204
Marshall, George, 105
Marxism, 48
Massachusetts Institute of Technology, 153, 167, 189
Matthew, St., 244
Max, Andrew, 135
May-Johnson bill, 119, 122, 128, 153
Meitner, Lise, 67
Men and Decisions (Strauss), 161
Mesons, 55, 138, 185
Metallurgical Laboratory, 71
Meyer, Agnes, 250
Military Affairs Committee, 135
Military Liaison Committee, 135
Millay, Edna St. Vincent, 43-44
Millikan, Robert, 25, 26
Monet, Edouard, 9
Montgomery, Deane, 235-236
Moore, G. E., 236
Morgan, Thomas, 211, 222, 226-227, 231
Morrison, Phillip, 51-52, 56, 108, 123, 140, 224
Mozart, Wolfgang Amadeus, 53
Murray, Thomas E., 193, 228-229
Murrow, Edward R., 235, 238

Nabokov, Nicholas, 250
Nagasaki, 112-114
National Academy of Science, 66, 124

National Bureau of Standards, 128, 148
National Research Council, 24, 199
Nedelsky, Leo, 36
Nedelsky, Mrs. Leo, 36
Nehru, Motilal, 233
Nelson, Steve, 62, 64, 82, 180, 182-183
Nelson, Mrs. Steve, 64
Neumann, Johnny von, 142, 175, 236
Neutrons, 38, 45, 55, 67, 87, 127, 143, 160
New Deal, 43, 46
New World, The, 131
New York *American*, 38
New York Herald Tribune, 128
New York Times, The, 128, 142, 212-214, 228
Newsweek, 123
Newton, Alberta, 7
Newton, Isaac, 201, 238
Nichols, Kenneth, 75-76, 193, 198, 204, 206-209, 212, 227-228
Nimitz, Chester W., 130
Nitrogen, 75
Nixon, Richard, 147, 154, 181, 197
Nobel Prize, 16-17, 20, 25, 31-32
Nobel Prize Committee, 45
Norman Bridge Laboratory, 25, 32
Nuclear rockets, 138
Nuclear warheads, 138

Office of Defense Mobilization, 229
Office of Scientific Research and Development, 68
Office of War Information, 96
Official Secrets Act, 225
Oliphant, Marcus, 66-67
Oppenheimer, Ben, 2, 5
Oppenheimer, Frank, 4, 8, 10, 15-16, 24-25, 27-33, 39, 42, 44, 45, 48, 56, 58, 60, 64-65, 75, 80, 82, 94, 101, 111, 115, 122, 134, 141-142, 147-148, 164, 197, 210, 215-216, 218, 224, 233, 253, 255
appears before the House Committee on Un-American Activities, 149, 150-151
dismissed from University of Minnesota, 151
joins Communist Party, 46-47
marriage of, 46-47
Oppenheimer, Mrs. Frank, 47-48, 64-65, 80, 94, 134, 149-151, 197, 215
See also Quam, Jacquenette
Oppenheimer, J. Robert
addresses Columbia University bi-

Oppenheimer, J. Robert (*cont.*)
  centennial celebrations, 233-235
antipathy toward Bernard Baruch,
    129, 132
appointed chairman of General Ad-
    visory Committee, 137
appointed chairman of State Depart-
    ment Advisory Committee on Dis-
    armament, 189-190
appointed head of Los Alamos lab-
    oratory, 78
arranges meetings at Mt. Kisco, 250-
    251
awarded the Enrico Fermi Award,
    247-249
awarded honorary doctorate of Ox-
    ford University, 203
awarded honorary doctorate of Science
    at Princeton University, 253
awarded Legion of Honor, 238
the Bernard Peters case and, 152-156
birth of, 3-4
birth of daughter, 88
birth of son, 65
boyhood of, 1, 4-5, 6, 7-11
campaigns for May-Johnson bill, 122
Chevalier incident and, 80-82, 92-93,
    95-97, 139, 141, 206, 208-209, 211,
    216
Communist movement and, 48-49, 180-
    182
death of, 254
death of father, 58
death of mother, 33
as Director of the Institute for Ad-
    vanced Study (Princeton), 141-142,
    235-236
early association with atom bomb, 67-
    72
education of, 25-33
the Eltenton affair and, 80-81, 93-97
as exchange physics professor at the
    Sorbonne, 241
first testing of atom bomb, 108-111
gives memorial address for Niels Bohr,
    252
influence on fundamental research and
    weapons, 138-139
the Kennedy administration and, 243-
    244
as leader of Journal Club, 41
lectures on British Broadcasting Cor-
    poration, 199-203
lectures in Japan, 241-242
lectures in Latin America, 242

marriage of, 63
memorial services for, 255
as physics teacher at University of
    California (Berkeley), 30-33, 36-38,
    51-57
plan for international control of
    atomic bombs, 127-128
purchases home, 65-66
reaction to detonation of atom bombs,
    113-114, 117
recommends international control of
    atomic weapons, 115, 119-121, 144-
    145
relationship with Jean Tatlock, 47,
    49-50
retires from General Advisory Com-
    mittee, 189
retires from Institute for Advanced
    Studies, 252
reveals names of Communists, 94-96
as security risk, 75-76, 195-198, 204,
    207-230
selects scientists for Los Alamos, 78-
    79
students of, 51-57
subpoenaed by House Committee on
    Un-American Activities, 149
suspected of being Soviet spy, 195-
    198
as symbol of trust, 83-85
views on building and use of hydrogen
    bombs, 172-178
views on cosmic rays, 42
views on use of atom bomb, 89, 105-
    107, 168
visits Europe in 1948, 143, 145
Oppenheimer, Mrs. J. Robert, 64, 70-
    71, 74-75, 78, 80, 82, 97, 111, 134,
    140-142, 151, 181-182, 184-185, 197-
    199, 203, 210, 222, 241, 245, 255
birth of daughter, 88
birth of son, 65
illness of, 239, 240
joins Communist Party, 61-62
marriages of, 61-63
  See also Puening, Katherine
Oppenheimer, Judith, 151
Oppenheimer, Julius, 2-9, 10, 24, 25,
    30, 33, 39-40, 58
Oppenheimer, Mrs. Julius, 3-4, 5, 8, 10,
    12, 14, 15, 24, 30, 33, 39-40, 73-74
Oppenheimer, Katherine (Toni), 88,
    184, 239, 241, 245
Oppenheimer, Louis, 4
Oppenheimer, Michael, 151

Oppenheimer, Peter, 65, 80, 183-184, 240-241, 245, 249
Oppenheimer: The Story of a Friendship (Chevalier), 140
Operation Candor, 190, 194
Organization of American States, 242
Osborn, Frederick, 144
Oxford University, 203

Page, Katherine, 10-11, 13, 26-27, 133
Parkhurst, Charles, 2
Pash, Boris, 89-90, 92-94, 99, 139-140, 216-217
Pauli, Wolfgang, 26, 28, 29, 34-35, 37, 143
Pearl Harbor, 71
Peters, Bernard, 95-96, 149-150, 152-156, 157, 178
Peters, Mrs. Bernard, 95
Phillips, Melba, 36, 38-39, 45
Phosphorus, 138
Physical Review, 25, 35, 57, 67, 69
Pike, Sumner T., 136
Pitzer, Kenneth, 170, 189
Placzek, George, 57, 209
Plutonium, 86-88, 103, 108, 110, 112, 127, 136, 171
Plutonium bomb, 102
Poland, 59
Potsdam Conference, 106, 108, 111, 115, 122
Princeton University, 45, 149, 241, 249, 253, 255
Project Lincoln, 188, 190, 192
Project Trinity, 103, 109, 111, 114
Project Vista, 188, 190, 192
Protons, 38, 42, 45, 55
Proust, Marcel, 17
Puening, Katherine, 61
  See also Oppenheimer, Mrs. J. Robert

Quam, Jacquenette, 45-47
  See also Oppenheimer, Mrs. Frank
Quebec Agreement (1948), 98

Rabi, I. I., 29, 52, 137, 138, 171-172, 192, 206, 223
Radiation Laboratory, 68, 70, 80, 82, 91, 101, 134, 141, 151
Radin, Max, 70
Radioisotopes, 137
Radium, 159
Reith Lectures, 199-203, 238, 250
Remembrance of Things Past (Proust), 17

Research and Development Board, 186, 193
Reston, James, 212-214
Riefenstahl, Charlotte, 22, 23, 24-25
Rilke, Rainer Maria, 58
Robb, Roger, 207-209, 211-221, 223-226, 237
Rochester *Times-Union*, 153, 154
Rockefeller Foundation, 20-21
Rogers, William, 207
Rollander, Arthur, 212
Roosevelt, Eleanor, 177
Roosevelt, Franklin, 43, 48, 67-68, 98, 100, 103-104, 121, 146
Roosevelt, Theodore, 3
Rothfeld-Stern Company, 3, 5
Round Table (radio program), 177-178
Rousseau, Jean Jacques, 251
Rowe, Hartley, 137, 167, 170-172
Rusk, Dean, 243
Russell, Bertrand, 242
Russell, Kay, 173, 208
Russell, Louis J., 147
Rutherford, Ernest, 16, 25
Ryder, Arthur, 39, 52

Sanskrit, 43, 209
Sartre, Jean Paul, 146
Schiff, Leonard, 53
Schlesinger, Arthur, Jr., 243
Schwinger, Julian, 53, 55-56, 157, 254
Science Advisory Committee, 229
Seaborg, Glenn, 86, 137, 167, 170, 173, 219, 247
See It Now (TV program), 235
Serber, Robert, 79, 82, 95, 140, 218
Serber, Mrs. Robert, 80, 82, 95, 218
Shawcross, Sir Hartley, 81
Shoupp, William, 160-161
Silva, Peer de, 90-91, 150, 197
Slotin, Louis, 108
Smith, Cyril, 78, 137, 171-173
Smith, Herbert, 10
Smyth, Henry D., 193, 227-230, 255
Smyth, Mrs. Henry D., 228
Snyder, Hartland, 54, 67
Socrates, 14-15
Sodium, 160
Sommerfeld, 34
Sorbonne, the, 241
Spanish Civil War, 76, 182-183
Spellman, Cardinal, 183
Sperry Corporation, 211
Stalin, Joseph, 42, 97, 103, 105-106, 108-109, 111-112, 115, 121-122, 187

Stalingrad, Battle of, 81
State Department Advisory Committee
on Disarmament, 189-190
Steinbeck, John, 145
Stendahl, 146
Stern, Alfred, 47, 58, 213
Stern, Hedwig, 5, 47, 58
Stewart-Harrison, Richard, 60, 62-63, 182
Stewart-Harrison, Mrs. Richard, 60, 63
See also Oppenheimer, Mrs. S. Robert
Stimson, Henry L., 104, 106, 111, 115,
119-120
Strassmann, Fritz, 67
Strategic Air Command, 166, 187-189,
191-192, 195
Strauss, Lewis L., 136-137, 141, 159-164,
168, 173-175, 192-193, 197-198, 204,
211, 213, 228-229, 232, 235, 239
Subatomic elementary particles, 163
Szilard, Leo, 100, 107

Tatlock, Jean, 47-50, 52, 63, 89, 95, 197,
209, 217, 232
Teachers' Union, 64
Teller, Edward, 74-75, 79, 102, 107, 114,
138, 151, 157, 168-171, 174, 175, 176,
187, 190, 192, 193, 214, 220, 232,
247-248
testifies at Oppenheimer's hearing,
224-225
Tenney, Jack, 147
There Will Be No Time (Borden), 163
Thermonuclear bomb, 114-115, 138
See also Hydrogen bomb
Thomas, Charles, 125
Thomas, Dylan, 199
Thomas, J. Parnell, 135, 147-148, 152
Thomas, Norman, 46
Thompson, Dorothy, 123
Thomson, Joseph, 16, 17
Through These Men (Brown), 242
Tibbets, Paul, 108
Time, 155
Tinian, Island of, 108, 112
Tokyo, fire bomb raids on, 104
Trimethy (boat), 8, 9, 15
Tritium, 169
Truman, Harry, 104, 106, 108-109, 111-
112, 115, 119-122, 124-125, 130, 136,
140, 146, 158, 166, 170, 173-176, 187,
195-197, 211, 249
Truman, Mrs. Harry, 121
Truman Administration, 189

Uhlenbeck, George, 21, 24

Uhlenbeck, Mrs. George, 24
Ulam, Stanislaw, 175
Union of Soviet Socialist Republics, 57,
58, 81, 97, 99-100, 103, 105, 144, 167,
168, 170, 171, 173, 187, 210
first test of atomic bomb, 166
first test of hydrogen bomb, 194
Klaus Fuchs spies for, 98, 104, 112,
175
reaction to proposed international con-
trol of atomic weapons, 131-132
United Nations, 104, 131, 144, 195
United Nations Educational, Scientific
and Cultural Organization, 203
United Nations General Assembly, 125,
194
United Nations Security Councio, 129-
131
U.S. Air Force, 166, 169, 176, 186-188,
190-192, 199
U.S. Army, 186, 188, 210
U.S. Congressional Record, 158
U.S. Defense Department, 186, 189, 193,
198
U.S. Department of Commerce, 148
U.S. Navy, 186, 188
U.S. Senate Permanent Subcommittee on
Investigations, 195
U.S. State Department, 104, 144, 159,
180, 198
U.S. State Department Advisory Com-
mittee on Disarmament, 190
U.S. Treasury, 196
University of California, 60, 117, 168
University of California (Berkeley), 29-
33, 36-38, 45, 51, 53, 55, 57, 69-70,
75, 76, 81, 89, 91, 93, 106, 115-117,
123, 134, 160, 213, 224, 248
University of Chicago, 71
University of Göttingen, 19-20, 21, 22,
24, 26, 57
University of Illinois, 35
University of Minnesota, 141, 149, 151,
155
University of Munich, 61
University of North Carolina, 158, 211
University of Pennsylvania, 62
University of Pittsburgh, 61
University of Rochester, 57, 149, 153, 155
University of Washington, 232, 238, 242
University of Wisconsin, 61, 71
Uranium, 43, 67, 86-87, 113, 127-128,
131, 139
Uranium gas, 86-87

Uranium isotope 235, 68, 86-88, 108, 127-128, 136, 158, 171
Uranium isotope 238, 87
Uranium oxide, 158
Urey, Harold, 71, 122, 135, 148, 176, 189

Van Gogh, Vincent, 6
Vandenberg, Hoyt, 186, 191, 193
Vanity Fair, 120
Vassar College, 24
Volkoff, George, 52
Volpe, Joe, 161, 207-208, 219
Voorhis, Jerry, 135-136

Wall Street Journal, 189
Walter, Francis E., 149
Washington Times-Herald, 148
Washington Post, 228, 250
Waste Land, The (Eliot), 16
Waymack, William W., 136, 158, 174
We Accuse (Alsop), 232
Wedgwood, Veronica, 238

Weinberg, Joe, 51-54, 91, 95, 149, 155
Weisskopf, Victor, 57, 79, 153-154, 157, 170, 176, 209
White, Harry Dexter, 196, 205
Who's Who of American Science, 68
Wilson, Carroll, 137
Wilson, Charles, 193, 197-198, 214
Wilson, Robert, 79
Wilson, Roscoe, 197
Winne, Harry, 125, 221-222
Winslow, Art, 184
Worthington, Hood, 137, 167
Wyman, Jeffries, 15, 17, 203

Yale University, 29
Yang, 237
Young Communist Leaguers, 46
Yukawa, Hideki, 55

Zacharias, Jerrold, 192
ZORC, 192
Zuckert, Eugene, 193, 227-229